Tort Law for AC AS and A-Leve

plus an introduction to the nature of l... substantive law

(the English legal system and the nature of law)

Sally Russell LLB (Hons), PGCE

©Copyright Sally Russell 2017. All rights reserved.

Key features

Tasks and self-test questions throughout (with answers at www.drsr.org)

Key cases with key principles highlighted

Examples to bring the law to life

Links between the law and the English legal system

Links between the law and the nature of law in relation to various concepts

Summaries with diagrams for the main points of each area

Examination and evaluation pointers

Examination guidance and question practice

Free interactive exercises at www.drsr.org

Free guide for teachers also at www.drsr.org

My main objective has been to combine legal accuracy with a style that is accessible to all students, so I hope you will find this book both stimulating and helpful. Fully updated with recent cases and laws it is written in a lively, clear and accessible way and is designed to help students of all learning styles to understand the subject. AQA would only give approval to one publisher so this book does not carry an official badge of approval. However the AQA Portfolio Curriculum team kindly gave help and advice on content and assessment and I am grateful to them.

Although aimed at A-Level the book provides a good base for 1st Year LLB, CILEx and other courses, and can be used as a self-study guide.

Other books by Sally Russell

As new books may be available by the time you read this I have not listed my other books by title. They currently include crime and tort at AS and A2 level for both the AQA and OCR examination boards. Also *'the law explained'* series offers a more in-depth coverage of individual areas with additional tasks, examples and examination practice. These cover much of crime and tort as well as the various concepts of law. This means you can pick those topics for which you need more guidance (all the answers to tasks are included in the booklets).

For the most up-to-date list of what is available please check my author's page on Amazon or visit my website at www.drsr.org. All my books are available in both Kindle and paperback.

Table of contents

Table of contents	ii
Introduction: things you need to know and links to other areas	1
Part 1: Tort for AS and Year 1 A-Level	6
Chapter 1 Rules and theory of tort law	8
The nature of law	8
Linking the concepts with the law	12
Chapter 2 Duty of Care for physical harm and damage to property	14
The Caparo test	15
Police, councils and sporting bodies	18
Lawyers	21
Liability for omissions	22
Chapter 3 Breach of duty	24
The standard of care expected	24
The factors	25
Objectiveness, children and professionals (subjective considerations)	28
Chapter 4 Causation (damage was caused by the breach)	35
Successive and multiple causes	36
Loss of chance	40
Causation in law: Remoteness of Damage	41
Chapter 5 Occupier's Liability for visitors	46
The duty	46
Children s 2(3)(a)	48
Professionals s 2(3)(b)	50
Independent contractors s 2(4)(b)	50
Warnings s 2(4)(a) and 'obvious risks'	52
Exclusions s 2 (1)	55
Defences	56
Chapter 6: Occupier's Liability for trespassers	58
The duty s 1(1), s 1(3) and s 1(4)	59
Warnings s 1(5) and 'obvious risks'	61

Dangerous activities or dangerous premises	*62*
Defences	*63*

Summary 1: Negligence, occupier's liability and remedies — 67

Chapter 7: The AS examination (7161) — 70
About the exam	*70*
Examination guidance	*72*

The Bridge — 79
Key criticisms of negligence at common law	*79*
Key criticisms of occupiers' liability under the two statutes	*79*
The nature of law (concepts)	*80*
The nature of law links	*85*

Part 2: Tort for Year 2 — 88

Chapter 8 Duty of Care for economic loss — 90
Economic loss and negligent misstatements	*91*
The special relationship from Hedley v Byrne	*91*
Assumption of responsibility	*94*
Economic Loss by acts	*98*

Chapter 9 Duty of Care for psychiatric harm) — 103
Primary and secondary victims	*105*
Rescuers	*107*
The control mechanisms	*108*
Law Commission proposals for reform	*111*

Summary 2: Economic loss and psychiatric harm, — 115
Key criticisms	*116*

Chapter 10 nuisance — 118
The definition of private nuisance	*119*
What is unreasonable interference?	*120*
Claimants: who can sue?	*124*
Defendants: who can be sued?	*124*
Defences	*127*
Remedies	*129*

Chapter 11 Rylands v Fletcher (the escape of dangerous things) — 135
- The rule in Rylands v Fletcher — 135
- Is liability strict? — 140
- Defences — 141

Chapter 12 Vicarious liability — 144
- What is vicarious liability? — 144
- Test for an employee — 146
- In the course of employment — 147

Chapter 13 Contributory negligence and consent — 153
- Contributory negligence — 153
- Contributing to the damage or loss — 154
- Contributing to the accident itself — 154
- Consent — 157
- Implied consent — 159

Chapter 14 Remedies — 163
- Damages: Compensation for the harm caused — 163
- Special damages — 163
- General damages — 164
- Mitigation of loss — 165
- Injunctions — 166

Summary 3 Nuisance, Rylands v Fletcher, vicarious liability, defences and remedies — 169
- Key criticisms of nuisance and Rylands — 169
- Key criticisms of vicarious liability — 170

Chapter 15: The A-level Examination (7162) — 174
- **About the exams** — 174
- Examination guidance — 176
- **Examination paper Task 50** — 180

Index of cases — 185

List of abbreviations — 188

Introduction: things you need to know and links to other areas

This book covers all the tort law for AQA for both Year 1 and Year 2 (AS and A-Level), as well as an introduction to the nature of law. AS tort is much the same as the first year of A-level, but it is not identical. You may well share your lessons so I have included a little more evaluation of the substantive law (tort and crime) than is needed for AS, where evaluation is mainly limited to the advantages and disadvantages of various legal institutions and procedures. However, the evaluation pointers will often also include matters which relate to these, because a particular law may raise issues about e.g., different types of law-making, influences on Parliament or how judges have interpreted the law.

Part 1 covers Year 1. Firstly, the general rules for liability in tort are explained, then the tort of negligence in respect of physical harm to a person or damage to property is covered. Then there are two types of liability which are similar but occur when the harm is caused on somebody's property, a special form of negligence. There is liability for lawful visitors and a more limited liability for trespassers, under the two **Occupiers Liability Acts**. Finally, we look at the remedy of damages, which is compensation for the harm caused. This is the material you need for both AS and A-level tort Year 1.

Part 2 covers Year 2 for the A-level. It continues negligence to look at liability in relation to psychiatric harm and economic loss. We then look at two new torts, nuisance and liability for the escape of dangerous things. Then we look at a slightly different situation, rather than a tort in its own right, where someone is liable for someone else's torts, called vicarious liability, and finally defences. This is the additional material you need for A-level tort Year 2.

More on how the key features can help:

Examples help you to see how the law relates to real-life situations

Tasks and self-test questions help you to check your understanding

Examination pointers help with application

Evaluation pointers help you to see problems with the law, which are relevant to the development and reform of the law as well as to the rule of law and justice (both of which require fairness and clarity)

Key cases show you the important cases to know, and where a principle of law is established this is clearly stated

Summaries and diagrams help to make the law clear and accessible

Links between tort and the English legal system show you how to deal with questions which mix these

Links between tort and the nature of law show you how to deal with questions which mix these

At the end of Part 1, there is a summary and examination practice. Although there is no need to take an external examination at the end of Year 1, you may wish to do so if you are not 100% sure about doing the full A-Level. The AS won't count towards the A-level but if you decide to go no further you will have a law qualification at AS level.

Part 1 is followed by 'The Bridge'. This section links Year 1 and Year 2. It includes an evaluation of the law so far, along with proposals for reform where appropriate, which you will need for Year 2. The Bridge also explains the nature of law and the role of law in society, and provides examples to illustrate these from within the areas already covered. This will set you up for Year 2, where you will need to be able to discuss the nature and role of law in relation to all areas of law, including the new law you will meet in Year 2. Examples are given in each chapter for Part 2.

It is a bit early to talk about examinations (covered at the end of Parts 1 and 2) but there are a couple of things you need to know now, firstly so you can use the book effectively and secondly so you can understand the links to other areas required throughout the course.

In some questions you will be asked to apply the law to a set of facts, in others to evaluate it. There are 'pointers' throughout the book to help with this. Two questions on each paper are mixed, linking tort (the substantive law) to the English legal system and, for A-level only, to the nature of law (the non-substantive law). Throughout this book references to the English legal system refer to both this and to law-making.

There are links in each chapter to help with this. Throughout this book references to the English legal system refer to both this and to law-making.

These three aids to learning include:

Examination pointers

These relate to legal rules and application of the law. For application of the law you need to identify the specific legal rules that apply to the given facts. Then you need to apply those rules logically to the facts in order to reach a sustainable conclusion. The law for application is the current law and latest case developments.

Evaluation pointers

These cover criticisms of the law. They are for evaluation questions where you may be asked to provide a critique of the law on a particular topic or a particular legal rule. The evaluation pointer may show the law has improved in some way too, as any critique should include the good points. For evaluation, you may need to include developments or advantages and disadvantages, not just the latest cases and principles.

Links

In Part 1 the links are to the English legal system. In Part 2 the links are to both the English legal system and the nature of law (concepts of law such as morals). The links are needed for the mixed questions on each paper. There is more on this under 'more on the two mixed questions'.

A few terms need explaining.

Substantive law means the particular topic, like crime and tort.

Non-substantive law means the nature rather than the substance of law. This includes the English legal system and various legal theories. The first is needed for both AS and A-level, the second only for A-level.

Extended writing questions can be on the application or evaluation of the law, or a mix of both of these. They require that you provide "an extended answer which shows a clear logical and sustained line of reasoning leading to a valid conclusion". There are two extended writing questions on each of the AS papers and three on each of the A-level papers.

Application: You will need to explain the relevant rules of law and then apply those rules to decide whether a person is liable. You will need to support what you say by using cases and principles to illustrate your points and then reach a conclusion based on your application.

Evaluation: This could require e.g., a discussion of how far the rules on a certain area of law or procedure are satisfactory (for both AS and A-level) and/or whether the rules reflect the appropriate level of fault (for A-level). You may need to discuss whether there is a need for reform of the law in a particular area, or whether proposals for reform have been suggested (especially any by the Law Commission as this body was set up to investigate the law and suggest reforms).

Whatever you need to discuss, try to produce a balanced argument. Where there is debate on an issue there are usually valid arguments on both sides, so don't strive to write what you think examiners want to see; they will be much more impressed by independent thought. Have an opinion, but look at the issue from the other point of view too to show that you have considered the arguments before reaching that opinion.

For more detail on what non-substantive areas are in each of the examination papers see the two 'examination practice' sections at the end of Parts 1 and 2 of this book. However, you need to be able to link tort to the non-substantive areas as you work through the course, so here is a short guide to get you started.

More on the two mixed questions

You will have to link the substantive law to the English legal system for the AS examination (there are two mixed questions on each paper). Here is a diagram to show how the links might work between tort and the parts of the English legal system which are on Paper 2 AS. This means you can start thinking about these as you work through your course.

I have not included delegated legislation and the European Union as these are on the AS but not the A-level tort paper. So is statutory interpretation, but I have included that so you can consider it when you study the two **Occupiers Liability Acts**. Bear this in mind depending on which examination you are taking. For more information on the links for the A-level paper, see the examination guidance in Part 2.

At the end of each chapter is a reminder to look back at this diagram to see what parts of the English legal system the particular topic you have just studied could link to (look for the linked rings symbol). Think of the topic as being in the central box and see how it can link to any of the outer boxes (adding delegated legislation and the European Union as appropriate). There may not always be a strong link in a particular examination question, but there will be one. However, as most of the substantive law can link to any part of the English legal system there is no way of knowing where the link will be made, so it is best to think about it for all areas. Also note that any cases establishing new principles are indicative of the development of the law and can be related to many areas of law-making.

Examples

If someone is taken to court they may need to obtain legal advice and representation (access to justice). Funding may be needed to help pay for preparing the case (access to justice) or in lodging an appeal (appeals). To avoid the cost of going to court it may be appropriate to try to find an alternative (alternative dispute resolution). The amount of the claim will determine which court (civil courts) and which type of judge, and will also involve the role of the judge in the case (judges and their role). If the case comes under one of the **Occupiers Liability Acts (OLA)**, the judge may need to interpret that **Act** (statutory interpretation). These **Acts** are examples of both law made in Parliament (parliamentary law-making) and the Law Commission as an influence on that law (influences on Parliament). They also illustrate that both the common law and statute law are important sources of law and show how they can interconnect. The **OLA 1984** developed from a decision by a judge (common law). The statute included some other aspects of common law too, such as the definition of an occupier. Once an Act is passed, the courts then have to interpret it in order to apply it to the particular facts e.g., the extent of the duty the occupier owes.

The above examples apply to all areas so are not repeated in every chapter. In the 'links to the non-substantive law' I have added a little, but reminded you to look back at this diagram and these examples.

A final few things before you start the book.

It is important to try to learn plenty of cases as these help to show you how the law works in practice. If you have trouble remembering them then do the best you can, but be sure that you at least know the 'key cases' well.

Civil cases are between the *claimant* (C) and the *defendant* (D), e.g., Smith v Jones 2017, although you will still see the use of the old word *plaintiff* in cases before 1999, when it changed to *claimant*.

Criminal cases are usually in the form *R v the defendant (D)* e.g., R v Smith (usually abbreviated to just Smith in textbooks).

There is a list of some common abbreviations in the appendix at the end of the book.

Part 1: Tort for AS and Year 1 A-Level

Chapter 1 covers some general principles of liability in tort. The word tort comes from French and means a civil wrong. Unlike criminal law, civil law is based on people's responsibility to each other rather than to society as a whole. The role of the law in tort is compensation for the claimant (C) rather than punishment for the defendant (D).

The next three chapters cover liability in negligence for physical harm and how it is proved in court.

Negligence is an important area of tort. You have probably seen cases reported in the paper or seen them on television. Negligence includes situations where, e.g., a person sues a hospital for negligent treatment, or the council for uneven pavements causing injury, and even a case of suing McDonalds because the coffee was too hot and scalded someone – this one failed, but you see the type of thing that negligence involves. As it is such a big area of law and has been developed by judges through the common law (rather than written down in an Act of Parliament), there are a lot of cases to look at. You can't learn every single one but you do need to know the law and to give examples of how it applies in practice. Make sure you know the 'key cases' well because these are especially important, usually because they have established a new principle of law which then applies in later cases, or a principle of law has been confirmed by a higher court. Then pick a few examples in each area which make sense to you and learn those, in particular regarding how the principle of law has been applied.

To be able to claim compensation for harm caused by D's negligence, C must prove 3 things:

- **D owes C a duty of care**
- **D has breached that duty**
- **D's breach caused the harm**

These *all* need to be applied to the facts of a case to prove liability in negligence.

After negligence, we will look at a similar type of situation, but where the harm or damage to property occurs on someone else's property, this is occupiers' liability.

Occupiers' liability is a form of negligence but there are special rules governing liability contained in two Acts of Parliament, the **Occupiers Liability Act 1957** and the **Occupiers Liability Act 1984**. The first deals with people who have permission to be on the property and the second with those who don't. The difference with the two **Occupiers Liability Acts** is that the duty is automatically owed by an occupier if the requirements of the Acts are met, so there is no need to prove a duty in the same way as for negligence under the common law. The rules on breach of duty and causation are the same though.

Example

The council is building a new swimming pool and there is a large hole on the site with no barriers. Fred is delivering materials to the site and falls into the hole and is injured. Fred can sue in negligence or under the **Occupiers Liability Act 1957**. In the latter case, he will not have to prove he is owed a duty by the council. Anyone in control of a property owes visitors a duty of care despite not being present at the time. If Fred had not been delivering, but had been trespassing on the site, he can still sue but he will have to use the **Occupiers Liability Act 1984**. The liability is more limited under this Act, and there are special rules.

A punctuation note: you may see the two Acts with and without the apostrophe. The government website uses an apostrophe in the **Occupiers' Liability Act 1957** but not in the **Occupiers Liability Act 1984**. For the sake of consistency, this book will not use the apostrophe when referring to either Act.

The final chapter for Year 1 is remedies. The usual remedy in tort is called damages, which is compensation for the harm or damage to property. This is the only remedy needed for the AS paper. The other remedy you need for A-level (an injunction) is discussed in the chapter on nuisance in Part 2 as that is where it applies.

Finally, there is a practice examination paper for AS. Although there is no external examination at the end of Year 1 if you are taking the full A-level this will help you to practise what you have studied.

Chapter 1 Rules and theory of tort law

This chapter covers an introduction to the nature of law (theories of law) in general, and in relation to tort specifically. The rule of law is part of the English legal system and needed for both AS and A level. I have included it here because, as with the other theories which come within the nature of law, you will need to be able to relate this to all areas of study. I have also included the other theories very briefly, so you can think about these in relation to the law of tort as you work through the book.

You may already have covered this part of the English legal system, this is just a summary.

The nature of law

The nature of law is essentially that it is based on rules. Legal liability occurs when the rules have been broken. To understand the nature of law we need to know a bit more about where the law comes from, what distinguishes a legal rule from other rules of behaviour, how a person may become liable in law and what differences there are between civil and criminal liability.

Sources of Law

We are governed by rules imposed by the state. This includes the courts, which produce common law through cases heard in court, and Parliament which produces statute law. Some (not many) laws come from custom, i.e., they have been going on for so long they are accepted as law even though not set out in a case or statute. These are all sources of law. Other sources of law today include European law and human rights law.

All these areas are covered elsewhere in the A level course under law-making and the English legal system. Here we are specifically looking at the (civil) law of tort, but remember nothing should be viewed in isolation so as you look at cases think about law-making (what was the source of law, was a precedent set, did a statute need to be interpreted?) and the English legal system (which courts were involved, which judges, was it an appeal case?).

Legal rules and liability in tort

Social rules are often referred to as norms. A norm can be described as the expected standard of behaviour within a society. However, both legal rules (law) and social rules (morals) are called norms by academics and lawyers. That is why it is important to be able to differentiate between law and morals (see Nature of law below). It is possible to say all rules are norms, but social norms are not enforced in a court of law whereas legal norms are.

There is no agreed definition of law. Essentially it is a matter of rules, but so is much a life. Therefore, a distinction needs to be made between enforceable legal rules and other rules of behaviour. There are many rules governing our lives but not all are enforceable. There may be rules governing how you behave in school or college, and there will be rules at home too. None of these rules have the force of law. A teacher or parent may punish (sanction) you for breaking these rules but there will be no such sanctions from a court of law.

Law is based on liability. A person is legally liable when accountable in law for something done/not done. There are two types of liability, criminal and civil, and both are based on the principle of individuals being responsible for their conduct.

Criminal liability is based on an individual's responsibility to the state and society as a whole

Civil liability is based on an individual's responsibility to other individuals

The main differences between criminal and civil liability are seen in the *consequences* not the deed. Harming someone is against the criminal law, but the victim (V) may want to sue in civil law to claim compensation for any injuries, so there is both criminal and civil liability. Here is a summary of the different types of action in court:

Criminal Law

    Proceedings are initiated by the Crown (Crown Prosecution Service)

    Proceedings are paid for by the State

    Cases commence in the Magistrates' Court

    Serious crimes are heard in the Crown Court

    The accused is prosecuted

    The burden of proof is on the prosecution

    The standard of proof is beyond reasonable doubt

    The primary purpose is punishment

    The case is in the form of R v Smith (R stands for Regina i.e., the Crown)

Civil Law

    Proceedings are initiated by the individual (the claimant)

    Proceedings are paid for by the parties (usually the loser)

    Cases commence in the County Court or High Court depending on the amount claimed

    The Defendant is sued

    The burden of proof is on the Claimant

    The standard of proof is the balance of probabilities

    The primary purpose is compensation, called damages

    The case is in the form of Smith v Brown (i.e., the parties to the dispute)

If you prefer diagrams:

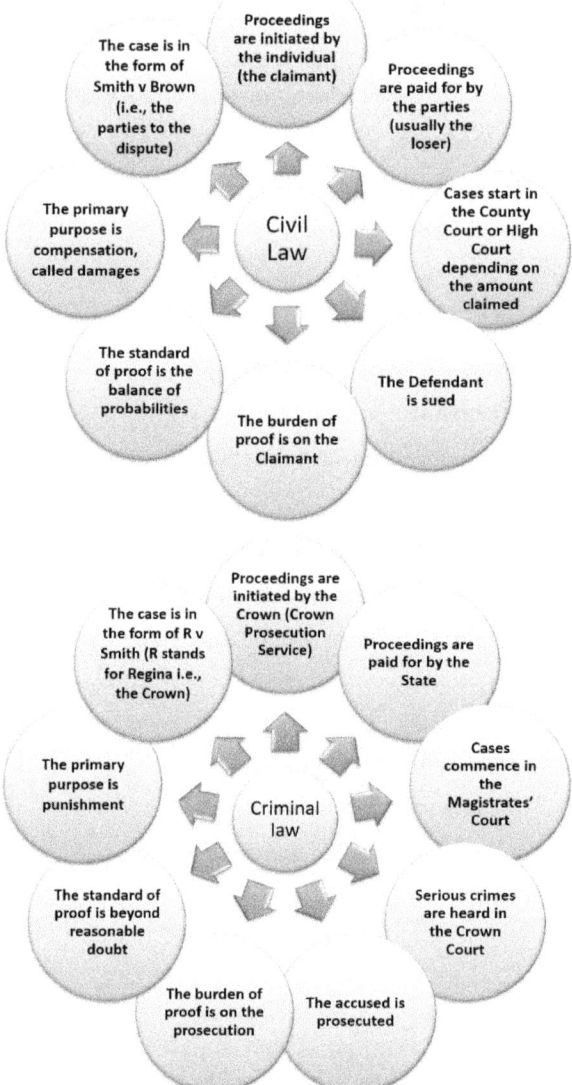

As this book deals with the civil law a little more on the background of civil liability is needed.

Civil liability occurs when someone has infringed the rights of another, e.g., the right not to be harmed or to enjoy one's property without interference. Both criminal and civil law are usually based on the principle of fault, so a person is not liable unless blameworthy. Both are also based on the principle of individual responsibility. However, both these principles are just that, principles not rules. There are exceptions and you will meet these when studying the law of tort in more detail. The main purpose of the civil law is to compensate the claimant (C) by awarding a remedy against the defendant (D). This is usually in the form of monetary compensation (called damages) but may also be an injunction (to stop the wrongdoing).

Tort is an important part of the civil law and protects a wide range of interests. These include physical harm (to a person or to property), psychiatric harm, financial interests and the use and enjoyment of land. Negligence is the most relevant tort in today's society and you will see examples of it daily in newspapers and other media. Negligence is based on not taking enough care to ensure people are kept safe from harm. I said in the introduction that a council could be liable for uneven pavements. This is because the council should take care to ensure residents are not harmed, so should fix the pavement or put up a sign. I am sure you have seen plenty of 'uneven pavement' signs. This is because the council wants to show it has taken sufficient care so cannot be successfully sued in court.

Example

I also mentioned suing McDonalds because the coffee was too hot and someone was scalded. The claim in the English courts failed, but in 2017, a woman successfully sued Starbucks in America because she was badly scalded when the lid popped off her coffee. The same could happen here because although you would expect coffee to be hot, so should take care yourself when drinking it, you would not expect the lid to pop off. Starbucks should have taken more care to ensure the lids were safe.

The theory and nature of law for A-level

The nature of law not only covers what law is and where it comes from, as well as the differences between civil and criminal law, but also includes how law operates in society, involving different theories (or concepts) of law which are studied for the full A-level. These are covered in depth in my book 'The Nature of Law for AQA and Eduqas A Level', as legal theory is a subject in its own right. The book also contains links to the legal system and the substantive law e.g., tort, crime, contract and human rights. The theories and concepts of law need to be related to all your other areas of study (i.e., they are synoptic) including what you study in Year 1, and not only to the substantive law but also to the legal system. The new A-level requires that you can use the substantive law to illustrate the concepts, and can discuss the concepts in the context of the substantive law. It is therefore a good idea to think about them, at least briefly, as you work through the rest of your studies, so I have included a short introduction here. There is a little more detail in 'The Bridge' between Parts 1 and 2 of this book to prepare you for Year 2.

Liability in tort is usually based on responsibility. However, sometimes it is based on policy. This means looking at the wider picture and at what is best for society as a whole. You will see this in particular with proving a duty of care in negligence. It also comes into the remedy of an injunction.

The other theories, or concepts, you will need for the A level are law and morals, law and justice, balancing competing interests and fault. These will not be tested at AS but for the A-level you will need to apply these theories to the areas of law studied in Year 1 as well as Year 2.

Here is a very brief explanation of each so that you can consider how they might apply in practice as you work through your course. Thus, if you see a case which you think was decided unfairly you can ask yourself whether the law is achieving justice, or whether the level of fault involved was properly reflected in the decision. This is just a taster; for examples which relate to the civil law studied in Year 1, and more on these concepts, see 'The Bridge' between Parts 1 and 2. For the rest of the course (Part 2 of this book) examples are given in each chapter under the heading 'Links to the non-substantive law'. These illustrate how the law works in practice in relation to such concepts as justice, morals, fault, and balancing competing interests. You will then have a store of cases you already know to use as examples in a question on any of these concepts in the A-level examination at the end of your course. I have not done this for Part 1 because if you are planning to stop at the AS you don't need to study these concepts.

Balancing competing interests – the law must balance different interests (or rights) between individuals (private interests), and between an individual and the state or society (the public interest), to achieve justice.

Fault – both civil and criminal liability is based (usually) on fault, or to put it another way a person is not liable unless blameworthy. Fault is an indicator of blame so it justifies the imposition of liability. You will see that the usual level of fault in tort is being negligent, not reaching the expected standard of someone in the same position and thereby causing another person harm or loss.

Morals – the law is only involved when someone breaks legal rules, not social (or moral) ones. However, legal rules and social rules share many characteristics. This is what law and morality is about: how far social and legal rules overlap and whether the law should be involved in moral issues. Sometimes the law must get involved because a moral issue comes up in court (examples are whether life support can be withdrawn from a patient in a coma and whether an anorexic teenager could be force-fed against her wishes).

Justice – justice is in the very nature of law e.g., when taking a case to court a person is hoping to achieve justice. Fairness and equality in the law are what justice means to most people, but there are other, more formal views of what justice means. One view of justice (called positivism) is that justice depends on legal rules. A law that is made properly using the correct procedures will be a just law whether or not it is moral. Another view of justice (called natural law) is that it is based on moral rules, so if a law is not moral it is not a true law. This shows the overlap between justice and morality.

Note that these concepts are not all on all papers (see the examination practice sections for a table of what goes where in each paper as regards the non-substantive law). For tort, you need fault and morals (and also balancing competing interests in regard to remedies) so concentrate on these. As you work through this book, ask yourself the following questions.

- *What is the fault element here?*
- *Is the level of fault reflected in the judge's decision on liability?*
- *Does the law involve morality?*
- *What interests are competing and how has the law balanced them?*

Linking the concepts with the law

AQA have confirmed that *"where appropriate, irrespective of the Paper to which a Nature of Law/ELS topic is assigned, examples may be drawn from the substantive law in other Papers"*. For the nature of law this means that although fault and morals are assigned to the tort paper (and balancing competing interests in regard to remedies), you can also use examples from crime, contract and/or human rights to illustrate these concepts. It is anyway a good idea to have a basic idea of each of the concepts as not only is there an overlap, but it will also give you a better understanding of how the legal theories can be related to the law in practice. The overlap can be seen in the case example in Task 1, where the court had to **balance the competing interests** of the public at large and the cricket club against those of the woman who was injured by a cricket ball. The public interest prevailed, as the availability of recreational sports is in the interests of society as a whole. The court found that the club had not been negligent so they were not at **fault**. This was because they had erected a high fence and taken other precautions to try to prevent balls going out of the cricket ground. When balancing interests the judge will try to achieve **justice**, but there is no agreed definition of what justice is and there is unlikely to be agreement on whether it was achieved. Finally, the woman may have felt she had a **moral** right to be compensated but she did not have a legal one because the club was found not to be blameworthy.

This first task gives you an idea of how you might think about these concepts as you read a particular case.

Task 1

In **Bolton v Stone 1951**, a woman was walking down a street near a cricket ground when she was hit and injured by a cricket ball. She sued the club and claimed compensation for her injuries. The court ruled that the club had not been negligent because they had erected a high fence and taken other precautions to try to prevent this happening.

Do you think the decision achieved justice?

What interests were balanced?

What role did fault play in the case?

What role did morality play?

The rule of law

When rules of law and procedure are formulated they should conform to the rule of law. This involves equality, clarity and fairness.

The law should apply to everyone equally and no-one should be above the law.

The law must be clear so that people know the rules (then if the rules are broken it will be fair to punish those at fault).

The law must be accessible so that if a person is accused of a crime it is only fair that access to justice and legal advice is possible.

This is a simplified description of the rule of law, and it applies not only to Paper 1 at AS but also to Paper 3 for the A level, so needs further discussion.

 **The Rule of Law**

The **Constitutional Reform Act 2005** refers to the rule of law, and the Lord Chancellor's oath requires the Lord Chancellor to respect the rule of law, but there is no agreed definition of it. An early view of the rule of law is that formulated by Dr Thomas Fuller in 1733: "Be you ever so high, the law is above you". This view has continued for centuries. In **Evans v AG 2015**, the SC ruled that correspondence between Prince Charles and government ministers should be made public under the **Freedom of Information Act** and said it was "fundamental to the rule of law" that decisions and actions of the executive are subject to review in a court of law.

The rule of law was popularised by A. V. Dicey (a constitutional lawyer) the following century who, in summary, said "everyone, whatever his rank, is subject to the ordinary law of the land". A little more recently, Lord Bingham said "If you maltreat a penguin in the London zoo, you do not escape prosecution because you are the Archbishop of Canterbury". So, an important part of the rule of law is that everyone is subject to it, with no exceptions. There is more to it than that, and opinions differ on what it means in the modern sense. Although the rule of law is a somewhat abstract notion, to try to explain it today a good place to start is with Lord Bingham's 2014 lecture on the subject, taken from his book 'The Rule of Law'. The core principle is as above, that no-one is above the law, including those who make it. He notes that the rule of law has evolved and continues to do so, and sets out eight sub-rules which he feels describe the rule of law in its current form. These are:

Law must be accessible. This means that if people are bound by the law they must be able to know what the law is.

Questions of legal rights and liabilities should be resolved by application of the law and not be a matter of discretion. This does not mean there is absolutely no discretion. A judge must exercise a certain amount of discretion when deciding on an appropriate sentence or remedy – the point is that any such discretion is limited by law, e.g., statutes or earlier decisions.

The law should apply equally to all. This is accepted by most people as being part of any rule of law but Lord Bingham points out that in practice it is not always apparent. An example is the various **Terrorism Acts** where non-nationals suspected of terrorism are subject to being locked up without trial, but nationals are not – even though they pose the same threat. It is arguable that anyone subject to national laws should be entitled to the law's protection. Even where the law appears to apply equally it may not in practice. It is true that the Archbishop of Canterbury is not above the law – but if he does mistreat a penguin he can probably afford a decent lawyer to help his case! The **Legal Aid, Sentencing and Punishment of Offenders Act 2012 (LASPO)**, has severely reduced access to justice and legal aid, especially in civil cases.

The law should adequately protect fundamental human rights. This is perhaps a more recent addition to the concept of the rule of law. The preamble to the **Universal Declaration of Human Rights** says that if people are not to be compelled to rebel against tyranny and oppression that "human rights should be protected by the rule of law".

The state must meet its obligations under international law. Thus an act by a state that is unlawful would be against the rule of law. He referred to the war against Iraq and whilst not saying whether or not he believed it to be illegal, he did say that if it *was* illegal then it would be against the rule of law "if this sub-rule is sound".

Means must be provided for resolving civil disputes. He says that if people are bound by the law they should receive its benefits and should be able to go to court to have their rights and liberties determined "in the last resort". He does not rule out less formal methods of resolving disputes but sees access to the courts as a "basic right" adding that legal advice should be affordable and available without excessive delay. Where the first sub-rule requires law to be accessible in the sense of clarity, this sub-rule requires accessibility in terms of cost. It has been said that justice is open to all "like the Ritz hotel" – meaning that everyone may be entitled to it but many are unable to use it in practice due to lack of money. Going back to the mistreatment of penguins, the Archbishop is more likely to be able to afford to go to the Ritz and to gain access to justice than the average person on the street is, especially since **LASPO**.

All public officials must exercise their power reasonably and not exceed its limits. As with the second rule, this rule is against the arbitrary use of power. An example of its application is that everyone has the right to apply for judicial review of a decision made by public officers and government ministers – a judge cannot overturn such a decision, but can rule that it is unreasonable.

Adjudicative procedures must be fair. This means open court hearings, the right to be heard, the right to know what the charges and evidence against you are, that the decision maker is independent and impartial, and that in criminal cases D is innocent until guilt is proved. Fairness would also cover access to justice in both the earlier senses of clarity and cost.

Lord Bingham sees the rule of law as depending on an unspoken bargain between the individual and the state. The citizen sacrifices some freedom by accepting legal constraints on certain activities, and the state sacrifices some power by recognising it cannot do all that it has the power to do. He concludes that this means those who maintain and protect the rule of law are "guardians of an all but sacred flame which animates and enlightens the society in which we live".

To sum up the rule of law:

No-one is above the law

Everyone is subject to the law, not the arbitrary exercise of power

The law must encompass clarity, access to justice, fairness and an independent and impartial judiciary

The law must apply equally

In Lord Bingham's view, the rule of law should also protect human rights and comply with international obligations if it is to apply to a modern state with national and international commitments. Bear that in mind if you will be studying human rights for Paper 3.

As you study the law try to consider whether the rule of law is being upheld.

Chapter 2 Duty of Care for physical harm and damage to property

"You must take reasonable care to avoid acts or omissions which you can reasonably foresee would be likely to injure your neighbour" – Lord Atkin

By the end of this chapter you should be able to:

- **Explain the rules on how to prove a person is owed a duty of care by another**
- **Show how the law applies by reference to cases**
- **Identify problems with the law and/or discuss its development in order to evaluate it**

Here we will look at how to prove a duty of care in relation to physical harm caused by someone's negligence. This is important because if there is no duty, the claim will fail. There will be no need to consider breach of that duty or causation.

Whether there is a duty is based on what is called the 'neighbour principle' from **Donoghue v Stevenson 1932**. This case is famous for establishing liability in negligence, and is often referred to as 'the snail in the ginger beer case'. Ask anyone who has ever studied law and they will know it.

Mrs Donoghue was in a café with her friend. She drank some ginger beer with her ice cream, and later she emptied the rest of the contents into a glass. To her horror a decomposing snail came out. She was ill (whether from drinking the beer or from seeing the snail in its state of decomposition is not clear) and sued the manufacturer. As her friend had paid, there was an important legal issue to consider. Mrs Donoghue was owed no duty under contract law because she did not buy the drink herself. The case eventually went to the HL on the issue of whether the manufacturer could owe a duty to a consumer who did not buy the goods. Lord Atkin gave the leading and produced the now famous 'neighbour test'. He said that the biblical requirement that we must 'love our neighbour' became, in law, that we must not injure our neighbour. He said, *"You must take reasonable care to avoid acts or omissions which you can reasonably foresee would be likely to injure your neighbour"*. He then goes on to pose the question *"who then, in law, is my neighbour?"* and answers, *"persons who are so closely and directly affected by my act that I ought reasonably to have them in contemplation as being so affected when I am directing my mind to the acts or omissions which are called in question"*

So a precedent was set. Tort law now protects those without a contract.

Example

I am baby-sitting for someone at work and being paid. I have a contract so there is no problem – I owe a duty under the contract and can be sued if the baby is harmed due to my negligence. However, if I am doing it for free, perhaps for a friend, then there is no contract. Since

Donoghue, I can be sued in tort, as I owe a duty to anyone affected by my acts or omissions. The baby would be someone I would have in mind when I am contemplating, or thinking about, doing (or omitting to do), whatever is being questioned – my negligent action (or inaction).

In **Grant v Australian Knitting Mills 1935**, a man had bought some underpants and contracted a skin disease due to a chemical in the material. In deciding the manufacturer owed him a duty of care the court followed the case of **Donoghue v Stevenson**. A person (the consumer) wearing a manufacturer's products (in this case the underpants) is someone likely to be *closely and directly affected* by the manufacturer's actions (producing the underpants). The manufacturer, therefore, ought *reasonably to have them in contemplation* when making the product, so the consumer satisfies the 'neighbour' test and the manufacturer owes them a duty of care.

The test is essentially one of foreseeability. If the result of your actions may foreseeably harm someone, you will owe that someone a duty of care.

Task 2

You may not be able to remember the entire quote so write out Lord Atkin's neighbour test in full, but then put it in your own words so it is clear to you. Then note how it would have applied in **Donoghue v Stevenson**.

Over the next few decades the courts were reluctant to extend the law further. Then, in the 60s, they became more expansive, and a high point was reached in **Anns v Merton LBC 1978**. I am not repeating the facts here as what followed was a retreat from this case and it was later overruled in **Murphy v Brentwood BC 1990**. It is mentioned to highlight the turning point from the wider to the narrower tests for proving duty. In **Anns** a claim had been allowed where no damage had been done but negligent building inspections had led to a reduction in the value of the property. In **Murphy**, which was also a claim for loss of value, the HL specifically rejected such claims and ruled that **Anns** was no longer good law.

Later judges then began to use an incremental approach, i.e., not expanding in great leaps but bit by bit, case by case. A line from an Australian case has been quoted with much approval. The case is **Sutherland Shire County v Heyman 1985**, and the Judge, Brennan J, said,

> "It is preferable, in my view, that the law should develop novel categories of negligence incrementally and by analogy with established categories."

In **Caparo v Dickman 1990**, these words were approved by the HL. The HL said that there was no general principle which applied to all cases and it was necessary to consider whether imposing a duty was 'just and reasonable' in the circumstances. A three-part test was established.

The Caparo test

For a duty to arise:

- **there must be foreseeability of harm**

- there must be proximity between C and D
- it must be fair, just and reasonable to impose a duty on D

Key case

In **Caparo**, C had claimed that the auditors of a company's books owed him a duty of care. They had produced inaccurate accounts and he had lost money by investing in the company. Arguably, it was foreseeable that people in his position, who had relied on the accounts, would suffer loss. The HL held, however, that there was no proximity between him and the auditors. The auditors produced the accounts for the company, to comply with the legal requirements to produce annual accounts, not for potential investors. Nor was it fair, just and reasonable to make the auditors liable for losses to unknown investors.

Key principle: The three-part test was established to decide on whether a duty is owed, adding to the principle from **Donoghue v Stevenson 1932**.

The first two parts of the **Caparo** test are similar to the neighbour test from **Donoghue**. The third is a matter of what is fair in the circumstances of the particular case.

In brief:

Caparo	Donoghue	Meaning
It must be foreseeable that someone will be harmed by D's actions	D should have that someone 'in contemplation' when acting	'someone' is a group, or class, of people not an individual. Thus a duty was owed to all consumers, not to Mrs Donoghue in particular. It is foreseeable that a consumer will be affected by the act or omission of a manufacturer.
There is proximity between C & D	C is D's 'neighbour'	There is some kind of legal connection or relationship between C & D
It is fair, just and reasonable to impose a duty on D	Not specifically mentioned, although it was arguably the attempt to achieve justice that extended the law	A matter of policy, of what is right in the circumstances

The **Caparo** case involved economic loss rather than physical harm, but the 3-stage test applies to all types of harm. It is applied more strictly in relation to economic loss and psychiatric harm, and we will look at these in Part 2. In **Caparo** itself, Lord Roskill recognised that *"there is no simple formula or touchstone"* for deciding whether to impose liability. The third part of the test allows for a certain amount of flexibility, based on what is 'fair' in the circumstances.

Evaluation pointer

Do you think that the incremental approach is a good one? Arguably it is leaving a lot to the individual judge on the particular facts of a case leading to uncertainty in the law. The fact that **Caparo** provides a test, but at the same time makes it clear that it may not always apply, is also somewhat problematic. Should there be a clearer set of rules? Would this make the law too rigid? There is always a need for a balance to be struck between certainty and flexibility. People need to know what the law is so that it can be relied on, but at the same time the law may need to adapt to the circumstances.

Let's look at the 3 issues established in **Caparo**.

Foreseeability

It must be foreseeable that D's act (or omission) could cause harm to someone in the same circumstances, or in the same position as C, not necessarily the particular C. Thus in **Donoghue v Stevenson 1932**, it can be said to be foreseeable that the manufacturer's act (of allowing a snail to get in the bottle), or omission (the failure to clean the bottles properly), could harm someone in Mrs Donoghue's position (a consumer of ginger beer).

Despite Lord Atkin's words in **Donoghue** that you should avoid acts or omissions which *"you"* can foresee might injure your neighbour; the test for foreseeability is an objective one. It is what the *reasonable person* foresees, not what D foresees.

Example

In **Kent v Griffiths 2000**, a doctor called an ambulance for a woman who had an asthma attack. Despite only being a few miles away, it took nearly 40 minutes to arrive and she suffered respiratory arrest. The ambulance service argued that there was no duty of care. The CA held that it was reasonably foreseeable that a person could suffer further harm as a result of a delay and there was no good reason for the delay. A duty was owed.

In **Topp v London County Bus Ltd 1993**, a driver had left the bus with the keys in it and someone stole the bus! The bus company was found not liable as this was not foreseeable.

Task 3

Read the **Donoghue** case and answer the following questions.

Why couldn't Mrs Donoghue sue the shopkeeper?

Whom did she sue and what did the HL decide?

In what way do you think the manufacturer was negligent?

Proximity

The concepts of foreseeability and proximity overlap. The more proximate you are to someone, the more foreseeable it is that his or her actions may harm you. In **Bourhill v Young 1943**, a woman heard a motorcycle crash and went to the scene after the rider's body had been taken away. She saw blood on the road and then claimed that the shock caused her to miscarry and lose her baby. She failed in her claim, as she hadn't actually seen the accident. It was not *foreseeable* that she would be harmed nor was she in close *proximity*. It would be different for a passenger, who would be affected by a driver's actions so would be owed a duty of care. Also for a pedestrian near to where someone is driving, who could also be affected and so be owed a duty. However, she was not in the vicinity so would not be foreseeably affected by the driver's actions. It is not just physical proximity, however, but whether the *relationship* between the parties is proximate enough.

Examples

In **Donoghue v Stevenson**, the relationship was one between a manufacturer and consumers. In **Caparo v Dickman**, there was proximity of relationship between the auditors and the company whose accounts they did, but not between the auditors and investors. The latter relationship was not sufficiently close, or 'proximate'.

In **Kent v Griffiths** the CA also held that the ambulance service was in sufficiently close proximity to a patient once it had accepted the call and sent an ambulance to collect that patient.

Fair, just and reasonable to impose a duty

The last point is a matter of public policy. This is perhaps the most difficult of the three. It means that the court looks at what is best for society as a whole and/or may restrict the duty to avoid 'opening the floodgates' to claims, especially where these would be paid by public funds. Some examples should help clarify this. In each area I have included a case where it was held to be fair to impose a duty and another where it was not, so you can compare these.

Examination pointer

You don't need to learn all the cases, there are a lot in tort as it is mostly based on case law. However, the more examples you know the more you can see how the law is applied in practice. It is also useful to be able to cite a case where there was a duty and another where there was not, as this will help you support your answer in an examination whatever your conclusion is. Do make sure you understand all 'key cases' though, these are the 'must know' cases.

Police, councils and sporting bodies

The courts are reluctant to impose a duty on those providing a public service. Actions against public bodies such as the police, hospitals, rescue services and local councils may therefore fail on this point. This means that the courts may refuse to impose a duty on such groups, even though harm is foreseeable, as a matter of public policy.

Key case

In **Hill v CC for West Yorkshire 1988**, a consequence of the 'Yorkshire ripper' case, the police were held not to owe a duty to potential victims of a crime after releasing a suspected killer through lack of evidence. When he killed again the mother of the victim sued the police, claiming they owed a duty to her daughter. The HL refused to find a duty, partly on lack of proximity between the police and an unknown member of the public. However, the policy issue also arose. The HL felt that the threat of being sued could make the police less efficient in carrying out their duties. This would not be in the public interest.

Key principle: It is not in the public interest for the police to owe a duty to unknown members of the public.

In **Smith v CC of Sussex Police 2008**, (full name **Van Colle and another v CC of Hertfordshire Police**; **Smith v CC of Sussex Police 2008**, as it was a joint appeal), a claim was brought by the victim of a violent attack, who had told police about threats to him by his ex-partner. When the attack materialised, he argued that the police owed him a duty to take reasonable steps to prevent the injury occurring. Harm was foreseeable as the police knew about the threats and the whereabouts of the person from whom they came. The CA held that the police were liable. The HL considered the 'policy' element of the three-fold test as stated in **Caparo v Dickman 1990** and applied in **Hill**, and noted that the 'core principle' of such cases was that imposing a duty would be detrimental to good policing, as it might make the police defensive and unwilling to take risks. The HL declined to move away from this principle and reversed the decision of the CA. No duty of care was owed.

The police do not, however, have immunity from owing a duty. There have been several successful claims against the police where there has been a greater degree of proximity between them and C. This shows that all three parts of the test are connected. The more foreseeable something is, and the greater the degree of proximity, the more likely it is that it will be fair, just and reasonable to impose a duty. In **Reeves v MPC 1999**, the police were held to owe a duty to a prisoner who committed suicide while in their care and whom they knew to be a suicide risk. The police had left the door flap open and he used it to hang himself. An important factor in **Reeves** was that the police *knew* that he was a suicide risk. In another suicide case, **Orange v CC of West Yorkshire Police 2001**, a similar claim failed. In this case a man, who hanged himself while in custody after being arrested whilst drunk, was *not* a known suicide risk.

Example of applying the test

Reeves can be used to illustrate all three parts of the test. Harm was *foreseeable* because the police knew that he was a suicide risk. There was *proximity* between C and the police because he was in one of the police cells. In such circumstances it seems *fair, just and reasonable* to impose a duty on the police to the group of people – prisoners – who are in their care. There were no policy reasons to exclude a duty as it was to a limited, and known, group and imposing a duty in these circumstances would not lead to a flood of claims.

Kent v Griffiths an also be used to illustrate all three parts of the test. We saw above that there was foreseeability of harm because of the delay, and there was proximity between an ambulance service and the person it was sent to collect. In deciding there was a duty of care, the CA also considered this last factor and held that where no good reason for a delay is given it is fair, just and reasonable that an ambulance service should owe a duty of care as regards the promptness of the pickup of a patient. This case distinguished cases against the police such as **Hill v CC for West Yorkshire** as here there was a specific patient who would be affected by the delay, not the public in general. Again it would not lead to a flood of claims.

The issue of policy and references to several other cases seen in this chapter were raised in the next case, the principles of which could also apply to other public bodies.

Key case

In **Michael v CC of South Wales 2015**, the SC followed **Hill** in slightly different circumstances. Here the victim had telephoned the police to report an attack by a former partner, the police had failed to respond in time and she died. The majority felt that **Hill** should be followed and said that the public at large should not bear the burden of compensating a victim for harm caused by a third party for whom the state was not responsible, adding "to impose such a burden would be contrary to the ordinary principles of the common law". The question was not whether the police should have a special immunity, but whether an exception should be made to the common law principles which had been applied in many cases involving public authorities of some kind. Two dissenting judges felt that **Hill** could be distinguished because there was a closer proximity, as she had called the police. Overall, the SC noted that the concepts of proximity and fairness overlapped but that public policy considerations (placing too much of a burden on the police and on the public purse) outweighed the fact that there was a closer proximity in this case than in **Hill**. The SC suggested the problem was an inadequate criminal compensation scheme, not a failure of the common law, concluding that it was for Parliament to act if the law should be changed, not the courts.

Key principle: The public should not bear the cost of compensating a victim injured by a third party.

This was followed in **CLG v CC of Merseyside Police 2015**, where the police had allowed the address of witnesses in a case to be made available to the accused. The witnesses had moved because they feared violence from the accused and sued the police for negligently allowing their new address to be obtained by the accused. The CA restated that no duty was owed to members of the general public unless there were special circumstances, such as the police taking on an assumption of responsibility for the victim (as in **Reeves**).

Local councils also have some immunity, again depending on the circumstances. In **Fernquest v Swansea CC 2011**, a man sued the council after slipping on ice at a bus stop. The judge applied **Caparo v Dickman 1990** and held that there was proximity between the parties and the risk of injury was foreseeable as the council knew about the ice. However, the CA reversed the decision and held that although injury was foreseeable, it was not fair, just and reasonable to impose a duty of care on a council for 'normal hazards' which members of the public could be expected to be aware of.

Again, as with the police, immunity is not absolute and the higher the risk of harm (foreseeability) and the closer the proximity, the more likely a duty will be owed. In **Vernon**

Knight Associates v Cornwall CC 2013, the CA held that a council owed a duty to local residents to keep drains clear to prevent flooding. It was therefore liable when it failed to do so. The council knew the risk of flooding during times of heavy rainfall and had previously taken steps to keep the drains clear. Flooding was highly foreseeable and there was a close relationship between a council and local residents. It was therefore fair, just and reasonable to impose a duty.

Evaluation pointer

In deciding whether imposing a duty is 'fair, just and reasonable' the courts are presumably taking into account how far councils with limited budgets should be expected to use their funds in a particular way. The money would have to come from another area. The courts are balancing the rights of people harmed to compensation, and the burden to the council – and therefore to local residents – of imposing too strict a duty. How far do you think the courts should decide such matters of public policy? Arguably, this is a job better suited to an elected government.

Although sporting activities are seen as for the public benefit, it has been held to be 'fair, just and reasonable' to impose a duty in many situations. In **Watson v British Boxing Board 2000**, the boxer Michael Watson suffered head injuries during a fight against Chris Eubank. He sued the Board on the basis that had proper medical treatment been given at the ringside he would not have suffered brain damage. The CA found that it was 'just and reasonable' to impose a duty on the Board to ensure adequate medical facilities were available, and upheld his claim. A similar decision was made in **Vowles v Evans 2003**, where a player was injured in an amateur rugby match when a scrum collapsed. Without going into the finer details of the rules of rugby, the essence was that the scrum collapsed due to the referee not applying the rules properly, and the player sued. Allowing his claim, the judge said that the rapport between referee and players is crucial to a good game of rugby, and would not be lessened by the knowledge that the referee owed a duty of care for the players' safety. (Unlike **Hill v CC for West Yorkshire 1988** where it was thought police efficiency *would* be lessened by such knowledge.) Applying **Caparo v Dickman 1990**, the CA held that as a matter of policy it is 'just and reasonable' that the law should impose a duty to take reasonable care for the players' safety. This could be achieved by the sensible and appropriate application of the laws of the game. Thus, there will usually be a duty in sporting cases, mainly because in most sporting situations there is foreseeability of harm and a close relationship (proximity) so that it is fair to impose a duty.

Task 4

What type of relationship might there be in a sporting situation? See if you can think of three people who would be likely to owe an injured player a duty of care.

Hospitals will owe patients a duty of care in most cases (there are several examples in the next two chapters showing a duty was established, but where the claim then failed on either breach or causation). However, it is clear from the following case that this is not an unlimited duty, and individuals are expected to take some responsibility for their own actions.

In **Darnley v Croydon NHS Trust 2017**, a man attended an Accident and Emergency department after being injured in an attack, and was told he would have to wait for up to four or five hours. He was in pain so left after only a matter of minutes, not realising that he would have been seen by a triage nurse earlier than that. His condition later got worse and he sued the hospital, saying that his decision to leave was based on incorrect information and had he stayed he would not have suffered a greater degree of harm. The court applied the **Caparo v Dickman 1990** test and held that it would not be fair, just and reasonable to impose a duty on the hospital for the failure by the receptionists to inform him of the likely waiting time to be seen by a triage nurse. He should take responsibility for the consequences of his decision, not the hospital or its reception staff. The CA agreed and rejected C's appeal.

Lawyers

Lawyers acting for a client in court enjoyed immunity from being sued in negligence but the law has developed over time. In **Rondel v Worsley 1969**, lawyers were held not to owe a duty of care to a client for negligent advocacy work in court. In **Hall v Simons 2000**, the HL used the 1966 Practice Statement to overrule its decision in **Rondel** and removed this immunity. This effectively means that a negligent lawyer will be treated in the same way as any other defendant, so that if there is foreseeability and proximity the lawyer will usually owe a duty and there is no longer a policy reason to exclude such professionals.

Evaluation pointer

Again, the courts are deciding cases on grounds of public policy rather than merely applying the law. Matters of policy are what democratically elected governments are for, and it is debatable whether it should be the role of non-elected judges. However, there is also an argument that the law needs to keep up with the times and that it has to react immediately to a given situation – and that is something governments can take too long about.

Liability for omissions

In **Donoghue v Stevenson 1932**, Lord Atkin referred to *"acts or omissions"*. This means D can be liable for *not* doing something, as well as doing something negligently. There may be liability for an omission when there is a particularly close relationship, such as that between an employer and employee, or where there is a high degree of control by one person over another. There will be a duty to take care of that person's safety, and failure to do so may result in liability, e.g., not preventing a suicide in **Reeves v MPC 1999**.

Where there is a risk of harm and that risk was created, or known about, by D there is a duty to take steps to avoid harming anyone. This is true even if the danger has actually been created by a third party, as long as D knew of it. In **Smith v Littlewoods 1987**, an owner of a disused cinema had left his property unsecured and vandals broke in. They caused a fire which spread to a neighbour's property. The omission here was not locking up properly. The neighbour sued the cinema owner on the basis that this omission had caused the fire damage. The claim failed but had the owner known of the vandals he would have been obliged to act to prevent harm to others. The claim also failed on the issue of causation (D successfully argued that the act of the vandals had broken the chain of causation between the omission and the fire). We will look at this case again with causation but it illustrates that there can be liability for an omission as well for an act.

The issue of omissions connects with foreseeability. If D had known of the vandals breaking into the cinema then the damage would be more foreseeable and so a greater obligation to take care would arise. However, the court made clear that a property owner is not expected to put a 24-hour guard on the property to ensure nobody enters it and creates of risk of damage to neighbouring property.

Examination pointer

Note the words of Brennan J. He said that the courts should develop *novel* categories of negligence incrementally and by analogy with established categories. This means that you should only need to use the 3-part test where it is a new situation, one which has not been to court before. If this is the case (e.g., it has already been established that a manufacturer owes a duty to a consumer), deal with the test very briefly. An examiner may use a scenario where there is a clear duty because you are expected to focus on another issue, like breach or causation.

Summary of duty of care for physical harm

Donoghue v Stevenson 1932 – the neighbour test on foreseeability

Caparo v Dickman 1990 – the 3-part test

- *Is there foreseeability of harm?*
- *Is there proximity between the parties?*
- *Is it fair, just and reasonable to impose a duty? This is a matter of public policy.*

Links to the non-substantive law

For links to the English legal system, look back at the diagram and examples in the introduction to Part 1. In particular, where a principle of law has been established the system of appeals is relevant, as these principles are established in the higher appeal courts, i.e., the CA and SC. Alternative dispute resolution (ADR) is always relevant to tort cases too, as is access to justice, because cases can be expensive to take to court so alternatives or help with expenses may be needed.

Self-test Questions

1. What did Brennan J say in **Sutherland Shire County**?
2. What is the 3-part **Caparo** test?

3. Who might be immune from owing a duty?

4. Why was there no duty in **Bourhill v Young**?

5. Why was no duty owed in **Caparo**?

Answers to the tasks and self-test questions are on my website at www.drsr.org. Please click on 'Answers to tasks'. For a range of free interactive exercises, click on 'Free Exercises'.

Chapter 3 Breach of duty

"We must not look at the 1947 accident with 1954 spectacles" – Denning LJ

By the end of this chapter you should be able to:

- *Identify the standard expected of people in deciding whether there is a breach*
- *Explain what factors are considered in assessing this standard*
- *Recognise that it is an objective test, but also identify the subjective element*
- *Show how the law is applied by reference to cases*
- *Identify any problems to evaluate the law on breach*

A breach of duty occurs when D has not taken sufficient care, i.e., has been negligent. There is no set standard by which a person's conduct is measured. It is an objective test, and the courts will consider what a reasonable person would have done given the same circumstances.

The standard of care expected

In **Blyth v Birmingham Waterworks Co. 1856**, Baron Alderson said:

"Negligence is the omission to do something which a reasonable man ... would do, or doing something which a prudent and reasonable man would not do."

We would say 'reasonable person' now, and it is a reasonable person in the particular circumstances D is in.

We saw in **Vowles v Evans 2003**, that a referee in an amateur rugby match owed a duty of care for the players' safety. By allowing an inexperienced player to play in a scrum position for which he was not trained the referee was in breach of his duty. He hadn't reached the standard expected of a reasonable person in those circumstances, i.e., *a reasonable referee.*

In **Harris v Perry 2008**, a couple hired a bouncy castle for a birthday party and a boy was seriously injured by another child while playing on it. The judge held they had breached their duty of care by not supervising the children at all times. There was a higher risk of harm because children of different ages, and sizes, were playing together. The CA reversed the decision and held the standard of care required was that of a *reasonably careful parent*. Would a reasonably careful parent have acted in the same way and what precautions should reasonably have been taken to protect against risks which ought to have been known? The CA held that it was impossible to avoid all risk that children might injure themselves or each other when playing together. It was impractical for parents to keep children under constant surveillance or supervision and it would not be in the public interest to impose a duty upon them to do so. In deciding they were not in breach the CA referred to the incident as *"a freak and tragic accident"*.

In **Daw v Intel Corp (UK) Ltd 2007**, an employer knew an employee was suffering from severe stress but did little to remedy the situation. The CA upheld the decision that help had not been adequately provided so the employer had not reached the standard expected of a *reasonable employer* and was in breach of duty. The CA also restated the factors which apply in establishing breach and said an employer is only in breach of duty if there is a failure to take the steps which are reasonable in the circumstances, bearing in mind the magnitude of the risk of harm occurring, the gravity of the harm which may occur, the costs and practicability of preventing it, and the justifications for taking the risk.

You should be able to explain and apply these four factors, with a case on each.

The factors

The magnitude of risk

The greater the risk of harm, the greater is the obligation on D to take precautions. However, no breach will have occurred if the risk was impossible to foresee. In **Fardon v Harcourt-Rivington 1932**, D's car was parked on a street with a dog inside. As C walked past the dog jumped up and broke the window and some glass went in C's eye. The HL held there was no duty to guard against "fantastic possibilities". Similarly, **in Scott v Gavigan 2016**, C had run into the road and been hit by D, who was riding a moped. C had given no indication of any intention to cross the road and his progress down the pavement had indicated the opposite. The CA upheld the judge's finding that it was not foreseeable, and said D did not have to take steps to avoid a risk of which he neither had been, nor should have been, aware.

Whether something is foreseeable is judged at the time of the incident. In **Roe v Ministry of Health 1954**, contamination of an anaesthetic left C paralysed. Medical knowledge at the time was not such that this could have been expected; in fact, it was this event that alerted the medical profession to the problem. There was no known, or foreseeable, risk, so the Ministry of Health was not liable. The court will not use hindsight to assess this. In **Roe**, Denning LJ made the comment opening this Chapter. It is whether the risk of harm was foreseeable *at the time*. A more recent example is **Maguire v Harland & Wolff plc 2005**. C's husband was exposed to asbestos dust at work, but he did not become ill, *she* did. She claimed damages on the basis that she was exposed to the dust he brought home. The judge found in her favour, saying that it was reasonably foreseeable that there was a serious risk to her health. The CA allowed D's appeal. At the time of C's exposure the risks of secondary exposure were unknown. The injury to a member of C's family was therefore not foreseeable. In **Williams v University of Birmingham 2011**, a physics student who had been exposed to low levels of asbestos over 30 years before he became ill, sued the University. The CA held that the lack of knowledge of the dangers of exposure to small amounts of asbestos at the time meant the University had not breached its duty.

If the risk is foreseeable, but small, the other factors will be relevant in deciding whether D had done enough. In **Bolton v Stone 1951**, a woman was hit by a cricket ball whilst walking near a cricket ground. The cricket club had taken precautions by erecting a 17-foot fence and the ball had gone over it only a matter of 5 or 6 times in some 35 years. There was thus a foreseeable, but only very small, risk of a ball going over and, balanced against the other factors, the club had done all that was expected of it. Similarly, in **Gray v Workington Golf Club 2016**, a man hit by a golf ball failed in his claim because the trajectory of the ball could not have been foreseen so the consequences could not reasonably have been prevented.

This shows that where the magnitude of risk is low there is unlikely to be a breach. In **Blair-Ford v CRS Adventures Ltd 2012**, C took part in a 'welly-wanging' contest at an activity centre. He was throwing a wellington boot backwards between his legs when he overbalanced and broke his neck. He sued for compensation. The judge ruled that it was a freak and tragic accident and rejected his claim. In **Uren v Corporate Leisure 2013**, a man who was injured during a game at an RAF base sued the organisers of the game and the Ministry of Defence in negligence. The game involved running to an inflatable pool and then getting over the side to retrieve a piece of fruit floating in the water. C dived in head first and broke his neck. He argued that as the water was shallow going in head-first should have been prohibited. At trial, the court found that although there was some risk of harm from such an activity it was very small, and the existence of such a small risk along with the fact there was some social value to outdoor activities, meant there was no breach of duty. This seems similar to **Blair-Ford v CRS Adventures Ltd**. However, after an appeal a retrial was ordered and the decision reversed, this time the court said the harm was more than minimally foreseeable and D should have taken precautions to avoid it.

The gravity of the potential harm

A higher standard of care may be required where, although the *risk* is small, the *consequences* may be serious. This can be seen in **Paris v Stepney BC 1951**, where C was a garage worker who was already blind in one eye. Whilst trying to loosen a rusty bolt on a car axle he was injured by a chip of metal in the other eye. His employer had goggles on the premises but only issued them to welders. C's job only involved a slight risk of injury, but the HL held that although a failure to provide goggles would not always make the council liable to their employees, in this case the seriousness of the harm that *could* occur was very great. There was therefore a duty to take greater care to ensure the worker was safe by providing him with goggles.

Examination pointer

The **Paris** case shows that a greater duty is owed to those suffering under a disability. This would also apply to children or the elderly, so look for clues in the scenario. What may be doing enough in respect of a fully able person may not be so in other cases. Note also that it is *potential* harm that is looked at. Don't be tempted to say that there is a breach because the harm actually suffered is very great. It is what harm *might* occur that is relevant, not what *has* occurred.

The cost and practicality of taking precautions

D may argue that avoiding a risk altogether would be too costly. The courts are unlikely to accept risk-taking based *solely* on the cost of avoidance, but it may tip the balance when considering the other factors. In **Latimer v AEC 1952**, the HL found a factory owner not liable for the injury to an employee who slipped on a wet floor. It was wet due to exceptional rain and flooding, and the owners had put down sand and taken other precautions. On the facts they had done enough. Shutting the factory would not only have been costly, but also impractical.

Example

If everyone drove at 5 mph. there would be fewer road accidents, but no one would expect the government to rule that such precautions should be taken. That would be impractical. In **Bolton v Stone**, the cricket club had already built a high fence – arguably, it would be impractical to do more than they had done, as in **Latimer**. By comparison, in **Paris v Stepney BC**, it would have been neither costly nor impractical to provide goggles.

If it is relatively simple to take precautions against the risk then these will be expected of a 'reasonable person' so D will be more likely to be found in breach if precautions are not taken. In **Vernon Knight Associates v Cornwall CC 2013**, the CA held the council owed a duty to do "*that which was reasonable in all the circumstances to minimise the known risk of flood damage*". What was reasonable would be assessed by reference to all the circumstances, including the extent of the foreseeable risk, the available preventive measures, the costs of such measures and the parties' resources. Although precautions had usually been taken to minimise the risk of flooding by clearing the drains, on two particular occasions these precautions had not been taken. The council was therefore in breach of duty.

In **Uren v Corporate Leisure 2013**, discussed above, the court held that even though the risk was small and there was some social benefit, more precautions should have been taken such as banning diving head first. This can be compared to **Bolton v Stone 1951** and shows how the factors are balanced against each other.

The **Compensation Act 2006 s 1** provides that in deciding whether D should have taken steps to meet the standard of care (e.g., taken precautions), a court may consider whether a requirement to take those steps might prevent a desirable activity from being undertaken or discourage people from undertaking functions in connection with a desirable activity. This means a higher level of fault may be acceptable when the activity in question is desirable, such as school trips and sporting events. This brings us to the final factor.

Whether the risk was justifiable

Even where the other factors are present, the taking of a risk may be justifiable in certain circumstances. A risk which is of some benefit to society, for example, may be deemed acceptable even though it could be foreseen. In **Watt v Hertfordshire CC 1954**, a fireman was injured when a heavy car jack fell on him. The vehicle he was in was not adapted to carry such equipment, but it was held that this was an acceptable risk in the circumstances because they were on their way to rescue a woman trapped under a car. Taking risks may also be justifiable in sporting situations and similar activities, but this will still need to be balanced with the other factors.

Many sports and games have a social benefit which may make a risk of harm justifiable, as in **Blair-Ford** above. However, risk-taking for the sake of it will not be acceptable even where there is a social benefit.

In **The Scout Association v Mark Barnes 2010**, the CA considered several breach factors in assessing whether the Association had breached its duty of care by allowing a game to be played with minimal lighting. The game involved running around and grabbing an object in the dark. The main lights were off but the emergency lighting was on and therefore there was some light. When a boy collided with a bench he injured his shoulder and sued. The trial judge found the Association had breached its duty of care and they appealed. On appeal the CA held that, balancing the risk of injury, the foreseeability of harm, the cost of preventing harm and the social benefit of the activity, there was a breach. The CA said that it was not the function of the law of tort to eliminate all risks but that the social value was limited and excitement for the sake of it did not justify the risk of harm.

In **Ahmed v MacLean 2016**, C was seriously injured at a mountain biking instruction course. The court found that the instructor had breached his duty to C because, although there is a risk in such sporting situations, and sports has social benefits, the instructor had failed to carry out his tuition with reasonable skill and care.

Examination pointer

As you can see from the Scout case, these factors are balanced against each other when the courts are deciding whether D breached the standard of care expected of the reasonable person. Look for clues to see if one factor is particularly relevant, but be prepared to discuss all four if necessary. If you are short of time it may be possible to use the same case to explain each factor, as long as you change the emphasis depending on which you are discussing.

Task 5

Using **Bolton v Stone 1951**, apply each of the four factors and the **Compensation Act** to the facts.

Objectiveness, children and professionals (subjective considerations)

The standard expected is said to be objective. It is based on what a reasonable person would do, not the particular D. A striking illustration of this is **Nettleship v Weston 1971**. Here a learner driver was liable for injuries to her driving instructor due to her negligent driving. The CA said that a learner driver should show the skill of an ordinary, competent driver.

However, the standard is also measured by reference to the circumstances and the courts have developed the rules in relation to the standard expected of children and professionals. This makes it slightly more subjective. A child is expected to reach the standard of a child of similar age, not an adult. In **Mullin v Richards 1998**, a schoolgirl of 15 was injured during a play-fight using plastic rulers as swords. The CA found the other girl not to be liable in negligence. An adult may have seen the risk; a child would not. In **Orchard v Lee 2009**, two boys had injured a playground supervisor whilst playing tag. Both were 13-years-old and the judge followed **Mullin v Richards** and held that the test was whether a 'prudent and reasonable' 13-year-old would have expected any injury to occur from his actions. The CA agreed and held that the primary question was whether their conduct had fallen below the standard that should objectively be expected of a reasonable child of that age. In the circumstance, they had been playing in an authorised play area and not breaking any rules. This was a simple accident and there was no liability in negligence.

In **Palmer v Cornwall CC 2009**, a claim was brought in respect of another incident which occurred during play-time at a school. A boy of 14 hit another boy in the eye while throwing stones at seagulls. The play area was supervised by dinner ladies and at the time only one was one duty. The victim's claim was rejected at trial but the CA reversed the decision and held that only one supervisor for around 300 children was clearly inadequate. If better supervision had been provided the boys may not have been throwing stones because they knew this was against the school rules. This time the claim succeeded, but this may be because it was brought against the council and not the other boy. Had the claim been against the other boy it may well have failed on the basis of **Mullin**, as was the case in **Orchard v Lee**.

Evaluation pointer

In **Nettleship v Weston 1971** it was said that a learner should show the skill of a competent driver. Is this fair to learners? We all have to start somewhere and it does not allow for a lower standard for those attempting to gain experience. Arguably, in a driving case this is OK, because everyone must have insurance. It won't be D paying, but an insurance company, who can best bear the cost. In other cases it may be less justifiable.

Where D acts in a professional capacity the standard expected is that of a person in that line of work. Where D is not acting in a professional capacity the standard expected is that of a "reasonably competent" person doing that job, not a professional. An example is **Wells v Cooper 1958**, where a householder had fitted a handle to his back door. C was a visiting tradesman and when he pulled sharply on the handle to close the door the handle came off. He fell down several steps and was injured. Although there was evidence that D should have used longer screws he was found not liable. The court held that D was to be judged against the standards of a reasonably competent carpenter, but not necessarily against the standards that would be expected of a professional carpenter working for payment. It was the sort of job that any householder might do and the standard expected was not that expected of a professional. However, the court recognised in **Wells v Cooper 1958** that this work was a typical DIY job, if the work is specialist in nature or could be dangerous if not done properly (like rewiring the whole electrical system), then D would be expected to get an expert in so could be liable.

So the standard expected is that of someone reasonably competent doing the same work. However, for professionals D is compared to a person in that profession, so the standard expected is higher. Thus, if there is an error of judgment by a professional the court will consider whether other professionals in the same area of expertise might have done the same thing. If so, D will not be in breach. This is often seen in cases of medical negligence. I have included several examples here so you can see examples of the law being applied in different situations, but medical cases can be difficult so don't worry about learning the facts, just the principles – you are studying law not medicine!

In **Bolam v Friern HMC 1957**, it was accepted that if a doctor acted in accordance with "a practice accepted as proper by a responsible body of medical men" there would be no breach. Thus, a doctor must show the skill that medical opinion would expect of a doctor, not just any 'reasonable person'. This was restated in **Bolitho v City & Hackney HA 1998**, where the HL emphasised that the medical opinion relied on must have some logical basis (this is not really different from **Bolam**, which had included the word 'responsible'). In **Bolitho**, a doctor failed to attend promptly to a patient and the patient subsequently died from a blocked airway. The doctor argued that even if she had attended she would not have intubated the patient. The HL confirmed the **Bolam** test but held that if the medical opinion was not capable of withstanding logical analysis the judge would be entitled to hold it was not reasonable or responsible. On the facts of the case, although there was conflicting medical evidence, the HL held that her action was supported by a responsible body of medical opinion which was not illogical. Both **Bolam** and **Bolitho** were followed in **R v Royal National Orthopaedic Hospital NHS Trust 2012**, where the court held that in most cases the fact that distinguished experts in the field were of a particular opinion would demonstrate that the opinion was reasonable. However, the court also held that in rare cases, if the opinion was incapable of withstanding logical analysis judges were entitled not to use it to assess the standard of care expected.

A further point, made by the court in **Wilsher v Essex AHA**, is that although a junior doctor would be expected to show the standard of a qualified doctor (which accords with the principle in **Nettleship v Weston 1971**) the post the doctor is in will be relevant, so that the standard expected of a junior doctor will be less than that expected of a consultant.

Note that the 'balancing factors' are still relevant in cases where there is a subjective element such as age or professional competence. In **McDonnell v Holwerda 2005**, the question was whether a GP had fallen below the standard expected of a reasonably competent GP by not recognising the possibility of meningitis in a child, following an examination. The court held that she had not fallen below the standard expected on the first occasion that she assessed the child. However, the GP had seen the child on a second occasion and, as the degree of risk was high due to the fact that the meningitis infection spreads so quickly, the standard expected was higher. She had fallen below this standard because she had not carried out a full enough investigation.

In **Ministry of Justice v Carter 2010**, the court was concerned with whether a general practitioner in the prison service was negligent in not referring a prisoner for a specialist opinion after she reported feeling a lump in her breast. The doctor had conducted a breast examination without detecting any abnormality so no referral was made. When C later developed cancer she sued the MOJ. The court found D negligent but on appeal it was made clear that in determining what should have been done by the doctor, the judge should have applied the test from the cases of **Bolam** and **Bolitho**. On the evidence, there was a responsible body of medical opinion that would have done the same as D and not have made a referral. There was no breach of duty and D's appeal was allowed.

In **Evans v Wolverhampton Hospitals NHS Trust 2015**, C claimed when her left leg went numb following a hip replacement operation. A piece of the cement used had been left behind, and although this was then removed it had permanently damaged the sciatic nerve. The CA upheld the judge's decision that the surgeon had been negligent in failing to see and remove the cement. In this case it was clear that a reasonable body of medical opinion would have taken more care to remove all traces of cement.

An important development on this subject shows that there may be times when the **Bolam** test is not appropriate. However, the principles of **Bolam** and **Bolitho** still apply in most situations so all three cases are important. Here are the earlier principles and the new case.

Key cases

Bolam v Friern HMC 1957 key principle: the standard expected will be met if a doctor acted in accordance with "a practice accepted as proper by a reasonable body of medical men".

Bolitho v City & Hackney HA 1998 key principle: adds to the principle in **Bolam** that if the medical opinion was not capable of withstanding logical analysis the judge would be entitled to hold it was not reasonable or responsible.

In **Montgomery v Lanarkshire Health Board 2015**, C claimed against a hospital after her baby was born with serious disabilities. As a diabetic there was a higher risk of problems and she argued that had she been told of the risks she might have opted for a caesarean birth and the harm would have been avoided. The hospital argued that because there are benefits to the mother in having a 'normal' delivery the doctor did not owe her a duty to give her this information, or if she did then she had not breached that duty as other doctors would have done the same. The court and CA agreed but the SC allowed the patient's appeal. The SC held that the **Bolam** test did not apply in these circumstances because the doctor's view that caesareans are not in maternal interests was a value judgment and that "once the argument departs from purely medical considerations, the **Bolam** test is inapposite". This means that where the issue is one of telling a patient of risks of a medical procedure, rather than a purely medical decision the **Bolam** test does not apply. The patient should have been told of the risks so she could make up her own mind, regardless of what any reasonable medical opinion may be. The SC noted "we would accept that a departure from the **Bolam** test will reduce the predictability of the outcome of litigation, given the difficulty of overcoming that test in contested proceedings. It appears to us, however, that a degree of unpredictability can be tolerated as the consequence of protecting patients from exposure to risks of injury which they would otherwise have chosen to avoid". There was a good chance that had she known of the risks she would not have opted for a natural birth and it was agreed that in that case the baby would have been born unharmed. **Montgomery** was followed in **Webster v Burton Hospitals NHS Trust 2017** by the CA in similar circumstances. In referring to **Bolam** the CA held that it was now clear from **Montgomery** that "this is no longer the correct approach".

Key Principle: The **Bolam** test is only appropriate for medical considerations, not for value judgements.

Note that the **Access to Medical Treatment (Innovation) Act 2016** provides that a medical practitioner will not be found negligent when departing from standard practice when acting responsibly. This does not change the **Bolam** test but does protect professionals who pioneer treatment of which their colleagues may not approve but which is in the patient's best interests.

Evaluation pointer

The decision in **Montgomery** seems sensible, as patients should be given all the relevant facts so they know the risks. If they do not know the risks of a procedure they cannot give proper informed consent to going ahead with it. It should be the patient's choice regardless of what is seen as reasonable or normal practice. If a patient has been told of the risks and elects to go ahead with the procedure, the doctor will not be in breach even if medical opinion would suggest an alternative procedure. This seems fair to both parties. If a patient has given proper informed consent to the medical procedure the hospital should not be liable merely because that procedure goes against what is regarded as normal practice.

Examination pointer

It is clear from the numerous cases on breach that the standard expected will always depend on the circumstances. You may not be able to make an absolute decision on breach, but you should be able to explain what is most likely. Look at the facts for clues, e.g., mention of a high risk or a high cost of prevention, or reference to D's profession or age. Then apply the factors as appropriate and decide what you think is most likely. If there is a scenario involving medical treatment explain the tests from **Bolam** and **Bolitho** but note the decision in **Montgomery**, that these may not apply to cases where a doctor makes a value judgment without having told the patient of any risks involved.

Examination pointer

Medical cases are complex and so unlikely to be examined. However, the same principle will apply to other professions. If your examination scenario involves a professional person then you can use these cases to support an answer that says that the person will be judged against what is accepted practice in the opinions of others in that particular profession, as long as there is a logical basis for that opinion. If the person concerned is a learner or trainee you may also need to discuss **Nettleship v Weston**. An example seen in an examination paper was that of a trainee hairdresser, where you would be expected to explain that a trainee hairdresser should show the standard of care expected of a competent hairdresser (**Nettleship**) and that the standard will be judged against the opinion of other responsible hairdressers (**Bolam**) and this opinion must have a logical basis (**Bolitho v City & Hackney HA**).

Task 6

Choose any 3 cases seen so far and explain which factors were most relevant in deciding whether there was breach of a duty of care. Then see how many other factors you can apply, as you did with **Bolton v Stone 1951 in task 5**.

Summary

The standard of care expected is essentially an objective one but there is a subjective element in that D is compared to a reasonable person of that age or in that profession. The court will look at what a reasonable person in the particular circumstances would have done.

- Reasonable parent
- Reasonable employee
- Reasonable child
- Reasonable doctor

The standard expected is based on 4 factors:

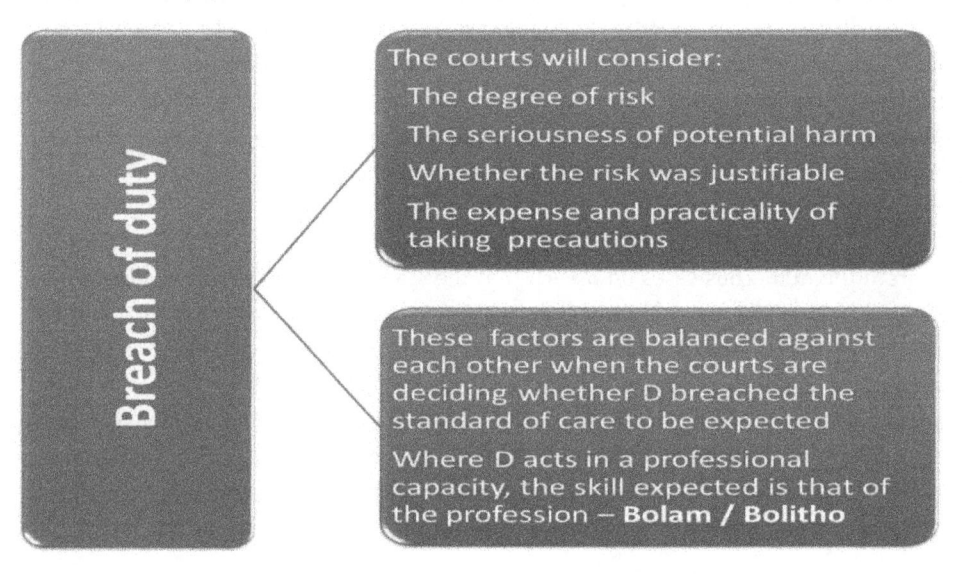

Breach of duty

The courts will consider:
- The degree of risk
- The seriousness of potential harm
- Whether the risk was justifiable
- The expense and practicality of taking precautions

These factors are balanced against each other when the courts are deciding whether D breached the standard of care to be expected

Where D acts in a professional capacity, the skill expected is that of the profession – **Bolam / Bolitho**

Task 7

Draw up the summary into a diagram, adding a case on each, and keep it for revision.

Links to the non-substantive law

For links to the English legal system, look back at the diagram and examples in the introduction to Part 1. In particular, where a principle of law has been established the system of appeals is relevant, as these principles are established in the higher appeal courts, i.e., the CA and SC.

ADR is always relevant to tort cases too, as is access to justice, because cases can be expensive to take to court so alternatives or help with expenses may be needed.

Self-test Questions

1. In which case was the objective standard explained, and by whom?
2. State the 4 factors which the court may consider when deciding what is reasonable
3. Give a case example for each of the above
4. What standard is expected of a professional? A child?
5. Why had the employers not breached their duty in *Maguire v Harland & Wolff plc 2005*?

Answers to the tasks and self-test questions are on my website at www.drsr.org. **Please click on 'Answers to tasks'. For a range of free interactive exercises, click on 'Free Exercises'.**

Chapter 4 Causation (damage was caused by the breach)

"… children's ingenuity in finding unexpected ways of doing mischief to themselves and others should never be underestimated" – Lord Hoffmann

By the end of this chapter you should be able to:

- **Explain the rules on both factual and legal causation**
- **Show how the law applies by reference to cases**
- **Identify problems with the law in order to evaluate it**

After duty and breach, the third matter that must be proved is causation. C not only has to prove that damage occurred, but must also prove D was the cause of that damage, both in fact and in law. Damage must be factually caused by D's breach and be reasonably foreseeable.

Causation in fact: the 'but for' test.

The question here is whether D's breach in fact caused the damage. The courts apply the 'but for' test. This asks, "but for D's negligence would the harm have occurred?" If the answer is "no" then D is liable.

Example

Using an earlier case, **Paris v Stepney BC**, we can see that 'but for' the employer's breach of duty (not making sure the employee wore goggles) the employee would not have been injured in the eye. The breach therefore factually caused the harm. Had the worker been injured in the arm then wearing goggles would not have prevented this. In that case we would say that 'but for' the breach the employee would still have been injured, so the breach did not factually cause the harm.

However, if the damage would have happened regardless of the negligent act or omission, D will not be liable for it.

Key case

The leading case is **Barnett v Chelsea & Kensington HMC 1968**, where a man suffering from vomiting and pain called at a hospital but was sent home without being treated. He later died of arsenic poisoning and his widow sued the hospital management committee. The hospital clearly owed a duty to patients, and was found to be negligent, but they were not found liable because he would have died regardless of whether he was treated. Here the answer to "'But for D's negligence would the harm have occurred?" was "Yes, it would.", so D was not liable. Both duty and breach were proved, but the claim failed on the third issue, that of causation.

Key principle: If the damage would have occurred regardless of D's fault (breach of duty), then D's breach did not cause that damage. (To put it another way, if the damage would not have happened 'but for' D's breach, then that breach is the cause of the damage.)

Similarly, in **DS v Northern Lincolnshire and Goole NHS Trust 2016**, a baby had been born with brain damage. A delay of three minutes by the midwife in calling an obstetrician was found to be a breach of duty. However, the court held that C had not proved on the balance of probabilities that 'but for' the negligent delay he would have not sustained brain damage. The claim failed.

In **Bolitho v City & Hackney HA 1998**, discussed with breach of duty, the doctor had argued that the patient would have died even if she had attended promptly. The HL confirmed that the **Bolam v Friern HMC 1957** test applied to causation as well as breach. As there was a body of medical opinion that also would not have taken the particular action (intubation of the airway), it could not be said that her lack of doing so caused his death. It is likely that, as in **Barnett**, he would have died anyway.

In the majority of cases the 'but for' test works fine. However, the rules have been modified in certain situations.

Note: The following is not needed for AS but it is for A-level. I have not moved it to 'The Bridge' because it is part of factual causation so better for you to look at now. However, if you are not doing the A-level, you can move on to 'Causation in law: Remoteness of damage'.

Successive and multiple causes

In breaches that follow each other (successive causes) there is not too much of a problem. The court in **Performance Cars Ltd v Abraham 1962** held that in most cases the original person in breach will be liable. Thus, C could not claim from a later negligent driver for repairs to his car previously damaged in a similar accident by another driver. It was the original driver who had caused the damage (which had not yet been repaired), so it was that original driver who was liable.

In **Wright v Cambridge Medical Group 2011**, a GP was found liable in negligence for the late referral of a baby to hospital where, if she had received effective treatment in time, she would probably have made a full recovery. The doctor had argued that although negligent in the late referral this had not caused the harm (damage to her hip from an infection at the hospital) and that the harm was caused by the later negligent hospital treatment. The CA held that in cases of successive causes of harm, if it was foreseeable that harm could be caused by D's original breach of duty then it was right to hold D liable. It was foreseeable a late referral could cause harm and D's negligence significantly contributed to C's permanent injury. The same principle was applied in **Dalling v RJ Heale & Co 2011**. D was liable for C's head injury which caused him behavioural problems. Three years after the initial accident he fell over while drunk and injured himself. The evidence showed that he rarely drank before the first accident. The CA confirmed the judge's decision that D was liable for the later injury (although damages should be reduced by a third for C's contributory negligence). The second injury would not have occurred 'but for' the original head injury and injury was foreseeable because of his behavioural problems.

In cases where there is more than one cause, any one of which could have been the possible cause (multiple causes) the 'but for' test can be hard to satisfy, especially if the injury is indivisible.

In **Bonnington Castings Ltd v Wardlaw 1956,** C inhaled contaminated dust at work causing a lung disease. There were two possible sources of the dust, only one of which was due to D's negligence. So we can say there was 'bad' dust and 'good' dust. These combined to cause the disease and it was an indivisible injury. We cannot say either one caused the harm by itself, but we can say that the bad dust, even though only a partial cause was a partial cause of the whole injury. The HL made clear that where the disease is indivisible, such as lung cancer which you either have or you don't, D will be liable in full. Where the disease is divisible, such as asbestosis, which will worsen with greater exposure, D will be liable only in respect of a share.

Where there are several different breaches (rather than one breach and one innocent cause), a claim could fail if causation could not be proved in respect of any particular D. In **Fairchild v Glenhaven Funeral Services Ltd 2002**, the HL modified the rules in the interests of fairness to C and made clear that the 'but for' test is *necessary* but not always *conclusive*.

Key case

The facts of **Fairchild** were that C became ill (with mesothelioma) after exposure to asbestos dust in the course of successive employments. The CA had held that he could not recover damages from any of the employers, since he could not establish which period of employment had caused his illness. This seemed unfair to C, because each of the employers could be shown to be in breach of duty. It just wasn't clear which particular breach was the cause of the illness. The HL reversed the CA's decision and held that if C could show that any one of the Ds had *'materially increased the risk'* of harm then the causation test could be satisfied. The HL said that the causation rules might be modified on policy grounds *'in special circumstances'*.

Key principle: If D's breach materially increased the risk of harm to C, that breach can be said to have caused any resulting harm and each and every D is liable.

There are earlier cases on material contribution to the harm itself but **Fairchild** includes a contribution to the *risk* of harm. It also applies to cases where there is more than one breach of duty and is a HL decision, so we can start from there. There have been plenty of cases; here is a selection. You don't need to try to learn them all, just make some notes on the ones which you understand best so you can explain the rules on factual causation.

In **Barker v Corus UK Ltd 2006**, with similar facts to **Fairchild**, but where C also had a period of self-employment, the HL developed the rule. The HL held that **Fairchild** could apply when there is more than one possible cause of harm, even if these include causes which would not usually lead to an action in tort (his period of self-employment). Where there was more than one cause, damages could be apportioned according to how far each D had materially increased the risk of injury (measured on the duration and extent of the exposure), so excluding his period of self-employment. This idea of apportioning damages between different

Ds was reversed by an amendment to the **Compensation Act 2006**, which provides in **s 3** that in mesothelioma cases each person who contributes to the harm is liable for the *whole* of the damage. However, the Act only applies to mesothelioma cases so **Barker** will still be good law for other types of claim.

In **Sienkiewicz v Greif 2011**, the Supreme Court looked again at a case involving mesothelioma allegedly caused by asbestos. A woman was exposed to asbestos during her employment in a factory and when she died her estate claimed. The trial judge held that causation had not been proven because she had not proved the risk had been doubled by her exposure, it had only increased her risk of harm by 18%. The CA held that, as per **Fairchild**, it was only necessary to show the breach 'materially increased the risk' of harm. The Supreme Court agreed and held that **Fairchild** applied even in single exposure cases (where there was only one cause of harm and therefore only one D). Furthermore, a risk was material if it was more than '*de minimis*' (meaning 'about minimal things' with which the court does not concern itself). This means the word 'materially' is interpreted widely, and the breach need not be the main cause, or even a high percentage of it.

Fairchild involved different negligent causes and **Sienkiewicz** only one cause, but both showed that a claim could succeed where someone materially increased the risk of harm.

In **Mayne v Atlas Stone Company Ltd 2016**, the court applied the rule in another case of exposure to asbestos where there were three possible causes. It had been argued that C had to prove not only a material contribution but also that a particular contribution had caused a quantifiable amount of the harm. The court did not accept this argument and held that C did not have to prove a particular D had caused a quantifiable amount of the harm suffered.

Is Fairchild fair?

In cases like negligent exposure to some agency or material resulting in a cumulative disease the material contribution rule works fairly, because each exposure would have made the disease worse. It is less obviously fair where the disease is indivisible, which is why **Fairchild** is a major decision. Where a disease is indivisible, like cancer, which does not increase in severity over a period, C could have contracted the disease at any one of the periods of employment. C cannot say any one of them contributed to the harm at all, but under **Fairchild** it is enough to say they each contributed to the *risk* of harm by the negligent exposure. One argument in favour of **Fairchild** is that there was negligent exposure in each case, so none of the employers was entirely innocent. Without the extension of the material contribution rule to the risk of harm, C would not have received any compensation at all despite those breaches of duty.

Multiple causes are often seen in medical cases. In **Bailey v Ministry of Defence and another 2008**, hospital negligence had led to a woman becoming weak. She later had other treatment elsewhere and suffered brain damage. The first hospital argued that a contribution to the risk of injury was not enough to prove causation. The judge disagreed: the correct question was whether the negligence had 'caused or materially contributed to' the injury, and it had. The CA upheld the decision and held that as long as D's act made a material contribution to the harm, causation could be proved, even if there was another, non-negligent, cause which also made a material contribution (the later treatment). The point is that if she had not been in a weakened conditioned she may not have suffered brain damage, so her weakened condition made a material contribution to the brain damage.

In **Williams v The Bermuda Hospitals Board 2016**, the Privy Council held that it did not matter whether the causes were concurrent or successive, the 'material contribution' rule applied to both. The hospital had negligently delayed diagnosis and treatment of a ruptured appendix, and the patient suffered heart and lung damage caused by sepsis. The two causes of the heart and lung damage were the ruptured appendix (which he had anyway) and the delay (D's negligence). The PC held that if D had made a material contribution to an indivisible injury then that D could be fully liable for it even though there were other contributing causes. Although the decision was based on the 'thin skull' rule (discussed under causation in law below) rather than extending the 'but for' test, the result is the same. Where material contribution applies, D is liable for the full value of the claim. Where the injury is divisible, and it is possible to attribute particular damage to D, then D is liable only for that damage.

A different situation arose in **Milton Keynes Borough Council v Nulty 2013**. A fire had started in a recycling centre and one of the possible causes was a cigarette end dropped by someone working there. The CA said that in deciding whether something was the cause the court must ask itself whether the suggested explanation was more likely than not to be true. The judge had concluded that a cigarette end carelessly discarded by D was the most probable cause of the fire. There were other possibilities but these were unlikely. The evidence for believing that D had caused the fire was stronger than the evidence for not so believing. The CA upheld the decision. There may have been more than one *possible* cause, but, as there was only one *probable* cause, this sufficed to find D liable.

In **Henegham v Manchester Dry Docks Ltd 2016**, another asbestos exposure case, the CA summed up the rules. This is not down as a key case as it established no new principle, however it is important because the CA referred to most of the earlier cases and attempted to clarify the law. The CA noted that there are three ways of establishing causation in disease cases:

> **Where 'but for' D's negligence C would not have suffered the disease (the test from Barnett)**
>
> **Where D made a material contribution to a divisible disease (one whose severity increases with increased exposure to some agency) each D is only liable for the amount of the contribution, and is not liable for any part which did not involve a breach of duty (the rule from Bonnington)**
>
> **Where causation cannot be proved in either of these ways, for example because the disease is indivisible, causation may be established if it is proved that D materially increased the risk of the disease (the Fairchild exception).**

Note also that damages can be apportioned (**Barker**). However, any D who has contributed will be liable for the full value of the claim in mesothelioma cases (**Compensation Act**) or where the harm is indivisible (**Fairchild/Williams**).

Example

C works for X and is exposed to asbestos. C gets cancer. C uses the 'but for' test to show that but for X's negligence he would not have got cancer (**Barnett**).

D works for three employers, X, Y and Z, all of whom expose him to asbestos. C gets a lung disease caused by exposure. It is the type of disease which is made worse by greater exposure. Each employer exposed C to the harm. X, Y and Z are each liable as they contributed to the harm, but are only liable for the amount of the contribution, calculated by the amount of exposure at each employment (**Bonnington**). Damages are assessed at £90,000. Assuming the exposure was the same for each employment, each employer is liable for £30,000. If one is insolvent or cannot be traced the others still only pay their own shares of £30,000 each.

D works for three employers, X, Y and Z, all of whom expose him to asbestos. C gets cancer. C cannot prove whether he got the disease while working for X or for Y or for Z. However, each employer exposed C to the risk of harm even if it could not be proved that any made a material contribution to the cancer. X, Y and Z are each liable in full (**Fairchild**). Again, assuming the exposure was the same for each employment, each employer is liable for £30,000. However, under **Fairchild** if one is insolvent or cannot be traced the others pay £45,000 each, a total of £90.000. Under **Barker** if one is insolvent the others pay £30,000 each, a total of £60,000 but this does not apply to mesothelioma or to indivisible harm which is impossible to apportion.

Examination pointer

You will not be asked to discuss apportioning the blame/damages in an application question. I have included a little on this because not only is it the correct law, it is also an example of influences on Parliament through a judicial decision (**Barker**) and of supremacy of Parliament (the **Compensation Act** overruled Barker in certain cases). As regards the nature of law it is useful when discussing fault (one or more of the Ds may not have been the cause of the harm at all). The main thing for you to remember for application purposes is that where there is more than one cause, the 'but for' test can be modified following the precedent set in **Fairchild**. Thus, any one of several D's in breach of duty could be fully liable if that breach made a material contribution to the risk of harm.

Loss of chance

The HL refused to extend the idea of 'possible' rather than 'probable' causes to allow compensation for *loss of chance* in **Gregg v Scott 2005**. Here a doctor negligently misdiagnosed C's cancer. If treated earlier the cancer might not have spread. It was shown that he had previously had a 45% chance of surviving 10 years. This had fallen to 25%. The judge held that even though there was a reduced chance, the chance of survival was still under 50%. The late diagnosis had not made sufficient difference to the result. On appeal, the HL accepted that there *could* be a claim for a loss of chance 'when overall fairness so requires'. However, they held that a complete adoption of 'possible' rather than 'probable' causation was too great a change in the law and should be left to Parliament. The appeal was rejected.

In **Webster v Burton Hospitals NHS Trust 2017** the CA followed **Montgomery** (see breach) but this time the decision was based on causation because the hospital admitted breach (they had done insufficient ultra-sound tests) but had argued that the breach did not cause the harm. The facts were similar and the CA held that failure to give correct information to a pregnant woman prior to delivery was a causative factor in the baby suffering birth defects because there was a good chance that had the woman known of the risks she would have decided to have a different type of delivery (**Montgomery**) or an earlier one (**Webster**).

Collett v Smith 2008 involved a successful claim for loss of chance. In 2003, at age 18, C injured his leg after a tackle, while playing for Manchester United reserve team. He was still given a two-year contract with the club, but as he never regained the same level of competence it was not renewed in 2005. He played for other clubs abroad but retired when he realised he would never have a successful career. He then commenced a claim for his lost chance of a football career. The court had to decide whether, 'but for' D's negligence, he would have succeeded in making a career in professional football and, if so at what level and for how long. There was evidence, most significantly from Sir Alex Ferguson, that he would have done well at the club, quite likely playing at Championship and Premiership level. He won his claim and was awarded nearly four million pounds based on the lost chance of a successful career.

Even if D's act was found to be the factual cause of the harm, there is still one more hurdle.

Causation in law: Remoteness of Damage

The test here is one of foreseeability. If the loss or damage is not foreseeable it is said to be 'too remote' from the breach. This was established in **The Wagon Mound 1966**, which replaced the wider test in **Re Polemis 1921**, that you were liable for *all* the direct consequences of your actions.

Example

Your teacher negligently spills coffee over you and you have to change your clothes. This makes you late leaving college and by this time a storm has started. As you cycle home your bike is struck by lightning and you are injured. It can be said that 'but for' your teacher spilling coffee you would not have been delayed and so would not have been struck by lightning and injured. However the lightning is not foreseeable so is too remote from the breach. Causation in law is therefore not proved.

The later test asks whether it was *foreseeable* that the damage would occur. D is only liable for the foreseeable consequences of any breach of duty.

The full name of **The Wagon Mound** is **Overseas Tankship (UK) Ltd v Morts Dock & Engineering Co 1966**, but it is commonly called **The Wagon Mound**.

Key case

In **The Wagon Mound** oil was negligently spilt by the Ds. This oil caused a fire that damaged C's wharf two days later. The Ds were not liable because it was not believed that this type of oil could catch fire on water. The damage to the dock by *oil* was foreseeable, so C could claim for this, but not damage caused by the later *fire*. That damage was too 'remote' from D's act, because it was not foreseeable.

Key principle: D is only liable for the foreseeable consequences of any breach of duty.

Intervening act

Sometimes something happens between D's negligent act and C's injury. This is referred to by the Latin tag *'novus actus interveniens'* or in modern parlance, 'new act intervening'. Such an act may sometimes break the chain of causation between D's act or omission and the harm to C. In **Smith v Littlewoods 1987**, an owner of a disused cinema had left his property unsecured and vandals broke in. They caused a fire which spread to a neighbour's property. The neighbour sued the cinema owner. The claim failed. D successfully argued that the act of the vandals had broken the chain between the omission (not locking up properly) and the damage. An example of the argument failing can be seen in a case we looked at earlier, **Reeves v MPC 1999**. The police argued that the prisoner's suicide was an intervening act, which broke the chain of causation. The HL did not accept this. It was foreseeable that he would try to commit suicide, and a foreseeable act does not break the chain.

In **Corr v IBC Vehicles Ltd 2008**, a widow had claimed damages in respect of her husband's suicide six years after he had an accident at work. The issue was whether the suicide was foreseeable, i.e., whether the breach had *caused* the suicide or whether it was too *remote*. The trial court found that the suicide was not foreseeable and that, based on the **Wagon Mound**, foreseeability was an essential requirement of establishing both duty and damage caused. The CA reversed this decision and restated that as long as the type of harm was foreseeable, the particular outcome need not be (a principle established in **Hughes v Lord Advocate 1963** below). The HL upheld the CA's decision. Several issues arose, but the main ones concerned causation, specifically foreseeability and breaking the chain. The HL held that severe depression was foreseeable and as this was of a similar type of harm to depression there was no need for suicide itself to be foreseeable. The suicide did not break the chain of causation as it was not a conscious voluntary act, but a response to his depression.

Overlap

Note the overlap between foreseeability and intervening act. An intervening act will only break the chain of causation if it was itself unforeseeable.

Example

In **Reeves**, the prisoner was on suicide watch so suicide was foreseeable and didn't break the chain. If the police had left the door flap open and a mouse had crawled in through the hole and then bitten the prisoner who happened to suffer a rare allergy to mouse bites and died, this would be an unforeseeable event and so would be likely to break the chain between the negligence of the police and the death.

Type of damage

If the *type* of damage is foreseeable, then the fact that it occurred in an unforeseeable way, or that the consequences were more extensive than could be foreseen, will not affect liability. The first can be illustrated by **Hughes v Lord Advocate 1963**. A child knocked over a paraffin lamp which caused an explosion. He was very badly burnt. The court found that the *type* of injury was foreseeable (burns) even though the way this had occurred (an explosion) was not. D was liable.

The consequences being more extensive can be illustrated by **Bradford v Robinson Rentals Ltd 1967**. C was told by his employer to make a long trip in a van with no heater. C asked to postpone the trip because of severe weather conditions, but was refused. Due to the severe cold he suffered frostbite and claimed damages. Although frostbite is very rare in England, the court decided that some injury was foreseeable due to the extreme cold, so his employer was liable for the more extensive harm of frostbite.

The principles of both **The Wagon Mound** and **Hughes** were confirmed by the HL in **Jolley v Sutton LBC 2000**.

Key case

In **Jolley**, a 14-year old boy was badly injured when working with a friend on an abandoned and derelict boat on council land. The CA had held that the council were not liable. Whilst it may be foreseeable that children might *play* on such a boat it was not foreseeable that they would attempt to *repair* it. The HL reversed the decision and made the point in the opening quote that the ingenuity of children should not be underestimated. It was foreseeable that they would meddle with the boat in some way – it did not matter that they had been repairing it rather than playing on it.

Key principle: Children can be expected to do the unexpected, so their actions are more likely to be foreseeable.

In **Hadlow v Peterborough CC 2011**, a teacher was working at a secure unit for young women who could be prone to violence. She should have had a member of the unit's care staff with her during lessons. When she noticed that the staff who escorted the three women to the lesson had both left and locked the door behind them, she jumped up to call out to them before they were out of earshot. In her hurry, she tripped and injured herself. The issue to be decided was one of causation. It was accepted that had one of the women attacked her the unit would have been liable, as they were in breach of duty by not ensuring she had someone with her. However, the unit argued that their breach did not cause the harm because she had not been attacked – she injured herself by tripping over her chair. The CA, following **Hughes v Lord Advocate 1963**, held that as the type of injury was foreseeable (the breach of duty had exposed the teacher to the risk of harm) even though it happened in an unforeseeable way (her attempt to remove the risk by getting the attention of the staff) the unit was liable.

Evaluation pointer

The **Hughes** test seems much wider than **The Wagon Mound**. It suggests that the harm itself does not necessarily have to be foreseeable. It would appear, at least in the case of children, that the wider principle is correct because it was approved by the HL in **Jolley v Sutton LBC 2000**.

Examination pointer

It may be important to refer to **Jolley**, not just **The Wagon Mound** test, if the scenario involves children. Use **The Wagon Mound** as setting the test on foreseeability, but go on to mention that in the case of children something may be foreseeable that would not be in the case of adults.

Task 8

Use two cases that you remember from looking at duty or breach. Use the 'but for' test to apply causation *in fact*. Then add the rules from **The Wagon Mound** (and **Jolley** if appropriate) to see if D *legally* caused the harm.

The thin-skull rule

It is a common-law rule that D must take the victim as he or she is found. This means that if a disability in the victim means they are likely to suffer more serious harm, or die, D is still liable, even though a person without that disability would not have been so seriously harmed. It is an exception to the requirement for foreseeability, as D may be liable for a type of harm that was not foreseeable. An example is **Smith v Leech Brain 1962**, where D's negligence caused a small burn, which activated a latent cancer from which C died. His widow sued his employer and the court held that C's particular vulnerability (the pre-existing cancer) did not affect liability. C's wife did not have to prove that cancer was foreseeable, only that some harm was, even though it was of a different type. It is called the 'thin-' or 'egg-shell' skull rule because the essence of the rule is that if there is something which makes V more vulnerable than other people this will not affect D's liability.

Example

Jake is riding his bike too fast and knocks over a man who has a very thin skull. Most people would have only suffered a few knocks and bruises, but this man dies because as he fell his skull broke. Jake can be liable for the death, not just the foreseeable injuries, because of the 'thin-skull' rule.

To help to remember this, use the facts of **Smith v Leech Brain** and imagine a conversation between the widow (C), the employer (D) and the judge.

The widow (C): My husband died because of an injury at work and it's your fault.

The employer (D): I'm sorry about causing the injury, but it wasn't life-threatening so it wasn't my fault he died.

Judge: Yes, it was. Your breach caused the injury which set off the chain of events leading to his suicide. Although he had an existing vulnerability, under the thin-skull rule you are liable for the death.

In **Williams v The Bermuda Hospitals Board 2016** (see successive causes above), the PC held that D was liable for the full heart and lung damage as the negligent delay was part of the cause and the ruptured appendix was an existing vulnerability, like a thin skull.

This shows the overlap between the 'but for' test and the 'thin skull' rule. In **Williams**, the CA had based the decision on the former, effectively extending the **Barker** decision to cases other than mesothelioma. The PC preferred the 'thin-skull' approach but upheld the decision.

Summary of the principles

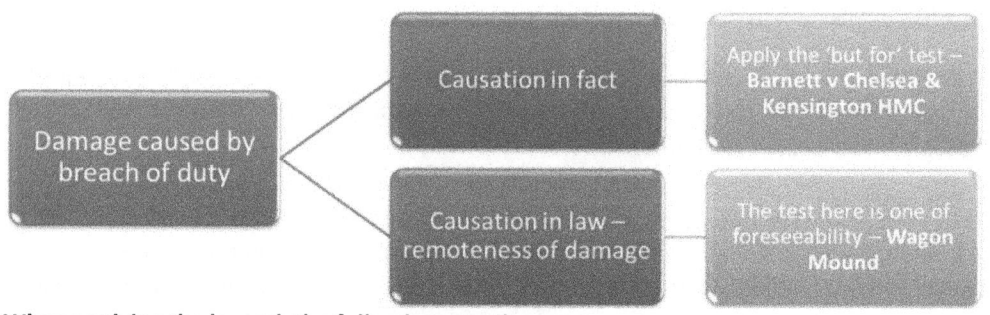

Damage caused by breach of duty
- Causation in fact — Apply the 'but for' test — **Barnett v Chelsea & Kensington HMC**
- Causation in law — remoteness of damage — The test here is one of foreseeability — **Wagon Mound**

When applying the law ask the following questions:

- Would the harm have occurred 'but for' D's act or omission?
- Is there more than one cause? If so the test may be modified.
- Was the harm foreseeable or was it too remote?
- Was this *type* of harm foreseeable?
- Does the thin-skull rule apply?

Task 9

Draw up a diagram as a guide for a problem question based on the summary of the principles. Add a case for each issue, briefly explaining the facts as far as they relate to the principle.

Links to the non-substantive law

For links to the English legal system, look back at the diagram and examples in the introduction to Part 1. In particular, where a principle of law has been established the system of appeals is relevant, as these principles are established in the higher appeal courts, i.e., the CA and SC. ADR is always relevant to tort cases too, as is access to justice, because cases can be expensive to take to court so alternatives or help with expenses may be needed.

Self-test questions

1. What is the 'but for' test and from which case did it come?
2. Which case established the rule on foreseeability?
3. What did **Hughes** add to this?
4. Can you explain the 'thin-skull rule'?
5. What was the point made in **Jolley** (in the HL) regarding children?

Answers to the tasks and self-test questions are on my website at www.drsr.org. **Please click on 'Answers to tasks'. For a range of free interactive exercises, click on 'Free Exercises'.**

Chapter 5 Occupier's Liability for visitors

"the responsibility for the safety of little children must rest primarily upon the parents" Devlin J

By the end of this chapter you should be able to:

- **Explain the special rules where harm was caused on someone's property**
- **Show how case law and statute law apply to visitors**
- **Identify problems with the law and/or discuss its development in order to evaluate it**

There are two Acts of Parliament which cover liability for harm caused on someone's property. The **Occupiers Liability Act 1957 (OLA 1957)** provides that an occupier of property owes a duty of care to lawful visitors to ensure their safety. Under **s 1(2)** this covers not only those people expressly invited, but also those who may have implied consent, or a right, to be on the property. The **Occupiers Liability Act 1984** covers those who are not lawful visitors, i.e., trespassers, and we will look at that more limited liability in the next chapter.

Examination pointer

Property is not defined but the **Act** refers to any "fixed or moveable structure including any vessel, vehicle or aircraft". A caravan or boat could certainly come within this so you should be prepared to consider more than buildings or land if necessary. If you decide the place where C suffers the harm is not 'property' then go on to apply the normal rules of negligence using the **Caparo** test. The rules for breach and duty are the same for both.

The **OLA 1957** covers liability for death, personal injury and damage to property (unlike the **1984 Act** which does not include damage to property).

Task 10

Other than invited friends, a regular window cleaner might be classed as a lawful visitor even though not expressly invited on one particular occasion. Make a list of 5 other people you think might be included.

We will now consider what the *duty* is, who the *occupier* may be, and who will be classed as a *lawful visitor*.

The duty

Under **s 2(2)** the duty on an occupier is to:

"take such care as in all the circumstances of the case is reasonable to see that the visitor will be reasonably safe in using the premises for the purposes for which he is invited to be there"

In **Poppleton v Trustees of the Portsmouth Youth Activities Committee 2008**, while at an indoor climbing premises, C fell and, despite the provision of matting, was badly injured. He claimed under the **OLA 1957** and in negligence. The court rejected his claim under **s 2 OLA** as the injury was not due to the state of the premises, but to his activity there. The CA upheld the decision and pointed out that D had no duty to protect C from risks which were obvious in an activity undertaken voluntarily. The risk of injury while climbing was obvious and it was also obvious that matting might not always prevent such injury. This case suggests that there will be no claim under the **Act** if the harm has not been caused by the state of the premises.

This is quite widely interpreted though. In **G4S v Manley 2016**, the court found the prison service liable when a prisoner had injured himself in his cell. There had been a power cut and the man had limited mobility following an operation. Due to a delay in restoring power the man was injured trying to use the toilet in the dark. The court held that the prison service should have taken more care in these circumstances. They should have responded more quickly to restore power to his cell so had not made the cell reasonably safe for him to use.

In **Lear v Hickstead Ltd and WH Security Ltd 2016**, C had been injured at a horse show while lowering the ramp on his horsebox which another person had raised in order to get past. C claimed against the occupier under the **OLA 1957** and the people running the parking arrangements in negligence. He argued that he should not have been allowed to park where he would be causing an obstruction. The court held that the occupier owed a duty even though the harm was caused by an activity rather than the state of the premises. However, that duty had not been breached because the system in place was "entirely reasonable" and the evidence was that he was not causing an obstruction as there were alternative ways past. It was foreseeable that someone might raise his ramp and that an injury could result, but to be liable it had to be shown that it was D's fault he was causing an obstruction and that was the reason someone lifted the ramp. As C was not causing an obstruction neither D was in breach of duty.

S 2 provides that the duty is to keep the *visitor* safe. **S 1(1)** refers to *'dangers due to the state of the premises or to things done or omitted to be done on them'*. The two sections together require that the harm is caused by the state of the premises (as confirmed in **Poppleton**) but the duty is to keep the visitor safe, not necessarily the premises.

Example

My shed is falling down and unsafe. I cordon it off securely and put up a large sign saying 'DANGER'. Although my **premises** are not safe, the fact that it is cordoned off and clearly marked will probably mean any **visitors** will be safe so I will not be liable.

The occupier

The occupier is the person *in control* of the premises. This was established in **Wheat v Lacon 1966**. C had fallen downstairs while staying at a pub. There was evidence to show that someone had removed a light bulb. The HL held that a duty was owed by the brewery who owned the pub, as well as the licensees who let the room to C. Lord Denning described the occupier as a person who had "*a sufficient degree of control over the premises*". Although it was found the brewers had not *breached* their duty, the principle is that there can be more than one occupier.

Lawful visitors

Who did you think might be a lawful visitor in the task? Many people have implied consent to enter, e.g., when making deliveries or reading the meter, professionals you have called in such as a doctor, plumber or electrician, as well as those who may have a right to be there such as the police – with a warrant – and fire-fighters attending a call-out.

Examination pointer

The **OLA 1957** makes provision for particular situations. It is important to know these, as examination questions often include a particular issue which you will be expected you to pick up on. Let's look at the provisions in relation to children and professionals.

Children s 2(3)(a)

This section provides that:

"an occupier must be prepared for children to be less careful than adults. If an occupier allows a child to enter the premises then the premises must be reasonably safe for a child of that age."

Not only is the degree of care higher in respect of children, but also age may be relevant in deciding whether someone is a visitor or a trespasser (and thus which **Act** applies). Cases before the **Acts** are still relevant on both these issues because legal principles have been established. In **Glasgow Corporation v Taylor 1922**, there was no warning or fence in front of a shrub containing poisonous berries in a public park owned by the corporation. A child died after picking and eating some. The council would probably not have breached its duty in the case of an adult, as an adult would probably have been treated as a trespasser on the basis that there was no right to take the berries. However, in respect of a 7-year-old, who would be fascinated by the bright berries, it **was** liable.

In **Phipps v Rochester Corporation 1955**, the court decided that an occupier could expect very young children to be in the care of an adult. This meant the council had not breached its duty when a 5-year-old C was injured on their land. He was with his 7-year-old sister, but no adult or responsible older person was present. The opening quote came from this case, but Devlin J also made clear that different considerations would apply *"to public parks or to recognised playing grounds where parents allow their children to go unaccompanied in the reasonable belief that they are safe"*.

In **Moloney v Lambeth LBC 1966**, a young child fell through a gap in some railings. The council was held liable even though an adult could not have got through the gap. The council should be prepared to take greater care as children could be around and are owed a higher standard of care.

Examination pointer

You should take special care if the scenario involves a child. Although D has to take greater care in respect of children (**Glasgow**), if the child is very young, D can argue that the parents should have been responsible (**Phipps**). Also, in **Glasgow**, the court said that such attractions can be 'fascinating but fatal' to children. This is referred to as an allurement. It means that a child who is attracted by something on D's land is being allured and thus, in a sense, invited. This means that even though a child is trespassing, an allurement can make that child a lawful visitor. Look out for clues such as 'a pile of sand', 'fireworks', 'a pond' etc., which might be attractive to a child. An implied invitation can make someone a lawful visitor and so come within the **OLA 1957,** rather than the **OLA 1984.** If in any doubt discuss both and explain why you are doing so. Note, though, that the duty to trespassers is more limited, so bringing an action under the **OLA 1957** may be better.

Task 11

Write a brief comparison of **Glasgow** and **Phipps** to show why one claim succeeded and the other didn't.

In **Jolley v Sutton LBC 1998**, the CA held that the council was not liable when a boat left abandoned and rotting on council land fell on a 14-year-old boy. He and a friend had been trying to repair it and had propped the boat up to work underneath it. The decision of the CA was based on the fact that, although the boat was both potentially dangerous and attractive, the injury was not foreseeable. There were indications that the decision may have been different if the boys had been playing rather than working. This distinction was not accepted by the HL, which reversed the decision.

Key case

In **Jolley v Sutton LBC 2000**, the HL found that there was a foreseeable risk of children meddling with the boat and injuring themselves. That they were working on it rather than playing on it was not important. There was a *foreseeable risk of some harm occurring*. Lord Hoffmann said that the ingenuity of children in finding unexpected ways of doing mischief to themselves should not be underestimated. The injury was also within the **Wagon Mound** test, i.e., it was *not too remote* from the danger (of a rotting boat). The council was liable.

Key principle: Children can be expected to do the unexpected, so their actions are more likely to be foreseeable.

Evaluation pointer

Read the cases and form your own opinion on how far an occupier should be responsible for the safety of children. This is a popular area for problem questions, but could also come into an essay. Consider whether parents should have responsibility for very young children, but also how to decide at what age this moves to the occupier. The extent of the duty under the common law and the **Act** is the same, so cases prior to the **Act** can be cited in support of an answer.

Professionals s 2(3)(b)

The duty of care for professional people is more limited in that they are expected to take their own precautions against risks that are incidental to their area of expertise. This section provides that:

"An occupier may expect that a person, in the exercise of his calling, will appreciate and guard against any special risks ordinarily incidental to it"

Example

You need to get your house rewired and call a qualified electrician to come and do it. The electrician gets a bad shock from a bare wire and is off work for several days. He is unlikely to win a claim for compensation, as he should have appreciated this type of risk.

In **Roles v Nathan 1963**, two chimney sweeps were not protected by the **Act** as they should have recognised the danger of carbon monoxide gas escaping from a boiler chimney. Similarly, in **General Cleaning Contractors v Christmas 1953**, a window cleaner was injured when he fell off a building after a defective window closed on his hand. He failed in his claim (then under common law) as he was expected to guard against that type of risk. It should be noted, however, that this does not mean that D is never liable to a professional doing his job. In **Salmon v Seafarer's Restaurant 1983**, a fire had been caused by D's negligence and a fireman was injured when he was thrown off the roof by an explosion. The court held it was foreseeable that the fireman would have to attend the fire and would be at risk of the type of injuries received due to D's negligence. D was liable. This principle was confirmed by the HL in the next case.

Key case

In **Ogwo v Taylor 1988**, D had negligently started a fire when using a blowtorch. C was a fireman who was injured trying to put it out. It was held that he was owed a duty as he was only there in the exercise of his calling because of D's negligence. Note that the fireman had taken normal precautions, i.e., he had *'guarded against the normal risks'*. Had he not done so, e.g., if he had not worn protective clothing or had taken unnecessary risks, it is unlikely that there would have been liability.

Key principle: D may be liable to a professional if the professional was only on the property and in the exercise of his calling because of D's negligence.

Independent contractors s 2(4)(b)

Occupiers are not usually liable for harm caused by independent contractors on their property. The **OLA** provides an occupier is not liable if:

"in all the circumstances he had acted reasonably in entrusting the work to an independent contractor and had taken such steps (if any) as he reasonably ought in order to satisfy himself that the contractor was competent and the work had been properly done"

Thus, if the occupiers did not take care in selection, or did not check on the work, then they may be liable. Much will depend on what type of work the contractor is doing. In **Haseldine v Daw 1941,** the occupier had discharged his duty by giving the job to a competent lift engineer, as he could not be expected to have the expertise to check such specialist work himself. In **Woodward v Mayor of Hastings 1945**, a pupil was injured slipping on an icy step, which a cleaner had left in a dangerous state. The occupier was liable for the cleaner's negligence in this case because he should have checked that the snow had been properly cleared from the steps. Note:

S 2(3)(b) relates to liability *to* **contractors and other professionals**

S 2(4)(b) relates to liability *for* **contractors whose negligence harms someone else**

Example

I have a very large tree in my garden, which is rotten. I get a tree surgeon in to remove it but while he is doing so a branch breaks and he falls. Unfortunately, he lands on my neighbour's son, Jim, who is playing in the garden with my kids. Both the contractor and Jim are injured. I am unlikely to be liable *to* the contractor. A branch breaking is likely to be seen as incidental to the job and he should have appreciated and guarded against such a risk, **s 2(3)(b).**

I also wouldn't owe a duty to Jim *for* the contractor's negligence (in working whilst children are nearby) if I had chosen a reputable tree surgeon. However, if he was just a mate from the pub, I may be liable *for* his negligence because I did not act reasonably in selecting him, **s 2(4)(b)**.

The CA considered the issue of liability for independent contractors in **Gwilliam v West Hertfordshire Hospitals NHS Trust 2002.** C was injured when using a "splat-wall" (if you've never heard of one it is where people bounce from a trampoline and stick – by wearing a Velcro suit – to a wall) at a fund-raising fair in the hospital grounds. It had been set up negligently by a contractor, and, as their insurance had expired, C claimed against the hospital. As the occupier, the hospital owed C a duty of care under **s 2(1)** to take reasonable steps to ensure that a contractor had public liability insurance. The hospital had specifically requested, and paid for, such insurance and the CA held that it would be unreasonable to expect them to check the terms of the actual policy. The duty had been fulfilled so the claim failed.

Task 12

Compare the **Woodward** case to **Gwilliam**. Can you identify the difference? Now look at the next case. Why was a duty owed by the cricket club but not by the hospital?

In **Bottomley v Todmorden Cricket Club 2003**, a cricket club hired an uninsured stunt team to perform firework displays on its land. An amateur helper was injured because of the team's negligence, and sued the club. The CA held that an occupier had a duty to take reasonable care in selecting a suitable contractor to carry on a dangerous activity over his land. This would include checking that insurance was in place. As they had not done so they were liable for the injuries sustained.

Warnings s 2(4)(a) and 'obvious risks'

The occupier can discharge liability by warning signs, but these must be sufficient to keep the visitor safe (as with my shed). The **Act** provides that such a warning is not enough *"unless in all the circumstances it was enough to enable the visitor to be reasonably safe"*. So the circumstances will need looking at. If you open your premises to children you would need to have clearer warnings than for adults. You would also be expected to consider the disabled. For example, a written notice would not be sufficient to keep a blind person safe. If the danger is obvious a warning may not be needed. Lord Shaw, in **Glasgow Corporation v Taylor 1922**, said that a duty to make premises reasonably safe *"does not include an obligation of protection against dangers which are themselves obvious"*. Although on the facts there was a duty to the child, the principle remains and there have been many cases since this which make clear that 'obvious risks' do not require a warning, at least in the case of an adult. This is particularly true in the case of trespassers (see next chapter).

In **Ratcliff v McConnell 1999**, a student was seriously injured diving into a swimming pool at his college. It was closed (and locked) for the winter and he had climbed in at night. He had been drinking but the evidence was that he knew what he was doing. The court found that the risk of hitting his head on the bottom would be obvious to anyone, so the occupier was not liable.

In **Darby v National Trust 2001**, a man had drowned whilst swimming in a pond on National Trust property. His widow sued the NT under the **OLA 1957** on the basis that they should have had signs warning of the danger. The CA held that the danger of drowning was an obvious risk and so there was no need to erect warning signs. However, if the danger is not obvious there is a duty to warn of any risks. This is shown in **Taylor v English Heritage 2016**, where C was injured when he fell down a very steep path on D's property. It was not part of the official route but D knew visitors sometimes used it and had put up warning signs in three places. There was no sign where C accessed the path and the CA said the sheer drop was not an 'obvious danger' so there was a duty to warn visitors. However, D should also have realised that descending any steep slope was risky so was 50% to blame. His damages were reduced for contributory negligence (for failing to take the safer option of going down on his bottom!). This case can be compared to **Edwards v London Borough of Sutton 2016** where a man slipped off an ornamental footbridge and was injured. The trial court had found the occupier liable as the bridge had no barriers and there were no warnings. However, the CA reversed this decision and held that the occupier was not liable because the danger was obvious so there was no need for a warning. The CA also commented that not every accident is the fault of another, however serious the consequences.

A warning is also only necessary if D knows a person is likely to be on the premises, so where C is trespassing there may not be a duty to warn. The CA and the HL decided on this matter in the next two cases. Although trespassers come under the 1984 Act (see next chapter) these cases are covered briefly here because the principle established applies to both Acts.

In **Donoghue v Folkestone Properties 2003,** a trespasser went swimming in a harbour late one evening in midwinter, and was injured by an underwater obstacle. At first instance the court found a duty was owed, but the CA allowed D's appeal. There were no reasonable grounds for knowing that he or anyone else would come into the vicinity of the danger late at night in midwinter.

In **Tomlinson v Congleton Borough Council 2002**, the facts were very similar. An 18-year-old dived into a lake and sustained injury. There were notices prohibiting swimming and at first instance the judge found the risks to be 'obvious' and so dismissed his claim. The CA reversed the decision and held that D was aware of the fact that people could be in the vicinity of a risk, so they might reasonably be expected to offer some protection against it. The appeal to the HL made the law clear on this, restating the principle from **Donoghue v Folkestone Properties** that no duty is owed if it is not reasonable to expect trespassers to be on the property.

Key case

In **Tomlinson v Congleton Borough Council 2003,** the HL reversed the CA decision. Lord Hobhouse expressed *"complete agreement with"* **Donoghue v Folkestone** and made the opening comment, adding *"The law does not require disproportionate or unreasonable responses"*. The HL held that there was no duty to C where the injury derives from the dangerous nature of a voluntary activity rather than the state of the premises. Lord Hoffman stated *obiter* that even if a duty had been owed, that duty would **not** have required the council to take steps to prevent C from diving or warning him against dangers which were *'perfectly obvious'*.

Key principle: There is no duty owed if it is not reasonable to expect trespassers to be on the property, nor where the injury derives from the dangerous nature of a voluntary activity rather than the state of the premises.

Evaluation pointer

It is always worth noting any conflict between the CA and HL because disagreement at this level is something that can be criticised as making the law uncertain. The CA had significantly increased the chance of an occupier being liable to a trespasser, and seemed to give a trespasser more protection than a visitor, so the HL view is probably to be preferred.

Also, it may not always be clear what amounts to an 'obvious' danger, especially if C is a child, and this can lead to inconsistent decisions.

In **Bourne Leisure Ltd v Marsden 2009**, the CA had to consider whether the owner of a holiday park had breached the duty of care owed to visitors to the site by not informing them of a pond nor of the pathway that could be used to get to it. A 2-year-old child had drowned and the judge ruled that the occupier should have done more to warn the parents of the dangers of the pond and of the access by path. The CA reversed this decision on the basis that an occupier does not have to give warnings where the danger is obvious. The CA held that in the exercise of a reasonable duty of care the occupier had no need to alert people to such an obvious danger.

In **Geary v Weatherspoon 2011**, C had tried to slide down some banisters in a pub and fell about 4 metres onto a marble floor, seriously injuring herself. She claimed against the owners of the pub. The court held that the injury was foreseeable because there was evidence that, because the banister was low, it had tempted customers to do the same thing on previous occasions. However, in referring to **Tomlinson**, the court went on to consider whether the law should interfere in the freedom of action of people who wished to take risks. Here, as in **Tomlinson** and also in **Poppleton v Trustees of the Portsmouth Youth Activities Committee 2008**, C had freely chosen to do something she knew was dangerous so the pub owners were not liable.

Tomlinson and **Poppleton** were cited with approval in **Grimes v Hawkins 2011**, where C had injured herself diving into a pool at her friend's house when the friend's parents were away. The judge said that the principle that D had no duty to protect C from risks which were obvious in an activity undertaken voluntarily had even greater force where C was a visitor to a private home. There was no duty to prohibit swimming in an ordinary pool which contained no unexpected hazards and the risk of injury from diving in any pool is an obvious one.

Evaluation pointer

Where harm is caused by an *activity* on the property rather than *occupancy* of the property it is unclear whether the **Act** or common law rules apply. The CA in **Bottomley** said that an occupier had an "activity duty" in respect of activities, permitted or encouraged on the land, and an "occupancy duty", for the state of the premises. This case shows that both *can* come under the **Act**, but, as in **Ogwo v Taylor 1988**, did not make it clear when. Is it satisfactory that such doubt exists? If I invite you onto my land should it make any difference if you are injured by something *done* on my property (an activity) or by the mere fact that I *control* the premises (my occupancy)? **S 1(1)** implies that both come under the **Act**.

You don't need to learn every case but these examples may help you to see how the law deals with different situations and you never know what may come up in an examination. Several other cases involving warnings and 'obvious dangers' were brought under the **OLA 1984**, because C was trespassing at the time. These are discussed in the next chapter.

Examination pointer

If C is harmed whilst lawfully on someone's property then you should consider a claim under the **OLA 1957**. However, you may need to look at negligence as an alternative. This is because there is some doubt as to whether the **Act** or common law rules of negligence apply when harm is caused by an *activity* on the property rather than *occupancy* of the property. The CA in **Bottomley** said that an occupier had an "activity duty" in respect of activities, permitted or encouraged on the land, and an "occupancy duty", for the state of the premises. However, the claim failed in **Poppleton** where the harm was due to a permitted activity. In **Ogwo**, the fireman claimed under both common law negligence and the **OLA 1957**. The first regarding the *activity* of starting the fire, the second regarding D's *occupancy* of the house. The HL held that the duty owed was the same, but they did not address the issue of which type of action was appropriate. It is likely an occupier will only be liable for an activity if the property is specifically used for such an activity (**Bottomley**) but even then a claim may fail (**Poppleton**). If in doubt, discuss both.

Breach of duty and causation

Once duty has been addressed you will still have to prove breach of duty **and** causation. Breach will depend on 'all the circumstances', including C's age and any warning signs. The normal negligence rules apply regarding the standard expected. In **Wells v Cooper 1958** the householder was compared to a competent DIY person not a professional carpenter so was not in breach. The factors looked at by the courts are the same too, such as the degree of risk and expense and practicality of taking precautions. Thus, in **Jolley**, the HL held that the risk was foreseeable and would take little expense to avoid. In not removing the boat the council had therefore not reached the expected standard, so had breached its duty.

Regarding causation, the normal 'but for' and 'remoteness of damage' tests will apply. This was confirmed in **Jolley**.

Task 13

Pete the plumber comes to mend Tim's water tank in the loft. Whilst there he falls through some rotten planking and is injured. Eddie, a qualified electrician, has also been called in to repair some faulty wiring. Whilst doing so, he is electrocuted. Is Tim liable for either injury? Why/why not?

Exclusions s 2(1)

Under **s 2 (1)**, an occupier can limit or exclude liability *'in so far as he is free to'*. Exclusion notices are subject to the **Unfair Contract Terms Act 1977 (UCTA)** as amended by the **Consumer Rights Act 2015 (CRA)**. **S 65 CRA** prohibits any attempt at excluding liability for death or personal injury caused by negligence. Excluding liability for damage to property is allowed, but the term must be fair. **UCTA** still applies to business to business and consumer to consumer dealings. The **CRA** applies to businesses dealing with consumers.

One problem that arose was that if an occupier could not exclude *liability*, then they were better off excluding *visitors* – no more school trips! An amendment to **UCTA** was therefore added by the **OLA 1984**. If the visit is for educational or recreational purposes then this doesn't come within 'business' – unless the occupier runs such a business. This is still the law and is now covered by **s 66 CRA**.

Example

You own an orchard. If you charge the public to come in to pick the apples, you are running a business. You are unable to exclude liability for injury by negligence, and any other exclusion, for example in respect of damage to cars, has to be reasonable. If you allow the public free access for recreational purposes, e.g., to park and picnic there, then you are able to exclude liability as you come within the exceptions under **s 66**.

Task 14

Walk around your school, college or work premises. Can you find any warning signs or signs that attempt to exclude liability? Look around the locality too.

Defences

Apart from warnings (which **discharge** liability) and exclusion notices (which **avoid** liability), the defences of contributory negligence and consent may apply. Contributory negligence is implied in **s 2(3)** of the **Act**, which says the courts may take into account the degree of care the visitor can be expected to show for their own safety. Consent is dealt with specifically. **S 2(5)** states: *"The common duty of care does not impose on an occupier any obligation willingly accepted as his by the visitor"*

Both defences are discussed in more detail in chapters 13 and 14 as you need them for the A-level examination but not for the AS.

Summary

the duty	To see that the visitor will be reasonably safe	S2(2)
occupier	The person in control of the premises	Wheat v Lacon
children	An occupier should be prepared for children to be less careful	S2(s)(a)
professionals	Are expected to take their own precautions against risks related to their trade	S2(3)(a) Roles v Nathan
warnings	Must be enough to enable the visitor to be reasonably safe	S2(4)(b)
	If the danger is obvious a warning is less likely to be needed	Darby v National Trust
exclusions	Can limit or exclude liability 'in so far as he is free to'. Thus any such attempt is subject to UCTA 1997	S2(1)
contributory negligence	Damages may be reduced if C fails to take reasonable care for their own safety	S2(3)
consent	Not liable in respect of risks willingly accepted	S2(5)

Links to the non-substantive law

For links to the English legal system, look back at the diagram and examples in the introduction to Part 1. In particular, where a principle of law has been established the system of appeals is relevant, as these principles are established in the higher appeal courts, i.e., the CA and SC.

ADR is always relevant to tort cases too, as is access to justice, because cases can be expensive to take to court so alternatives or help with expenses may be needed. Also for an area which is covered by statute law, parliamentary law making and sources of law are relevant as much of the **1957 Act** is based on common law principles from the cases before it. Also, judges must interpret the **OLA** as written by Parliament in cases after it.

Self-test questions

1. What test is used to find who the occupier is?
2. What is the extent of the occupier's duty under *s 2(2)*?
3. What is an 'allurement' and what effect does it have?
4. When may an occupier owe a duty for work done by an independent contractor?
5. Which cases will support your answers to each of the above questions?

Answers to the tasks and self-test questions are on my website at www.drsr.org. Please click on 'Answers to tasks'. For a range of free interactive exercises, click on 'Free Exercises'.

Chapter 6: Occupier's Liability for trespassers

"If the risk of serious injury is so slight and remote that it is highly unlikely ever to materialise, it may well be that it is not reasonable to expect the occupier to take any steps to protect anyone against it." – Lord Hobhouse

By the end of this chapter you should be able to:

- ■ ***Explain the occupier's duty in cases where the harm was caused to someone not lawfully on the property***
- ■ ***Show how the law applies by reference to cases***
- ■ ***Identify problems with the law and/or discuss its development in order to evaluate it***

What is meant by an occupier's liability for trespassers?

The **Occupiers Liability Act (OLA) 1984** deals with cases where harm is caused to someone not lawfully on the occupier's property. Usually this will mean trespassers but the expression non-visitor is used in the Act because there are a few other people exercising certain rights who are covered by this **Act** rather than the **1957** one. In particular, the **Countryside and Rights of Way Act 2000** increased access rights to land and an occupier of land owes the more limited duty under the **OLA 1984** to people exercising such rights. AQA use the term trespasser so I have referred to both non-visitor and trespasser here because in quoting from the Act I need to use the terminology contained in it.

Note that you can be a lawful visitor and a trespasser in different parts of the same building. For example, you are a visitor in a pub but would be a trespasser in the living area, which is normally marked private. Similarly, if you get a plumber in to mend the kitchen sink he would become a trespasser if he went into your bedroom.

Examination pointer

You should look at the scenario carefully. If the harm occurred on someone's property then consider a claim under the **OLA**. Look for clues as to whether C is a lawful visitor or a trespasser to decide which **Act** to discuss. You may need both. Don't forget **Glasgow Corporation v Taylor 1922** suggests that an allurement may bring a child trespasser within the **OLA 1957**. This could help if, for example, the claim is for damage to property, which is not covered under the **OLA 1984**. You can use the cases involving children from the previous chapter; the principles are the same for both **Acts**.

The **OLA 1984** followed a case where two boys were injured playing on a railway track. This case is important as it led to a change in the law.

Key case

The case is **British Railways Board v Herrington 1972**. The boys could not sue under the **OLA 1957** as they should not have got through the fence onto BR's land so were not lawful visitors. The HL held BR owed them a *'common duty of humanity'* because they knew of the danger, i.e., that the fence had many gaps in it, knew that children had been getting in, and had done nothing to prevent them entering.

Key principle: If an occupier knows of a danger there is a duty to take steps to avoid it and this protection extends to trespassers. This principle is now in statutory form under the **OLA 1984**.

The duty s 1(1), s 1(3) and s 1(4)

Parliament then passed the **OLA 1984** which confirmed this case. A person can sue under the later **Act** even if they are not lawfully on the property. **S 1(1)** provides that the duty applies to non-visitors for *"injury by reason of any danger due to the state of the premises or things done or omitted to be done on them"*. The duty is more limited than for the **OLA 1957**. There is no liability for damage to property, and a duty only arises under **s 1(3)** if:

D is aware of the danger or has reasonable grounds to believe it exists

D knows or has reasonable grounds to believe a 'non-visitor' is in, or may come into, the vicinity of the danger

The risk is one against which, in all the circumstances of the case, D may reasonably be expected to offer protection

Example

Bodgem Builders Ltd. is building a house on a site next to a children's playground. The workers finish at 5 p.m. and leave the site unlocked. A child goes onto the site and falls into a large hole, injuring herself. Applying the **s 1(3)** we can say that:

Bodgem know of the danger of having an open building site

Bodgem also have reasonable grounds to believe a non-visitor will come onto the site, as they know there is a playground next door

In these circumstances, it is reasonable to expect the company to protect against the risk by locking up.

In **Higgs v Foster 2004**, C was a police officer investigating a suspected stolen trailer which had been parked on D's land. There was an uncovered pit on the land and C fell into it and suffered knee injuries. The court held that D had not had reasonable grounds to believe that there was a non-visitor in the vicinity so was not liable.

In **Kolasa v Ealing Hospital NHS Trust 2015**, C had been taken to an Accident and Emergency department following an attack. He was drunk, and while waiting he climbed on to a wall outside the hospital and fell off, sustaining further injuries. The hospital was not liable. By climbing on the wall C had gone beyond his permission to be there so became a trespasser.

The hospital was not aware of the risk and anyway it was not one that it was reasonable to expect them to offer protection against, so no duty was owed under **s 1 (3)**.

If the three points under **s 1(3)** are satisfied then the actual duty is similar to that under the **OLA 1957**. Under **s 1(4)** the duty is to:

"take such care as in all the circumstances of the case is reasonable to see that ... (the non-visitor) ... does not suffer injury on the premises by reason of the danger concerned".

In **Platt v Liverpool City Council 1997**, a 14-year-old boy died when a derelict building collapsed on top of him. The CA held that by building an eight-foot fence the council had taken such care as was reasonable in all the circumstances to see that the boy did not suffer injury on the premises.

In **Scott and Swainger v Associated British Ports 2000**, D was the occupier of a railway. On two occasions, separated by several years, two teenagers had been 'train surfing' (jumping onto a moving goods train and riding it for a short distance). On the second occasion C lost a limb. In the first case, the court held that D did not owe a duty of care under the **OLA 1984** because they did not know (or have reasonable grounds to believe) that the trespassers were in the vicinity so the second part of **s 1(3)** was not satisfied. In the second case, D had knowledge of the first incident so that part of **s 1(3)** was now satisfied. However, the evidence was that the boys would not have been deterred even by a high fence, the trains were slow moving and easy to avoid had they wished to, but they chose not to. The risk was therefore not one that D could be reasonably expected to protect against. Again, there was no duty.

In **Mann v Northern Electric Distribution Ltd 2010**, a boy, aged 15, had tried to get a football from an electricity substation and received severe burns. The owners of the substation had taken steps to prevent unauthorised access, including high walls, railings and spikes. The boy had managed to negotiate these obstacles, but the CA held that this was not foreseeable. There was therefore no obligation on the occupier to guard against it, so D was not liable.

In the case of a younger child it may be more reasonable to expect an occupier to take precautions, but a teenager or adult is expected to be aware of risks and avoid them. In **Ratcliff v McConnell 1999** (discussed below), an occupier was not liable to a teenager who voluntarily took a risk. However, the CA made clear that the duty varied and that a child would not be expected to recognise the same risks as an adult would, so in these circumstances an occupier would be expected to take more care.

So there are three parts to the duty.

> **S 1(1)** provides that the duty applies for *"injury by reason of any danger due to the state of the premises or things done or omitted to be done on them"*
>
> **S 1 (3)** states the three matters which must be satisfied
>
> **S 1(4)** states that the duty is to *"take such care as in all the circumstances of the case is reasonable"*

Examination pointer

The occupier need not *know* of the danger or the trespasser, but there would need to be some evidence for there to be *"reasonable grounds"*. In an examination question, you should look for clues such as 'several times' or 'X knew that...' to indicate it had happened before as in **Scott and Swainger**. Also, reference to something like a nearby playground, as in my example, would give D *"reasonable grounds"* to believe a child might enter the site. Look too at the ages given. In my example, you could use **Glasgow Corporation v Taylor 1922** to suggest that Bodgems may be liable, as they should take greater care in respect of children. If told the child is very young use **Phipps v Rochester Corporation 1955** to say Bodgems may avoid liability as the parents should be responsible. However, then note it was suggested in **Phipps** that this may not apply to a playground, where it is more reasonable to expect children to be alone. Finally, consider 'allurements' as these may imply an invitation and thus the **1957 Act** as suggested by **Glasgow Corporation** and **Jolley**.

Warnings s 1(5) and 'obvious risks'

The occupier can discharge the duty by putting up warning signs, but as for the **OLA 1957** these must be adequate to protect C. **S 1(5)** provides that the occupier must take *"such steps as are reasonable in all the circumstances of the case to give warning of the danger"* so whether the warning is adequate will again depend on the circumstances of the case. If children could gain access you would need a clearer warning than for adults. However, if the danger is obvious there may be no duty to provide a warning at all. Again, this is the same as the **1957 Act**. In **Ratcliff v McConnell 1999**, a student was seriously injured diving into a swimming pool at his college. It was closed (and locked) for the winter and he had climbed in at night. He had been drinking but the evidence was that he knew what he was doing. The court found that the risk of hitting his head on the bottom would be obvious to anyone, including the student, so the occupier was not liable. In **Scott and Swainger** (above), the court approved **Ratcliff** and noted that young men often did rash things, especially after a drink, but that they could not blame others for the risks they voluntarily took and which were obvious.

In **Donoghue v Folkestone Properties 2003**, a trespasser went swimming in a harbour late one evening in midwinter, and was injured by an underwater obstacle. At first instance the court found a duty was owed, but the CA allowed D's appeal. Although D knew of the obstruction, and may have known that someone was in the habit of swimming in the harbour during the summer, there were no reasonable grounds for knowing that he or anyone else would come into the vicinity of the danger late at night in midwinter and there was no need to guard against obvious dangers. This shows the overlap between the third part of the test and warnings. If there is an obvious danger there is no need for a warning, and an obvious risk is not one 'against which, in all the circumstances of the case, D may reasonably be expected to offer protection'.

Key case

In **Tomlinson v Congleton Borough Council 2003**, an 18-year-old dived into a lake and sustained injury. There were notices prohibiting swimming and at first instance the judge found the risks to be 'obvious' and so dismissed his claim. Although the CA allowed C's appeal, the HL then reversed the CA decision, reinstating the judgment. Lord Hobhouse expressed *"complete agreement with"* **Donoghue v Folkestone** and made the comment opening this chapter, adding *"The law does not require disproportionate or unreasonable responses"*.

The HL also held that if the injury derives from the dangerous nature of a voluntary activity rather than the state of the premises no duty will be owed. Lord Hoffman stated *obiter* that even if a duty had been owed, that duty would not have required the council to take steps to prevent C from diving or warning him against dangers which were *'perfectly obvious'*.

Key principle: There is no need to warn of obvious risks and there is no duty where the injury derives from the dangerous nature of a voluntary activity rather than the state of the premises.

Dangerous activities or dangerous premises

As the HL said in **Tomlinson**, the occupier is not liable if harm is caused by what the trespasser does, rather than the state of the premises. In **Keown Coventry NHS Trust 2006**, an eleven-year-old child was injured when he climbed a fire escape in hospital grounds and fell. The hospital was not liable because the harm to the child occurred as a result of him climbing on the fire escape, not because the fire escape or building was dangerous. Similarly, in **Sidorn v Patel 2007**, some tenants of a flat had got onto the flat roof of the apartment building during a party, and were dancing. C fell through a skylight and was seriously injured. She sued the landlord for not ensuring the skylight was safe and not warning tenants of the danger. The tenants had no authority to go on the roof for any purpose so the relevant Act was the **Occupiers Liability Act 1984**. The defence argued that it was an 'activity' case, not a 'premises' case. She and her friends were adults who went outside when it was dark and they had been drinking. They had danced around the skylight without looking carefully at what they were doing. The danger was therefore to do with their activity and not the state of the premises. The court agreed. Neither the roof nor the skylights were dangerous within the meaning of the Act. Her claim failed. A case that succeeded on similar facts was **Young v Kent CC 2005**. A schoolboy was injured after climbing a wall and then onto a roof to get a ball. He fell through a skylight. By climbing on to the roof he became a trespasser so the 1984 Act applied. The school was aware that children had climbed on to the roof before. Also, unlike in the above two cases, the court decided that the state of the premises posed a danger. The roof was an inherently dangerous place for a child, particularly having regard to the brittle nature of the skylight. The council who ran the school was liable.

We also saw in **Kolasa v Ealing Hospital NHS Trust 2015**, that the injury was caused by his activity rather than the state of the premises so the hospital was not liable. The main difference seems to be that in **Young v Kent CC 2005**, it was a school with young children around so more care should have been taken. Also, the court referred to the fact that the skylight was brittle so arguably it was the state of the premises rather than his activity that caused the harm.

Examination pointer

You can see from these cases that the circumstances will be relevant, so it is important to look carefully at any given facts. If you are not sure you can use a case which goes each way, e.g., comparing **Keown Coventry NHS Trust 2006** to **Young v Kent CC 2005**.

Task 15

Paul has a very deep swimming pool in his garden. The neighbours' kids sometimes sneak in at night so he puts up a high fence and a big "KEEP OUT" sign. He knows you are studying law so he asks you if this will protect him from being sued if one of them is injured. What will you tell him?

After a few years Paul's fence has several gaps in it which he keeps meaning to fix. The neighbours' son climbs through a gap in the fence and drowns. Paul is surprised at being sued and asks you why. How will you explain why your advice might be different now?

Defences

Consent as a defence is implied in **s 1(6)** which states that no duty is owed to any person "*in respect of risks willingly accepted*". Contributory negligence may also apply. This is where any award of damages is reduced to take into account C's contribution to the harm. **Ratcliff v McConnell 1999** is a good example because at first instance the court decided D was liable but that damages should be reduced because C contributed to his own injuries. The CA reversed the decision and held that D was not liable because the effect of **s 1(6)** is that if C willingly takes a risk there is no duty. In this sense D is avoiding the duty, in another sense C is effectively consenting to the risk of harm.

These two defences overlap with the idea of warnings in that the bigger the warning the more likely the risk is 'willingly accepted', or at least that C was contributorily negligent.

Both defences are discussed in more detail in chapters 13 and 14 as you need them for the A-level examination but not for the AS.

Examination pointer

Look for clues that something is forbidden. *Doing* something without permission is equal to *being* somewhere without permission, so makes D a trespasser. **Tomlinson v Congleton Borough Council 2003** came under the **OLA 1984** because he ignored the 'No Swimming' signs, thus becoming a trespasser. Look carefully at any warning. Is it adequate to keep people safe? If children are involved will it keep *them* safe? If a warning is not adequate then it may actually make it *more* likely that the claim will succeed, as it shows the occupier *knew* of the danger. Clues like 'swimming at night', in a 'deep lake' or a 'busy harbour' should direct you to the 'obvious risk' issue, that D may avoid liability even *without* a warning sign. Note the overlap with **s 1(3)**. An 'obvious' danger is not one it would be *reasonable to expect D to protect against*. Finally, consider whether the defences apply.

Breach of duty and causation

Whether the duty is breached will depend on the facts of the case, including the age of the C and any warning signs. The usual factors looked at in assessing the standard of care at common law will also apply. In **Tomlinson**, Lord Hoffman said that what amounted to reasonable care depended not only on the likelihood of harm or the seriousness of potential injury, but also on the social value of the activity and the cost of preventative measures.

The law on both factual and legal causation is also as for common law negligence.

Evaluation pointer

Do you think D should be liable to trespassers at all? It can be argued that there should be no liability to those who should not be on your property in the first place. However, the **Act** is aimed at cases like **Herrington** where the railway company had been negligent and knew the fence had gaps in it, but the children were trespassing and so would not have been owed a duty under the **OLA 1957**.

Task 16

Read back over the last two Chapters and make a flow chart showing how to prove liability under both **OLA**s. Add a case in support of each point. Keep this to refer to when practising answering a problem question. Many of the cases, especially those involving children, are relevant to both areas.

Summary

S 1(1)	provides that a duty applies for injury by reason of any danger due to the state of the premises or things done or omitted to be done on them
S 1(3)	provides that for a duty to be owed:

(the occupier) must be aware of the danger or have reasonable grounds to believe it exists
(the occupier) must know or have reasonable grounds to believe a 'non-visitor' is in, or may come into, the area
the risk is one against which it is reasonably expected to offer protection

S 1 (4)	provides that the duty is to:

'take such care as in all the circumstances of the case is reasonable to see that ... (the non-visitor)... does not suffer injury on the premises by reason of the danger concerned'

S 1 (5)	provides that the duty can be discharged if the occupier takes:

'such steps as are reasonable in all the circumstances of the case to give warning of the danger'

S 1(6)	provides that no duty is owed where the risk is willingly accepted, i.e., C has consented to the risk

'Obvious dangers' overlap with the duty, warnings and consent

If the danger is obvious the risk may not be one against which it is reasonably expected to offer protection so S 1(3) is not satisfied (Scott and Swainger)
If the danger is obvious then a warning under s 1 (5) is less likely to be needed (Ratcliff/Tomlinson)
If the danger is obvious then s 1 (4) may be satisfied as 'in all the circumstances of the case' it is not reasonable to expect more of the occupier (Platt)
If the danger is obvious then C will be deemed to have consented to it (Ratcliff)

There is no liability for damage to property, only injury

Links to the non-substantive law

For links to the English legal system, look back at the diagram and examples in the introduction to Part 1. In particular, where a principle of law has been established the system of appeals is relevant, as these principles are established in the higher appeal courts, i.e., the CA and SC. ADR is always relevant to tort cases too, as is access to justice, because cases can be expensive to take to court so alternatives or help with expenses may be needed. Also for an area which is covered by statute law, parliamentary law making and sources of law are relevant. For the **OLA 1984** in particular, the Law Commission as an influence on Parliament can be linked because following the decision in Herrington the Government asked the LC to report and this led to the 1984 Act. Also, as with the **OLA 1957**, the **OLA 1984** is based on common law principles from the cases before it. Also, judges must interpret both the **OLAs** as written by Parliament in cases after them.

Self-test questions

1. What case led to the **OLA 1984**?
2. Which later case involving a railway, illustrates the more limited duty under the **1984 Act**?
3. What are the 3 points for proving the occupiers' duty under **s 1(3)**?
4. Why was there no liability in **Ratcliff**?
5. On what basis do cases involving children trespassers sometimes come under the **OLA 1957**?

Answers to the tasks and self-test questions are on my website at www.drsr.org. **Please click on 'Answers to tasks'. For a range of free interactive exercises, click on 'Free Exercises'.**

Summary 1: Negligence, occupier's liability and remedies

Duty of care: Whether a duty is owed is based on the Caparo v Dickman 1990 test

- there must be foreseeability of harm
- there must be proximity between C and D
- it must be fair, just and reasonable to impose a duty on D

Task 17

The last part is a matter of policy, what does this mean?

Task 18

Look up the tests mentioned above. Draw a diagram adding case examples. Keep this for revision.

Breach of duty: The standard expected of D is that of the reasonable person, an objective test **(Blyth)**

- **Nettleship v Weston 1971** – a learner driver should reach the standard of a competent driver

Note, though the subjective element:

- **Bolitho v City & Hackney HA 1998** – professionals
- **Mullin v Richards 1998** – children

Look at the four factors which apply in all cases:

- the degree of risk – Maguire v Harland & Wolff plc 2005
- the seriousness of potential harm – Paris v Stepney BC 1951
- whether the risk was justifiable – Watt v Hertfordshire CC 1954
- the expense and practicality of taking precautions – Latimer v AEC 1952

Damage caused by the breach: Causation in fact and in law

- would the harm have occurred 'but for' D's act or omission? Barnett v Chelsea & Kensington HMC 1968 but note also Fairchild v Glenhaven Funeral Services Ltd
- was the harm foreseeable or was it too remote? The Wagon Mound 1966
- was this type of harm foreseeable? Hughes v Lord Advocate
- does the thin-skull rule apply? Smith v Leech Brain

Note that foreseeability comes into all 3 areas, but becomes more specific at each stage.

Task 19

Add the rules on breach and causation to your diagram on the duty rules and keep this for revision.

Occupiers' liability summary

The first thing to establish is whether D is an occupier. This is the control test from **Wheat v Lacon** and applies in all cases.

The next step is to decide whether C is a lawful visitor or not a lawful visitor (e.g., a trespasser). There is a separate Act for each with different rules as regards whether a duty is owed to the visitor.

Here is a summary:

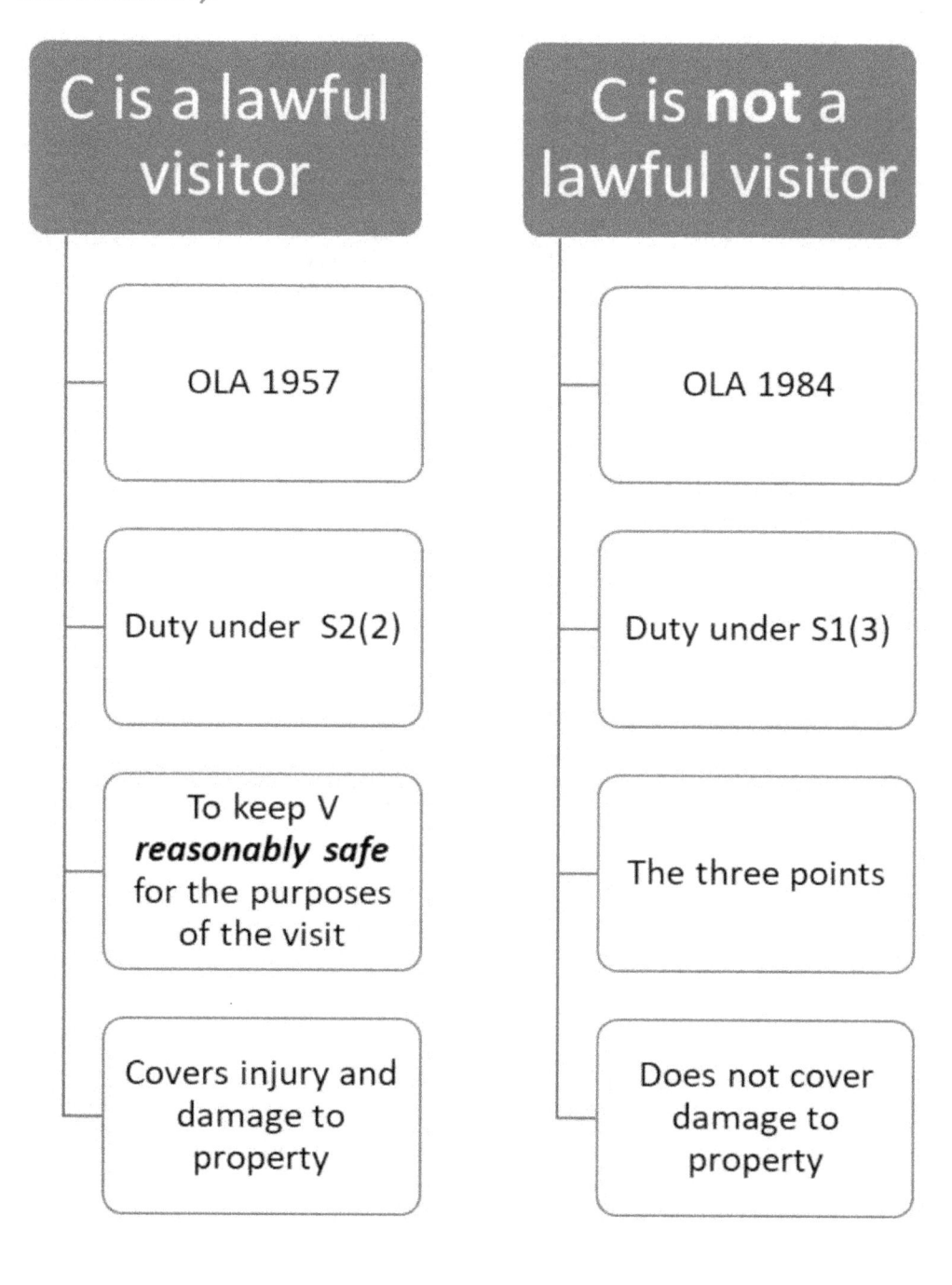

C is a lawful visitor	C is **not** a lawful visitor
OLA 1957	OLA 1984
Duty under S2(2)	Duty under S1(3)
To keep V *reasonably safe* for the purposes of the visit	The three points
Covers injury and damage to property	Does not cover damage to property

The rules on breach of duty and causation apply to both Acts. Here is another summary:

OLA 1957 and OLA 1984

Is there a breach of duty? – D must take reasonable care in all the circumstances of the case (apply the ordinary standard factors for breach)	Jolley
Children – greater duty Consider age and parental responsibility	S2(3)(a) Glasgow Phipps
Is there an allurement?	Glasgow Jolley
Contractors – lesser duty – they should guard against risks related to their jobs	Roles v Nathan
Is an independent contractor negligent? Occupier may be liable if the work is not checked	S2(4)(b) Woodward Haseldene
Did the breach cause the harm? – the but for test + foreseeability / remoteness	Barnet Wagon Mound Jolley

The last thing to do is to consider whether D can avoid or exclude liability. Here is a final summary:

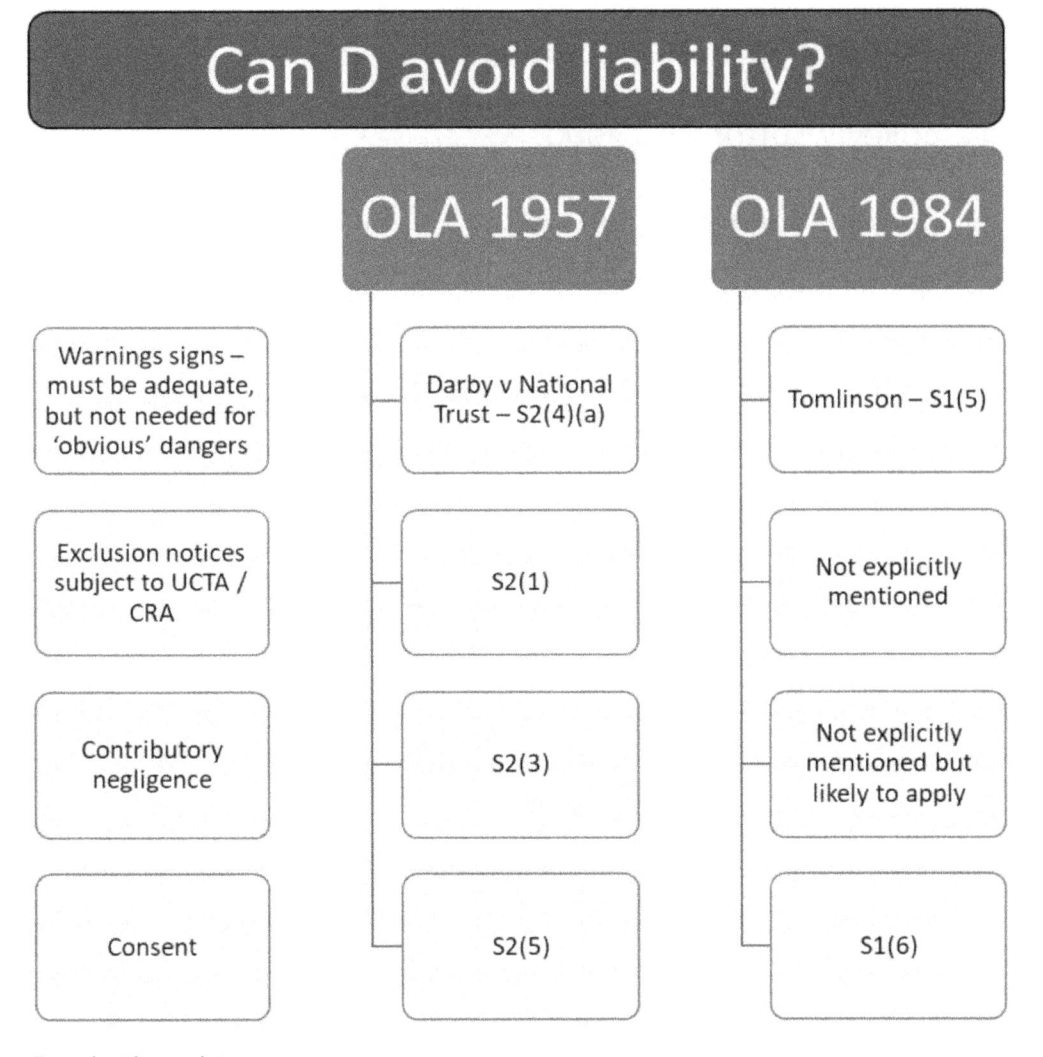

Can D avoid liability?

OLA 1957

- Warnings signs – must be adequate, but not needed for 'obvious' dangers — Darby v National Trust – S2(4)(a)
- Exclusion notices subject to UCTA / CRA — S2(1)
- Contributory negligence — S2(3)
- Consent — S2(5)

OLA 1984

- Tomlinson – S1(5)
- Not explicitly mentioned
- Not explicitly mentioned but likely to apply
- S1(6)

Examination pointer

Note that negligence and occupiers' liability overlap:

If the harm occurred to a visitor on someone else's property discuss **OLA 1957**.

If the harm occurred to a trespasser on someone else's property discuss **OLA 1984**.

If neither **OLA** is satisfied, discuss negligence and prove a duty is owed by applying the **Caparo** test. For all three you need to go on to prove breach and causation as well as the duty, and discuss defences if relevant.

Task 20

Note the brief facts and the principles of the cases below.

Glasgow Corporation v Taylor

Phipps v Rochester Corporation

Jolley v Sutton LBC 2000

General Cleaning Contractors v Christmas

Ogwo v Taylor

Bottomley v Todmorden Cricket Club

Tomlinson

Chapter 7: The AS examination (7161)

Remember, if you plan to do the A-level there is no need to take an external examination at the end of Year 1 and it won't count towards the A-level. However, if, you are not 100% sure about doing the full A-Level you should do it, then you will have a law qualification for AS. If you are doing the A-level you can treat this as a mock (but you will need to look at the remedy of damages which has moved to Chapter 15 at the end of Part 2 for this book).

All papers are a mix of multiple-choice, short answer and extended writing questions. The English legal system (non-substantive law) comes into both papers (see the table below for what is examined on each paper), the difference being the core substantive law. Each paper represents 50% of the AS examination.

Paper 1: The English legal system (40 marks) plus criminal law (40 marks)

Paper 2: The English legal system (40 marks) plus tort (40 marks)

About the exam

The assessment objectives (AOs)

These apply to all A-level courses and all examination boards. The examination will test you in the following ways.

AO1 tests your knowledge and understanding of the English legal system and legal rules and principles (23-25%)

AO2 tests your ability to apply legal rules and principles to given scenarios in order to present a legal argument using appropriate terminology (12.5-14.5%)

AO3 tests your ability to evaluate and analyse the legal rules, principles and concepts (11.5-13.5%)

The percentages total 50%, this is for each of the two papers so together totals 100% of the AS examination. You should be aware of these weightings so that you plan your time accordingly. A01 accounts for nearly half the marks. The other two are reasonably even.

For specimen papers and mark schemes visit the AQA site at www.aqa.org.uk. The following table relates to the AS examination.

For teachers: Please visit my website at www.drsr.org for a teacher's guide on the changes to the specifications and examinations.

The English legal system: What goes where for AS 7161?

Paper 1 Crime	Paper 2 Tort
The nature of law (legal and other rules, civil & criminal distinctions and sources)	The nature of law (legal and other rules, civil & criminal distinctions and sources)
The rule of law	Parliamentary law-making
Precedent	Delegated legislation
Law Reform (including Law Commission proposals and reforms)	The Law Commission as an influence on law-making
Criminal courts and process (including appeals and sentencing)	Statutory interpretation
Lay people	The European Union
Legal personnel	Civil courts and process (including appeals)
Judges and their role in criminal courts	Alternative dispute resolution
Independence of the judiciary	Judges and their role in civil courts
Access to justice and funding in the criminal system	Access to justice and funding in the civil system

Types of question and apportionment of marks

For each paper, there are:

5 multiple-choice questions on the substantive law and 5 on the English legal system at 1 mark each (total 10 marks).

2 short-answer questions (1 on substantive law and 1 on the English legal system) at 3 marks each (total 6 marks).

2 mixed questions covering BOTH the substantive law and the English legal system at 12 marks each (total 24 marks)

2 extended writing questions (1 on substantive law and 1 on the English legal system) at 20 marks each (total 40 marks).

Overall totals are 40 marks for the substantive law and 40 for ELS making a total for each paper of 80 marks.

Extended writing questions can be on the application or evaluation of the law, or a mix of both of these. They require that you provide "an extended answer which shows a clear logical and sustained line of reasoning leading to a valid conclusion".

The diagram below gives a brief idea about how the two mixed questions might work (repeated from the introduction). You would need to explain and apply the law on negligence and then explain the law on one of the other matters as appropriate, depending on the question asked. You would need to expand on these depending on the given facts; this is just a brief example to show how they can link to a question on negligence.

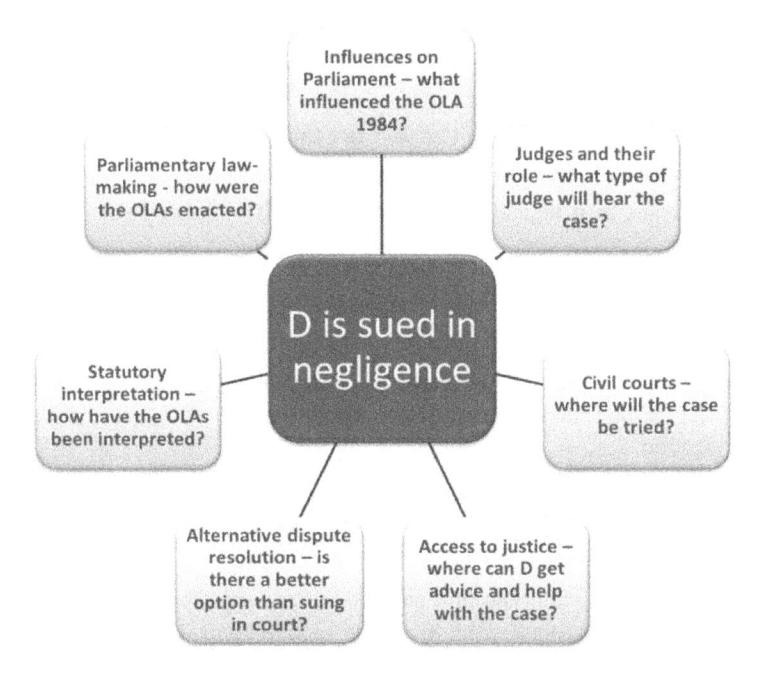

D is sued in negligence

- Influences on Parliament – what influenced the OLA 1984?
- Judges and their role – what type of judge will hear the case?
- Parliamentary law-making - how were the OLAs enacted?
- Statutory interpretation – how have the OLAs been interpreted?
- Civil courts – where will the case be tried?
- Alternative dispute resolution – is there a better option than suing in court?
- Access to justice – where can D get advice and help with the case?

Examination guidance

Application advice

Read the scenarios carefully to make sure you understand the questions. Sometimes you will be directed to a specific area of law and sometimes not. It may be necessary to discuss more than one as there is an overlap. However, if you are told to discuss a particular area you cannot get marks for discussing any other.

Try to summarise the facts in a few words. This is valuable when time is short. The principle of the case is the important part, although you may need to discuss the facts briefly to show why you have chosen that particular case.

Example

In **Reeves v MPC 1999**, one principle was that where there was a close proximity between the police and the victim the principle from **Hill v CC for West Yorkshire 1988** did not apply, so it was fair, just and reasonable to impose a duty. A second principle was that a foreseeable act will not break the chain of causation. You don't need all the facts, just what is relevant. If the scenario involves, e.g., a hospital and a patient, **Reeves** can be used to suggest that a duty may be owed and the relevant fact is the close relationship (police and prisoner is like hospital and patient). If the scenario involves something that D argues breaks the chain **Reeves** is an appropriate case to support the point that an act will not do so if it is foreseeable. Here the relevant fact is that he was a known suicide risk as this is the fact that relates to foreseeability.

If you can't remember the name of a case that is relevant don't leave it out but refer to it in a general way, e.g., 'in one decided case...' or 'in a similar case...'

You need to use *current* and *relevant* legal rules, which come from statutes or cases. **Key cases** highlight cases which are particularly important. Also use the ***examination pointers*** plus the ***diagrams*** or ***summaries*** at the end of each chapter as a guide. An answer should be rounded off with a conclusion as to liability where possible. You should never start an answer with "D will be liable ...." What you need to do is to use the law to prove it:

Identify the appropriate area of law – this will tell the examiner you have understood the focus of the scenario and will shape your answer.

Apply the relevant rules in a logical way to the facts – this will be the substance of your answer. Define the area of law then take each part of the definition in turn. Do this for each area if there is more than one. If you do this logically you won't leave anything out. If the area is covered by a statute, quote the law from that statute accurately and with section numbers if possible.

Add a little more detail if there is a particular issue shown by the facts – there will often be something particular to focus on so look for clues in the given facts to see if you need more on anything, e.g., causation.

Support your application with relevant cases – only use cases which are relevant to the particular scenario, and only state those facts that are essential to show the examiner why you have chosen that case e.g., because the facts are similar.

Conclude in a way that is sustainable and supported by what you have said and the cases you used – it is useful to look back at the question at this point. If it says, "Advise Mary ...", then make sure that your answer does so. In your conclusion, you should pull together the different strands of your answer and the say that based on that application "I would advise Mary that ...".

Try to refer to the facts of a scenario as often as you can when applying the law. This indicates that you are answering the specific question and have a sound enough knowledge to know which cases are relevant to the facts. It also helps to keep you focused.

Evaluation advice

Essays require more discussion and evaluation of the law or legal issues. The *key criticisms* in the summaries are designed to help with this, along with the *evaluation pointers*.

In an essay question, you may need to form an opinion or weigh up arguments about an area of law or legal procedure. Try to balance any arguments by referring to more than one viewpoint. Also round off your answer with a short concluding paragraph, preferably referring back to the question. This shows the examiner you are addressing the specific question and not one you would have preferred to have been asked.

As with application of the law, you should try to take a logical approach. The beginning should introduce the subject matter, the central part should explain/analyse/consider advantages and disadvantages of it as appropriate, and the conclusion should bring the various strands of argument together with reference to the question set.

The mixed questions

There are two mixed questions. The '*links to non-substantive law*' should help you to see how an area of law connects to the English legal system. The law spans various areas of process, procedure, rights and remedies as well as substantive laws such as crime and tort. These all interconnect and you will need to show you understand this connection between the substantive and non-substantive law.

Some questions may have a clear link although others may not. There will always be some type of link however, so try to connect the two parts, e.g., if asked to explain if Tom is liable in negligence and how any remedy would be calculated you would first need to apply the law you have learnt on negligence to whatever Tom has done. Depending on the exact information given in the question you can then discuss remedies reasonably separately, but you can tie the two together with occasional references to the harm that occurred to Tom's victim and what remedy seems appropriate in the circumstances.

The mixed question will cover both application (advise X) and evaluation (assess Y) so …

… here's a summary:

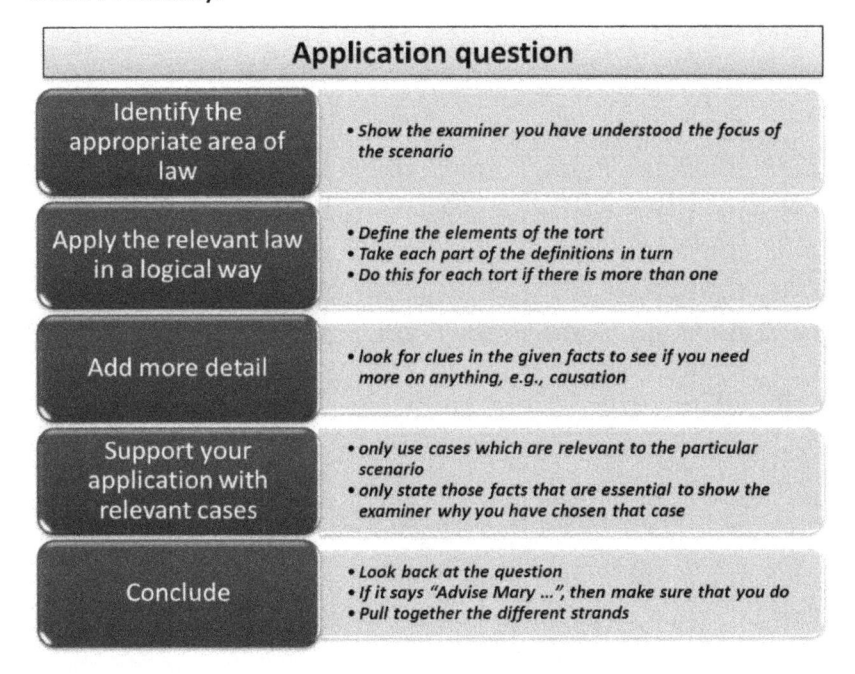

Application question

Identify the appropriate area of law
- Show the examiner you have understood the focus of the scenario

Apply the relevant law in a logical way
- Define the elements of the tort
- Take each part of the definitions in turn
- Do this for each tort if there is more than one

Add more detail
- look for clues in the given facts to see if you need more on anything, e.g., causation

Support your application with relevant cases
- only use cases which are relevant to the particular scenario
- only state those facts that are essential to show the examiner why you have chosen that case

Conclude
- Look back at the question
- If it says "Advise Mary …", then make sure that you do
- Pull together the different strands

Evaluation question

Introduce the subject matter
- *Identify the area of law*
- *State the main issue(s)*

Explain, Analyse, Consider
- *Advantages*
- *Disadvantages*
- *Either: take all the advantages and then all the disadvantages (AAA + DDD)*
- *Or: take advantages and disadvantages one at a time (A-D + A-D + A-D etc.)*

Conclude
- Bring the various strands of argument together
- Refer to the question set

Examination paper for AS

Although this book covers tort law I have included the English legal system in this paper because that is what you will get in the real examination. You should refer to your English legal system materials for revision on this area.

Task 21

For the AS examination, the marks are evenly distributed between the English legal system and tort. There are 80 marks in total and a time of 1½ hours.

Answer all questions

Tick the correct answer for multiple choice questions

[1] The test from Caparo v Dickman provides that a duty will only be imposed if it is fair, just and what? **1 mark**

A Negligible

B Foreseeable

C Reasonable

D Equitable

[2] In **Montgomery v Lanarkshire Health Board 2015** the Supreme Court held that the **Bolam** test for breach of duty did not apply to value judgments, only to professional considerations. Which profession does the test apply to? **1 mark**

A Driving instruction

B The legal profession

C The teaching profession

D The medical profession

[3] Which of the following statements is the most accurate description of causation in law? **1 mark**

A D is liable for all reasonable consequences of the breach

B D is liable for all direct consequences of the breach

C D is liable for all consequences of the breach

D D is liable for all foreseeable consequences of the breach

[4] When does an occupier not need to provide a warning about any risks on the premises? **1 mark**

A When the risk is obvious

B When C is a trespasser

C When the premises are not occupied

D When C is an adult

[5] Select the **one** true statement about an occupier's liability for harm caused by an independent contractor. **1 mark**

A An occupier is always liable for harm caused by an independent contractor

B An occupier is never liable for harm caused by an independent contractor

C An occupier is not usually liable for harm caused by an independent contractor

D An occupier is liable for foreseeable harm caused by an independent contractor

[6] In a judgment which **one** of the following aids to statutory interpretation gives the **least** flexibility? **1 mark**

A The literal rule

B The golden rule

C The purposive approach

D Hansard

[7] Which **one** of the following EU institutions is responsible for initiating new laws? **1 mark**

A The European Commission

B The European Parliament

C The European Court of Justice

D The Council of Ministers

[8] Which one of the following statements is most accurate? **1 mark**

A All bills start in the House of Commons

B All bills start in the House of Lords

C Most bills start in the House of Commons

D Most bills start in the House of Lords

[9] Which one of the following must be assessed by the court rather than included in a negligence claim? **1 mark**

A Loss of earnings

B Loss of amenity

C Damage to property

D Medical expenses

[10] Which one of the following institutions oversees legal aid provision? **1 mark**

A The Legal Aid Agency

B The Legal Aid Board

C The Legal Services Commission

D The Legal Aid Commission

[11] Both public bills and private bills may become an Act of Parliament. Explain these two main types of bill. **3 marks**

[12] A group of teenagers are playing football when the ball goes into the grounds of a derelict building owned by Mr Jones. Mr Jones was fed up with local boys playing around the building so put up an 8-foot fence and signs saying "Danger: Keep out". Shane, one of the teenagers, manages to get over the fence but is injured when part of the building collapses as he grabs the ball. Suggest why Mr Jones does not owe Shane a duty under the **Occupiers Liability Act 1984**. **3 marks**

[13] A bridge has collapsed and is in a dangerous state. Andy, a police officer, takes charge of the scene but then leaves it unattended without putting up cones, barriers or other signs. Sam, a passing motorist, is injured by the bridge further collapsing and has to spend a week off work. Advise Sam as to his rights and remedies in the tort of negligence against the police and assess the three tracks that a negligence case may be allocated to. **12 marks**

[14] Xavier was slightly injured in an accident and was taken to the accident and emergency department at a hospital. He later discharged himself without being attended to and climbed over a wall. He fell off and suffered injuries and torn clothing. Advise Xavier whether he has a claim against the hospital as occupiers of the premises and assess the role of the Law Commission as an influence on parliamentary law-making.

In Question 15 you are expected to provide an extended answer which shows a clear, logical and sustained line of reasoning leading to a valid conclusion.

[15]

Kevin manages a fitness club and had recently installed some equipment, which he bought second hand. He asked a local specialist firm to check the equipment to make sure it was safe. They said all was well except for the climbing wall which they judged was not safe. Kevin put up a sign on the door to the room containing the climbing area saying 'Danger: No admittance'.

The following day one of the members, Inga, injured her knee-cap when the treadmill she was using ran too fast and threw her off. Her brother Ian, who was also a member had wanted to go climbing but saw the sign saying No admittance. He thought he'd take a look and it seemed all OK to him so he had a go on one of the climbing walls. The wall partly collapsed and Ian broke his ankle.

Consider Kevin's liability to compensate both Inga and Ian for their injuries. **20 marks**

In Question 16 you are expected to provide an extended answer which shows a clear, logical and sustained line of reasoning leading to a valid conclusion.

[16] Explain the legislative process in Parliament and discuss the value of this process.

The Bridge

This section contains an evaluation of the law so far, along with an explanation and examples of the nature of law, which wasn't need for AS but which you will need for the A-level examination. The law plays an important role in settling disputes between individuals. An individual's liability is usually based on blameworthiness, or fault, so that the imposition of sanctions or compensation is justified.

In Part 2 of this book, ideas for links to the nature of law appear at the end of every Chapter so you can think about these as you go through each area. As before, look for the heading 'Links to the non-substantive law' which I have now split into the English legal system (ELS) and the nature of law. In these boxes the links to the nature of law specifically relate to the concepts of law and morals and fault which need to be linked to tort for the A-level examination. However, if appropriate, you can use tort cases in a discussion of the concepts which appear on other papers (justice and balancing competing interests). Therefore, if one of these is particularly relevant I have mentioned it.

Key criticisms of negligence at common law

- *It is arguable that the Caparo test is insufficiently clear because the third part allows too much flexibility. Judges make decisions based on public policy, arguably a job for an elected government*
- *The objective standard for breach of duty means that learners are treated in the same way as experienced drivers – Nettleship*
- *The thin-skull rule can be seen as unfair to D, who will be liable for unforeseen harm as in Smith v Leech Brain*
- *On a positive note, the harm must now be foreseeable which is fairer than the old rule that D was liable for all direct consequences – The Wagon Mound*

Key criticisms of occupiers' liability under the two statutes

- *It is not clear at what age a child becomes the occupier's responsibility rather than the parent's*
- *It may be difficult for an occupier to know whether the property contains an allurement, what is alluring to a child may be quite uninteresting to an adult*
- *It may not always be clear what dangers are 'obvious' so that no warning is necessary*
- *The HL overruling the CA in Tomlinson shows conflict in the higher courts, and thus uncertainty in the law*
- *How far should you be liable for trespassers? It seems fair where children are concerned but less so for adults, on the other hand it can be said it makes people take greater care for safety generally*

- *It is not clear whether UCTA applies to the OLA 1984. If not, it means trespassers have more rights than visitors as D will not be able to exclude liability*

Task 22

Look back at the **Evaluation pointer** boxes in Part 1. Write some notes on these with case examples. Add your own thoughts. Keep these notes for revision and as a guide to an evaluation question.

Links to the non-substantive law

For AS, you only needed to link the substantive criminal law to the English legal system, for A-level you still need to do that but you also need to link it to the nature of law, particularly in relation to fault and morals. I gave you a brief introduction to the nature of law concepts in Part 1 because you will need to do this for the Part 1 topics too, just not for the AS examination. Here is a bit more detail.

The nature of law (concepts)

The word law in phrases such as criminal law, human rights law, contract law etc., refers to the substance of the law (hence these topics are called substantive law). The word law in a wider sense is a more elusive concept, as it relates to the nature rather than the substance of law. It involves consideration of what academics and judges think the nature of law is (and what it should be). This in itself involves consideration of theories of law, such as law and justice, law and morality, the role of law in balancing competing interests and the role of law in punishing (criminal liability) or compensating (civil liability) based on fault. When considering the nature of law you need to look at the rest of your course from a different perspective. The examples given at the end of each Chapter should help you use cases and procedures you know to illustrate a discussion of any of these concepts. As a reminder, I repeat here what I said in Chapter 1.

Although only fault and morals are specifically assigned to the tort paper (plus balancing competing interests with injunctions), AQA have confirmed that "where appropriate, irrespective of the Paper to which a Nature of Law/ELS topic is assigned, examples may be drawn from the substantive law in other Papers". For the nature of law this means that you can also use examples from criminal law, contract and/or human rights to illustrate these concepts (unless you have been specifically asked to discuss tort cases only).

The law plays a role in society by regulating behaviour and establishing social control. It punishes those convicted of a crime and compensates the victims of any civil wrongdoing. It also facilitates (e.g., by giving powers to form contracts or get married) and protects (e.g., by laws against theft and violence, and consumer protection laws). The law plays an important role in society not only in providing **justice** but also in **balancing competing interests** (both public and private) in order to do so. It sometimes involves enforcing **moral** as well as legal rules, and legal liability usually relies on **fault**, e.g., one role of the law is to punish those found to be at fault, or blameworthy. The law of negligence is based on fault (breach of duty) so that if D is negligent the court will impose sanctions in the sense of ordering compensation to be paid. These are all concepts of law, or legal theories. Another area that comes into many negligence cases is that of public policy. We saw that with the third part of the **Caparo** test which is partly based on what is best for society. In the next two chapters you will see this again because the law imposes even stricter controls on proving a duty in cases of economic loss and psychiatric harm, again for reasons of public policy. Injunctions also involve public policy as well as balancing competing interests, and we will cover these in Chapter 10. We also saw when considering breach of duty that this is based on an objective standard. This means D is judged against what an average person would do, traditionally referred to as the 'man in the street' representing the public, and this is also part of the theory of tort law.

Most people recognise the role of law in punishing offenders who are found to be at fault in criminal cases, but the law has a less obvious role in many other areas. The following are all real cases and provide examples of the role that the law plays in society in relation to the above concepts. This covers a range so that you can get an idea of how the law in practice relates to the different theories. However, for the purposes of the final examination fault and justice come into Paper 1, fault, balancing competing interests and law and morality come into Paper 2, and balancing competing interests, justice, and law and morality come into Paper 3. I have included a little on all the concepts in the table below even though not specifically with Paper 2 because as stated above, you can use case examples from any substantive areas where appropriate. It also helps show you how to relate the substantive law in practice to the nature of law in theory, and there is an overlap between these concepts.

Case	Brief facts	The nature and role of law
Brown 1994 (See Chapter 7)	A criminal case where serious injuries had occurred during consensual sado-masochistic sex in private. Those involved were convicted of grievous bodily harm. A controversial case because they were all adults and no-one was forced.	In balancing the interests the law included the public interest (what was best for society) and also thought the moral wrong should be punished (society needs protecting from violent behaviour, even in private).
Re A 2001	A hospital sought a court order to allow an operation on Siamese twins to separate them. The result would be that one twin would die but without the operation they both would.	In granting the order the law had balanced many different interests. This not only included the people concerned but the public interest. The morality of the action also affected the decision in court. This shows the difficulty for the courts as society is divided on such issues.
Miller v Jackson 1977	A woman wanted the court to award an injunction to stop cricket being played nearby because she often had cricket balls landing in her garden.	In balancing the interests the court included the public interest and thought society would not be best served by granting an injunction to stop the cricket. The injunction was refused.
Murray v Express Newspapers 2008	The author of the Harry Potter books, JK Rowling, brought a case on behalf of her young son against a photographic agency for publishing secretly taken photographs of him.	The court had to balance the interests of the agency in freedom of expression against the child's right to privacy. The balance came down in favour of the child's right, but the court made clear each case would depend on its own facts and the decision could be different with an adult. This shows that in balancing interests the law is also protecting the vulnerable (the child).
Gemmell & Richards 2003 (See Chapter 3)	Two boys set light to some papers outside the back of a shop. Several premises were badly damaged. They were convicted of recklessly causing criminal damage by fire (arson) because the risk of damage was obvious to a reasonable person. Their ages were therefore not taken into account.	In order to achieve justice the HL overruled an earlier law and decided a person required a greater level of fault in order to be guilty of a crime. Thus to prove recklessness it must be shown that D is aware of a risk, but deliberately goes ahead and takes it. This shows the importance of proving fault in criminal law.

Some knowledge of these concepts is needed for you to understand how the links to the non-substantive law given in each Chapter apply, so here is a brief description of each with a couple of views and/or comments as a taster, using cases from the table above.

Balancing competing Interests

If one person has a right (an 'interest') this often conflicts with the rights of another person, as in the **Murray** case in the table. To decide whose rights are to be enforced the courts must balance the competing interests to arrive at a decision. The balance is not only between private interests (as in **Murray**) but may be between public and private (as in **Miller v Jackson 1977**). There may be several interests to balance, as in **Re A**, and the court may find the balancing act difficult – but that is part of the role of law, to consider difficult issues and decide what the legal position should be.

One view (that of Roscoe Pound) regarding competing interests is that law is an engineering tool which can be used to balance the different interests in society to achieve social control. However, he believed that public interests should not be balanced against private ones because the public interest will always prevail; a case example is **Miller v Jackson**. When you look at the cases in each Chapter consider what the interests involved are and how they conflict. Then consider whether the law achieved an appropriate balance (and therefore justice).

Fault

The meaning of fault in most cases is a sense of blameworthiness. The level of blame, or fault, is different in criminal and civil law. Criminal law usually requires a fairly high level of fault before someone is found guilty of a crime, this is that they acted with either intention or recklessness (you saw an example of the latter in **Gemmell** above). For civil law the most common type of fault is negligence, which is a lower level of fault.

In both crime and tort there may be strict liability. This means liability without proof of fault, which can seem unjust.

Some argue that strict liability is unfair, especially in criminal law, but others see it as necessary, especially in matters of social concern, because it protects the public. When you look at cases consider not only the meaning of fault, but the importance of fault and whether the law set the level of fault appropriately, as in **Gemmell** where the HL decided the level had been set too low and changed the law. You have seen that negligence is fault based (breach of duty) and will see later that some torts do not require fault, or require a lower degree of fault. In cases of vicarious liability fault is also a factor because this is where one person (usually an employer) is liable for the tort of another. Thus the person held liable is not necessarily the person that was at fault.

Law and morals

Both law and morals involve rules. As noted earlier, although they share many characteristics, there is a distinction between social rules and legal rules. The courts enforce legal, but not social, rules. An important question is whether moral issues should be a matter for society alone, or whether the law should promote and/or enforce morality. A law which makes immoral behaviour illegal is promoting morality, engineering the way society behaves. If the law makes a decision in court based on morality it is enforcing morality, as in **Brown 1994**. There has been much debate on this subject and there are opposing views. Here are simplified versions of three:

> **Professor Hart says that law and morals are separate and the law should not be used to enforce morality. If a law is made using the proper procedures, it is a valid law even if immoral, and so it must be obeyed. This is positivism.**

> **Lord Devlin said that law and morals are related and immoral acts, even in private, should be punished. Also, even if made using the proper procedures, if a law is immoral it is not a valid law and need not be obeyed. This is natural law.**

> **John Stuart Mill said that the law shouldn't normally be used to enforce morality but could if harm to others is involved. This is a type of positivism and also of utilitarianism (see under justice).**

The decision in **Brown** was partly based on the would see that as irrelevant, Devlin would not. others but it was by consent. The decision was judges disagreed on this issue too. Note the ove views on what justice involves.

The principle of not harming others was beh **Donoghue v Stevenson**. It is also seen in man matters of public policy which in turn will often in case usually involves what the judges see as mor rules because of a court judgment.

Consider whether the law should be involved in w pluralist society with diverse views, so there is no immoral, others don't (e.g., fox-hunting and smo society, or in one time, may not be so in another This makes legal involvement in morals a tricky i euthanasia and enforced feeding for anorexics.

Law and justice

One important role of the law is to achieve justice, s to illustrate this concept. As you saw in Chapter 1, th one meaning of justice, as is equality, another part o different things to different people and as you can se some but not all. There are different theories on what

The three theories under 'law and morals' are theori called utilitarianism, is that justice is achieved when th which produces a lot of benefit would be a just law. A the operation would save a life this was a big plus, so ju However, if you look back to the natural law theory moral content so an immoral law is not a proper law. Or achieve justice because it was immoral to operate knowi

When you look at the case examples consider whether t theory. You should also consider justice when studying th discuss whether the different legal institutions and proce

Let's finish on this by applying all the above concepts to English legal system thrown in. It is not specifically on any but it is an interesting example not only of the concep influences on Parliament.

Example

R v R 1991, involve moved back in with attempting rape. At was deemed to have Lords (now the Supr

The HL decided tha felt they achieved ju is part of the conce have been morally, the court had to ba been a legal act) ag interest (violence here there was th violence showed a should be punishe because the judge within marriage. H morality, and that immoral.

However, Devlin within marriage w

It is also arguable type of act is aga and changed the

A utilitarian wou greater number (unlike **Brown 19**

Links

For li diagram and exp Part 2 is a remi the particular to

The nature of la

Now you have the law that you interests is on t leave that until nature and theory of law. Part of the theory of tort law is based on public policy. The courts will consider what is in the interests of society as a whole. Tort law is often based on the reasonable person. This person represents society, effectively. If the reasonable person would not do something then that something is probably considered immoral (society in general thinks it wrong). The law is therefore enforcing morality by making it a legal wrong, such as breach of a duty of care.

Duty of care

Donoghue v Stevenson was based on the moral concept from the bible of 'love thy neighbour' but adapted by Lord Atkin to 'do not harm your neighbour'. Until this case there was a possible claim in contract but not in tort. It seemed immoral that if Mrs Donoghue's friend had suffered the harm she could have claimed (she bought the drink so had a contract with the café) but Mrs Donoghue couldn't. The HL put this injustice right; what had been morally wrong was now legally wrong. The decision accords with Mill's 'harm principle', that the law should only interfere in regard to actions which may cause harm to others.

The last part of the test from **Caparo** reflects the level of fault involved to the extent that the judge has flexibility when deciding if a duty is owed. It could be argued that this is not fair to C who therefore receives no compensation, as in **Hill**. In **Michael v CC of South Wales 2015**, the SC refused to find a duty owed by the police even though there had been direct contact. This case can illustrate both concepts. There was a higher level of fault because the police had received a call for help from the victim, so it seems unfair that no duty was owed. It seems morally right to impose a duty in these circumstances too.

Most policy decisions, such as that in **Caparo** and **Hill**, are connected to morality. Law and morality are both based on rules, but when we say something is a matter of principle we usually mean we believe it is morally right. In principle, it is wrong to put too much of a burden on health authorities and other public services.

Breach of duty

All breach cases involve fault because breach is the fault element of the tort of negligence. When linking the law to this concept it is a good idea to look for cases where there is a high or low degree of fault. Then it will be easier to produce an argument in favour of, or against, the decision. An example of the former is **Paris v Stepney** where the employer had a higher level of fault as he knew the employee was blind in one eye, so should have offered better protection. An example of the latter is **Nettleship v Weston** where she was a learner driver so her level of fault seemed lower than it would have been for an experienced driver. A compromise is seen in the case of children where the standard expected is lower than for an adult. A child is less likely to recognise the risks involved so has a lower level of fault, as in **Mullin v Richards**. There are plenty more examples you will find if you look back at Chapter 3.

As regards policy, we can say the decision in **Nettleship** was in part based on the principle that it is not in the public interest to exclude learner drivers from liability in negligence, as this would mean people injured would be left without compensation. A second point is that insurance has to be in place so it will not be the driver personally who has to pay.

Causation

The Wagon Mound replaced the test in **Re Polemis** that D was liable for all the direct consequences of the breach. This was recognised as too wide. **The Wagon Mound** test asks whether it was foreseeable that the damage would occur. Thus D is only liable for the foreseeable consequences of any breach of duty, which reflects the level of fault better than the earlier case.

The thin-skull rule is an example of liability with a low degree of fault. As in **Smith v Leech Brain** where the employer was at fault because his negligence caused the burn, but he was liable for the death. His fault did not seem sufficiently high for this amount of liability.

Occupiers Liability Act 1957

Fault can be discussed in relation to the provisions on liability for independent contractors. A comparison of **Haseldine v Daw** with **Woodward** illustrates the lower level of fault in the former case, where no duty was owed. The difference in **Woodward** was that the work was easy to check so the occupier was at fault for not doing this.

Both fault and morality can be related to the cases involving children. It was morally right to say the council was at fault in **Glasgow** because there should have been better protection from danger where children may be present. This was tempered by the decision in **Phipps** where it was held a young child should be in the care of an adult. This balances the interests of the parties in a fair way so the decisions are justifiable.

Occupiers Liability Act 1984

This Act was based on the decision by the HL in **BRB v Herrington** that occupiers had a moral duty (a duty of 'common humanity') to protect people from harm even if they were trespassing. Thus the court is promoting morality by making the occupier liable. The HL put what it saw as an injustice right, and what had been morally wrong became legally wrong.

Cases involving children can be used to link to both fault and morals here too. There was a duty in **Jolley** because children were involved. However, the older the young person is, the less likely a duty will be owed (you can use the swimming cases such as **Tomlinson** to illustrate this).

There is an element of public policy in ensuring that although people need to be kept safe there is a public benefit in occupiers opening their property to others. If the rules were too strict the occupier would e.g., exclude groups of school children from the premises.

The principle that there is no need to warn of obvious risks and there is no duty where the injury derives from the dangerous nature of a voluntary activity rather than the state of the premises (both confirmed in **Tomlinson**) further protects the occupier.

Part 2: Tort for Year 2

Part 2 continues negligence but for two different types of harm, psychiatric and economic. There are special rules for proving a duty of care in these cases, though the rules for breach and for causation are the same as for physical harm.

Example

In **Donoghue v Stevenson**, a woman suffered **physical** harm after consuming a drink containing a decomposed snail. You covered this case in Part 1.

In **Caparo v Dickman**, a purchaser of shares suffered **economic** loss having relied on the information provided by auditors who had negligently prepared a company's accounts. You saw this case in Part 1 as it provides the basic test for duty for all types of harm. However, where the harm is economic the test is more restrictive.

In **Bourhill v Young**, a pregnant woman suffered **psychiatric** harm having heard a crash and gone to the scene.

Each type of loss, or harm, has special rules for proving a duty of care. However, for all of them breach of duty is based on what a reasonable person would have done and causation in based on the 'but for' test and foreseeability of harm.

Then we look at two new torts connected to land. These are nuisance, where someone is causing a nuisance to someone else, e.g., by continually having noisy parties and the escape of dangerous things under the rule in **Rylands v Fletcher**, so called after the case of that name, where there is no need to prove negligence, liability is strict.

Example

Tina has a firework party every night. Her neighbours are fed up with the noise and one day a firework lands in their garden and sets fire to a shed. They can sue in nuisance in respect of the noise and under the rule in **Rylands v Fletcher** for the damage to the shed. If Tina has been negligent in the way she set up the firework display an action in negligence is also possible. Under **Rylands**, the neighbours won't have to prove Tina was negligent, just that the firework caused the damage, so this would be better for them.

Vicarious liability comes next, this is not a tort in itself but occurs where one person (usually an employer) is liable for torts committed by another (e.g., the employee).

The final step before C gets any compensation is to see if D has a defence. We cover some defences with these two new torts. In the last chapter we look at two defences which apply to *all* torts. It may be that C was partly to blame for the harm suffered, or consented to the action. These are the defence of contributory negligence and consent.

Example

John is injured when diving into the shallow end of his local swimming pool. He sues the council who owns it. The council can argue that John *consented* to the risk of injury. The effect would be that the council is not liable. Failing that the council can use the defence of *contributory negligence*, arguing that John was partly to blame for his own injuries by diving in at the shallow end, this leads to a reduction in the amount the council has to pay.

I have added a summary after psychiatric harm and economic loss as these are both part of negligence, they just relate to different types of harm with special rules on duty of care (but the same rules for breach and causation). There is a final summary at the end of tort for the rest of Part 2.

Chapter 8 Duty of Care for economic loss

*"... liability can, and in my opinion should, be founded squarely on the principle established in **Hedley Byrne** itself"* – Lord Goff

By the end of this chapter you should be able to:

- **Explain the special rules for proving a duty of care in cases of economic loss**
- **Show how the law applies by reference to cases**
- **Identify problems with the law and/or discuss its development in order to evaluate it**

Where the loss is financial rather than physical, liability is more limited. This is based on policy and what is known as the 'floodgates' argument. **Caparo** was an economic loss claim and established the 3-part test for proving a duty. This applies to all types of loss but other cases before and since have developed rules on what type of relationship (proximity) is needed and in what circumstances it will be fair, just and reasonable to impose a duty (the policy part of the test). In **Ultramares v Touche 1931**, Cardozo CJ said that allowing claims for pure economic loss would lead to liability "in an indeterminate amount, for an indefinite time and to an indeterminate class" – it would open the 'floodgates' to claims. This means it is necessary to limit liability in some way and the courts have developed certain rules which apply in cases where the loss is purely economic. A distinction is made between economic loss and *pure* economic loss. A great many claims involve economic loss of some sort, e.g., loss of earnings would be a result of many physical injuries and is included in the claim for damages for that injury. However, where there is no physical damage, either to person or property, any such claim would usually fail because the loss is *only* economic.

Example

You are walking to work when you see someone screaming that her husband has been hit by a car. You stop to help. As a result, you are late for a meeting, which means you lose an important contract. You also lose a day's pay. The husband can claim for his injuries and for loss of earnings whilst off work. The wife may have a claim for psychiatric harm, which will also include any loss of earnings. However, *your* loss of earnings was not a result of either physical or psychiatric harm so you cannot claim. In all three cases there is economic loss (earnings). Only in the last is it *pure* economic loss and so not recoverable.

The law also makes a distinction between economic loss caused by negligent statements (or, more correctly, misstatements), and economic loss caused by negligent acts. In this chapter we will look at the rules for finding a duty in respect of negligent misstatements and see that the law has established that there is no duty in respect of negligent acts.

Economic loss and negligent misstatements

The law has developed over the years and since 1963 the rule that no negligence claim involving pure economic loss could succeed has been eased in cases where the loss is a result of a negligent statement rather than a negligent act.

Key case

The leading case is **Hedley Byrne v Heller 1963**, where the HL approved a dissenting judgment by Denning LJ in **Candler Crane v Christmas 1951**. Lord Denning had argued that accountants owed a duty not only to their employer, but also to anyone to whom they showed the accounts. This would include people that they knew their employer would show them to but not *"strangers of whom they have heard nothing and to whom their employer without their knowledge may choose to show the accounts"*. This was accepted and developed in **Hedley**. A bank gave a credit reference in which they negligently stated that their client was sound. The Cs relied on this and consequently suffered heavy losses when the client went into liquidation. On the facts, the claim failed due to a disclaimer. However, the *principle* was established that there could be liability in tort for such losses if there was a 'special relationship' between C and D. The neighbour principle from **Donoghue v Stevenson 1932**, used for cases of physical harm, was held to be too wide. Lord Reid said statements had to be treated differently for the following reasons:

words can spread further than acts

people in a social situation may make statements less carefully than they would in a business one

Key principle: there can only be liability in tort for economic losses if there is a special relationship between C and D.

Examination pointer

Cases are always important when dealing with a problem question but a sound knowledge of them is also needed for an essay so that you can show how the law has developed. Although knowing the facts is useful as a guide to which case is most relevant when applying the law, it is the principle that is the important part so make sure you understand this. You will need to learn several cases as different cases have highlighted different principles. You'll see this as you read on.

The special relationship from Hedley v Byrne

Essentially a 'special relationship' means that:

- **D (the maker of the statement) possesses a special skill**
- **C reasonably relies on D's statement**
- **D knows that C is 'highly likely' to rely on the statement**

There is an overlap between these three points. The more special someone's skill is, the more reasonable it is for C to rely on it and the more probable it is that D will know C is likely to rely on it. Note that the word 'statement' is used in a wider sense than normal. It includes not only giving advice but also reports, references, accounts and other forms of providing information.

Special skill

Mutual Life and Citizen's Assurance Co v Evatt 1971 and **Esso Petroleum v Marden 1976**, illustrate the 'special skill' aspect. In the first case, the claim failed because D was in the insurance business and the advice was in respect of investments. The majority (3-2) held that only if they were in the business of giving that type of advice would a duty arise. The minority thought a duty could arise when D knew the statement would be reasonably relied on, even if they were not in that particular line of business.

The minority view was applied in **Esso**. Esso gave a negligent estimate of the potential turnover of a garage. This was not within their area of expertise, but the court held that they were liable to the buyer. They knew that the statement would be relied on and they had implied that they had expertise. It was also reasonable for the Cs to rely on it. This shows how 'skill', 'knowledge' and 'reasonable reliance' overlap. Again, in **Lennon v MPC 2004**, a personnel officer gave negligent advice to a police officer about the effect of a break in employment on his housing benefit. Even though the personnel officer was not skilled in giving advice about housing benefit, it was reasonable for the police officer to rely on the advice given to him and he had lost his benefit by so doing. The CA held that there was sufficient special relationship between them so that it was fair, just and reasonable to impose a duty.

Knowledge

In **JEB Fasteners Ltd v Mark Bloom 1983**, auditors prepared company accounts knowing the company needed finance. They knew that anyone considering a takeover would rely on the accounts. They were thus liable. Note that the court did not require that they should be able to identify a particular individual who would rely on them. It was enough that they knew *someone* would rely on them. However, D must know the *type* of person that would rely on the statement. This is best explained by looking at some cases to see how it applies in practice.

Key case

Caparo plc v Dickman 1990, established the 3-part test for proving a duty. This was a case of negligent misstatement. Auditors negligently prepared a company's accounts. They were held not liable to a purchaser of shares who had relied on them. This case shows how the 'knowledge' requirement can significantly limit cases. Because the auditors prepared the accounts for the company, not potential investors, they could not know Caparo, as potential investors, would rely on them.

Key principle: D must know that C is likely to rely on the advice (there must be a closer relationship, or proximity).

In **Smith v Bush 1989**, the HL held a surveyor owed a duty to a house buyer even though he prepared the survey for the building society lending them money. He owed a duty to the third-party buyers because it was quite obvious that they would rely on his survey, as this was the normal procedure for the majority of private buyers. There were *obiter dicta* in **Smith** to suggest a commercial buyer might fail. It is normal practice in commercial deals to have your own survey done, so a surveyor for the lender would not 'know' the buyer would rely on their survey – they would expect them to have done their own. The court felt there would only be a duty if it was "highly likely" C would rely on the statement.

In **Scullion v Bank of Scotland plc 2011**, in a claim regarding a negligent valuation, the trial judge relied on **Smith v Bush** in finding that a valuer owed a duty of care to the purchaser of the property. The CA however, reversed the decision and declined to follow **Smith v Bush**. That case could be distinguished because this was for a 'buy-to-let' property, rather than a domestic purchase, and thus was of a commercial nature. Most people who buy to let do not rely only on valuations prepared by a valuer instructed by their lender, but obtain their own valuation, unlike the case of a private buyer as in **Smith**. On these facts no duty of care was owed.

In **Stone & Rolls Ltd v Moore Stephens 2009**, the HL followed **Caparo v Dickman 1990** and held that the auditors of a company had a duty to take reasonable care in auditing the accounts, but this duty was owed to the company and did not extend to the company's creditors of whom they had no knowledge. Thus the creditors were in the same position as the shareholders in **Caparo** and were not owed a duty of care.

In **Law Society v KPMG Peat Marwick 2000**, a firm of accountants was hired to prepare annual reports on solicitors. This was a legal requirement and the reports would be passed to the Law Society. As the Law Society has to compensate any clients who are affected by a solicitor's misconduct, a duty of care was owed. The accountants knew the reports would be passed to the Law Society and that they would rely on them. Here **Caparo** could be distinguished.

In **Swynson Ltd v Lowick Rose LLP 2017**, a company had made loans based on a report by D. This had negligently misrepresented the borrower's capital. The borrower defaulted on the loan and the company sued D. D owed a duty of care; **Caparo** and **Stone** can be distinguished because the advice was provided for the company not a third party, there was clearly a close relationship.

In **Spring v Guardian Assurance plc 1993**, the HL held that an employer owed a duty to an employee in respect of a negligent reference, as they knew it would be relied on by a potential employer. In this case the advice was not given *to* C but was *about* C. This further extends the duty owed to third parties, i.e., someone other than the person to whom the statement was made, in this case the employee.

Task 23

Compare **Caparo** and **KPMG**. They aren't too different, so why was a duty found in one and not the other?

Reasonable reliance

Lord Reid said in **Hedley**, that there would be no duty of care for statements made on a social occasion. This seems fair. It would not be 'reasonable' to rely on a piece of information passed on in a drunken moment at the Christmas party! It isn't an absolute rule though. For example, in **Chaudhry v Prabhakar 1989,** a friend who negligently gave advice on buying a car was held to owe a duty to C. He had knowledge of such matters and she had reasonably relied on that knowledge.

Lejonvarn v Burgess 2017 also concerned advice from a friend. A couple wanted advice on landscaping their garden. A friend who was a qualified architect offered to help with the project management and to be the architect. This was done for free but she expected that she would get paid for other services on the project once some of the heavy work had been done, such as lighting and design. The couple were not happy with how the work progressed and sued her for damages. The CA held that this was not a social situation, it was almost contractual. She was held to owe a duty.

Evaluation pointer

It is arguably unfair for the court to have found the friend owed a duty in **Chaudhry**. In **Lejonvarn** it was fairer to impose a duty because although both cases concerned advice from friends the second situation was much more business-like.

Task 24

Give one argument for and one against the decision in **Chaudhry** to add to the evaluation pointer

In **Caparo**, it was not only who the information was for, but also the purpose of the information that was relevant. It is not likely to be found reasonable to rely on information intended for someone else (a third party) for a different purpose. However, in **Ross v Caunters 1980**, a solicitor was found liable to a third party, the beneficiary under his client's will, when he acted negligently and this resulted in the beneficiary losing financially. This was a major extension of the law at the time, because it appeared to relate to negligent *acts* rather than *statements*. In **White v Jones 1995**, the HL found a solicitor owed a duty to a third party but based their decision on an 'assumption of responsibility' for his professional advice. This concept brings in another part to the tests for establishing a duty in cases of negligent misstatement.

Assumption of responsibility

The principle of 'assumption of responsibility' was rooted in **Hedley Byrne** but more emphasis was put on it during the nineties. In **Henderson v Merrett Syndicates 1995**, the HL held that syndicate managers could owe their members (underwriters of insurance policies) a duty in tort as well as contract. That duty was to exercise reasonable skill and care. Lord Goff made the remark in the opening quote and added that where someone assumed responsibility for professional services, this would be enough to impose a duty.

Key case

In **White v Jones 1995**, two daughters had been cut out of their father's will. Before he died he changed his mind and instructed his solicitor to amend his will. Despite a reminder this was never done and the daughters did not receive their inheritance. The HL found the solicitors liable to the daughters for their losses. The emphasis was on the fact that the solicitor, as a professional, had 'assumed responsibility' for his work and thus was under a duty not to do it negligently. It is reasonable for beneficiaries of wills to rely on solicitors doing their jobs properly.

The majority based their decision on achieving "practical justice" and appear to be filling in a gap in the law to allow a third-party beneficiary (who has no contract with the solicitor and so cannot sue in contract law) to claim for the loss of their inheritance.

Key principle: It is fair, just and reasonable to impose a duty on professionals who have assumed responsibility for their work.

Task 25

Once you have proved a duty of care you need to prove that the duty has been breached. We have seen the different rules for professionals for proving a duty (mainly based on the assumption of responsibility). What difference will it make to proving breach of duty that D is a professional? Give a case example.

You can see from **White**, that the idea of 'assumption of responsibility' is related to the 'fair, just and reasonable' requirement when looking at professionals. A few case examples will help illustrate how this applies in practice. In **Phelps v Hillingdon BC 2001**, the CA held that an educational psychologist had not assumed responsibility for C when he failed to diagnose her dyslexia in a report made for the education authority. It was therefore not 'fair, just and reasonable' to impose a duty. The HL reversed this decision on the basis that a professional asked to work with a specific child could be liable to her for his lack of care and skill in the exercise of that profession. Similarly, in **Carty v Croydon LBC 2005**, C sued the council for damages for failing to assess his special educational needs properly and failing to provide him with a suitable education. The CA held that an education officer was a professional and so there could be a duty if he had 'assumed responsibility' towards a child. Dyson LJ said that this would be based on the normal **Caparo** 3-part test of foreseeability, proximity and whether it was fair, just and reasonable to impose a duty. The **Caparo** test was used again in the next case, this time without the assumption of responsibility angle.

In **Jain v Trent Strategic Health Authority 2009**, the Authority, concerned about both structural and health issues, closed a nursing home without prior notice. The proprietors successfully appealed against this but suffered economic loss to the business. At trial the judge held a duty of care was owed. The CA reversed the decision and allowed the appeal by the Health Authority, who successfully argued that the judge had erred in law in holding that it was fair, just and reasonable that it should owe a duty of care to the proprietors as it was well established that duties should only be held to exist either within existing categories or on an incremental basis, and that no similar duty had been found to exist. The CA approved **Caparo v Dickman 1990,** and held it was not fair, just and reasonable to impose a duty of care when the Authority's primary duty was to the residents of the nursing home and to the public interest. The urgency of the situation and risk of harm to residents outweighed the economic interests of the proprietors. The HL confirmed the decision of the CA and held that although the Health Authority owed a duty to the residents of a nursing home this duty did not extend to the proprietors.

So it is clear that the **Caparo** test is important but the other tests may also need to be considered.

Examination pointer

The law itself is not fully clear on which test to use so this is difficult. The next case can be used to explain that where there is an assumption of responsibility nothing else is usually needed, but in most other cases the **Caparo** test would need to be satisfied. Remember also that foreseeability, proximity and whether it is fair, just and reasonable to impose a duty will depend on satisfying the special relationship requirements from **Hedley**.

Key case

In **Customs and Excise Commissioners v Barclays Bank 2006**, a bank allowed money to be transferred out of two accounts, which had been frozen by Customs and Excise. This meant that the money owed to Customs by the companies involved could not be paid in full, so the Customs and Excise Commissioners sued the bank for the balance. The trial judge found that the bank did not owe a duty to the third party (Customs and Excise), mainly based on the lack of any 'assumption of responsibility'. In the CA, Longmore LJ had summarised the position. He said that the modern law derived from 4 cases, **Caparo, Henderson, White** and **Phelps**. In cases of economic loss it was appropriate to consider each of the following tests:

the 3-fold Caparo test (foreseeability, proximity and whether it is fair, just and reasonable to impose a duty)

the 'assumption of responsibility' test (White v Jones)

the 'incremental' test (liability is not extended in a giant leap but in short steps)

He said that the tests merged into each other, and that although an 'assumption of responsibility' may sometimes be enough for a duty to exist, it was not always a *necessary* ingredient. The CA found that the bank owed a duty to Customs and Excise. The HL reversed the decision of the CA, but confirmed the tests. Lord Bingham said an assumption of responsibility was "a sufficient but not a necessary condition of liability". If this test is satisfied, it may mean nothing further is needed, but if not, then the other tests may need to be considered. On the facts, the HL held that the bank had not assumed any responsibility towards the Commissioners. Nor was it fair, just and reasonable to impose a duty on the bank as it was not a party to the transaction between Customs and its creditors. Imposing a duty would not be analogous with or incremental to any previous development of the law. None of the tests was satisfied.

Key principle: an assumption of responsibility may be enough to justify imposing a duty but there may be a need to look at several different tests depending on the circumstances

In **Calvert v William Hill Credit Ltd 2008**, a gambler argued the bookmaker owed him a duty of care and had breached it by letting him continue betting after he asked them to stop taking his money. This had caused him both financial ruin and psychological harm. The High Court found William Hill owed him a duty to take reasonable care to exclude him after his request. Applying the 3-stage test, there was sufficient proximity between the parties (bookmaker and better), harm was foreseeable because gambling is a recognised psychiatric disorder, and there was no policy reason such as the floodgates issue to exclude such a duty. The court also accepted his argument that William Hill had voluntarily assumed responsibility by acknowledging his request for help as a problem gambler and undertaking to exclude him. This follows **Customs and Excise Commissioners v Barclays Bank 2006**, where the HL said the tests were to be looked at together, not in isolation. This case can be compared to **Ritz Hotel Casino v Al-Daher 2014**, where C claimed a casino had been negligent in not stopping her gambling after she lost £2 million in one night. The court held it was not fair, just and reasonable to impose a duty to prevent her cashing her cheques, adding that even if she had been stopped she would simply have gone elsewhere to gamble. The difference appears to be that in **Calvert** there had been a specific request to exclude him by C which led to a voluntary assumption of responsibility by the bookmaker.

Task 26

Once you have proved a duty of care and breach of duty you still have to prove that the breach caused the loss, whether physical loss or economic loss. Choose a case from this chapter and briefly apply the rules on causation to it.

Summary of negligent misstatement

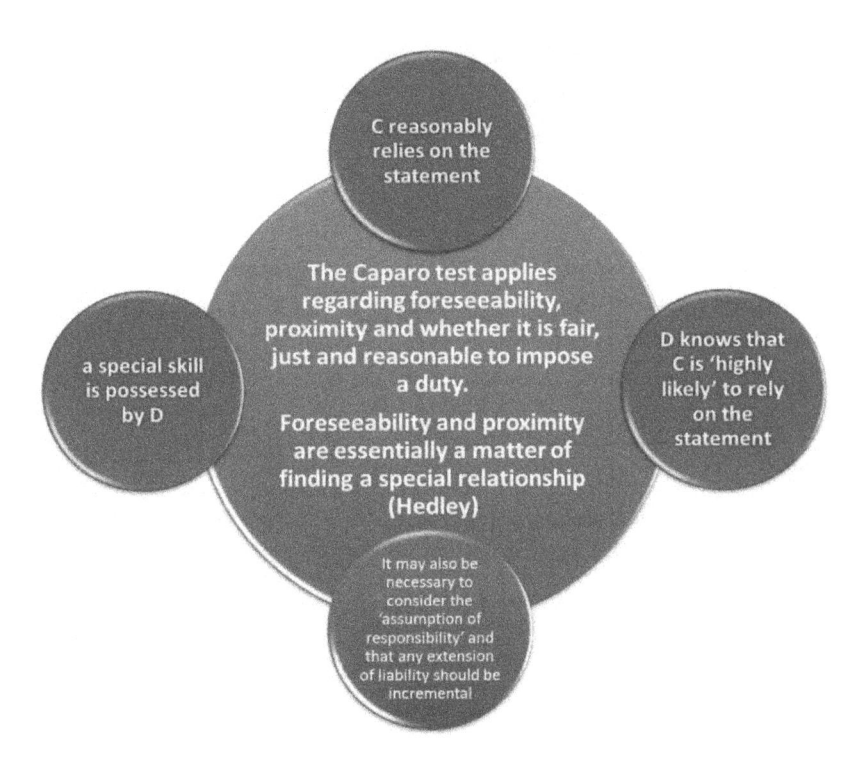

- C reasonably relies on the statement
- a special skill is possessed by D
- The Caparo test applies regarding foreseeability, proximity and whether it is fair, just and reasonable to impose a duty. Foreseeability and proximity are essentially a matter of finding a special relationship (Hedley)
- D knows that C is 'highly likely' to rely on the statement
- It may also be necessary to consider the 'assumption of responsibility' and that any extension of liability should be incremental

Economic Loss by acts

The question of whether economic loss could be claimed in respect of negligent acts was answered in the negative in **Spartan Steel and Alloys Ltd v Martin & Co 1973** by the CA.

Key case

In **Spartan Steel**, the Ds negligently severed a power cable to C's factory and caused damage to steel in production. The Cs were able to claim for the physical damage to the steel and for the consequential loss of profit on that steel, but not for further loss of profit due to other, undamaged, machines lying idle. This last sum was pure economic loss because it did not stem from any physical damage.

Key principle: there is no duty owed where the loss is purely economic and was caused by a negligent act rather than a statement

There is a case where a claim for pure economic loss has been successful, but this was where there was an exceptionally close proximity between C and D. In **Junior Books v Veitchi 1983**, a subcontractor was held liable to the owner of the premises he was working in and who had ordered the work (through the main contractor). This was almost a contractual relationship and so it sets no precedent for cases where the degree of proximity is less than this.

The rule against recovery for economic loss was reinforced by the HL in **Murphy v Brentwood DC 1990**. The Council's building inspector approved plans which meant C's property was poorly constructed and in a dangerous state. This led to a drop in its value. Reversing the decision of the CA, the HL held there was no duty. The judges appeared to have differing reasons for their decision but the result is that if there is a defect but it has not yet caused any damage, there is no duty. Of course, if the defect actually leads to damage then the usual rules for physical harm would apply.

Example

A property is built according to a set of plans that were negligently prepared. The balcony is unstable, thus making the property worth less than it should be. This is a defect but there is no damage yet. The owners cannot claim as their loss is purely economic – i.e., a lower value. However, if the balcony falls off then the house is now physically damaged and a claim can be made – make sense?

Examination pointer

Note that proving a duty is just the first step in a negligence case. To win, C will still have to prove that the duty was breached, *and* that the breach caused the loss suffered.

Summary of cases on misstatements

Hedley Byrne v Heller 1963 – to establish sufficient proximity there has to be a 'special relationship' between D and C. This means:
- D has a special skill
- C reasonably relies on D's statement
- D knows that C is 'highly likely' to rely on the statement

Mutual Life and Citizen's Assurance Co v Evatt 1971 – the Privy Council held that only if the defendants were in the business of giving that *type* of advice would a duty arise. The minority thought a duty could arise when D *knew the statement would be reasonably relied on.*

Esso Petroleum v Marden 1976 – Esso gave a negligent estimate of the potential turnover of a garage. This was not within their area of expertise but the court held that Esso was liable as they *knew* the statement would be relied on. It was also *reasonable to rely* on it.

Caparo v Dickman 1990 – the auditors prepared the accounts for the company, not potential investors so they could not *know* Caparo would rely on them. Thus it was not 'fair, just and reasonable' to impose a duty.

Smith v Bush 1989 – a surveyor owed a duty to a house buyer even if he prepared the survey for the building society, as he knew that the buyer would rely on his survey.

Chaudhry v Prabhakar 1989 – a friend who negligently gave advice on buying a car owed a duty to C as he had knowledge of such matters, so it was *reasonable* for her to rely on it.

Spring v Guardian Assurance plc 1993 – an employer owed a duty to an employee in respect of a negligent reference as they *knew* it would be relied on.

White v Jones 1995 – a solicitor, as a professional, had *'assumed responsibility'* for his work and thus was under a duty not to do it negligently.

Phelps v Hillingdon BC 2001 – a professional asked to work with a specific child could be liable to her for his lack of care and skill in the exercise of that profession.

Summary of cases on acts

> **Spartan Steel and Alloys Ltd v Martin & Co 1973** – C could claim for the physical damage to the steel and for the consequential loss of profit on that steel but not for further loss of profit due to other, undamaged, machines lying idle, which was pure economic loss.
>
> **Murphy v Brentwood DC 1990** – if no damage has yet been done, C cannot claim for the fact that the property is worth less than it should be because there is an inherent defect due to negligent building inspections.

Finally, don't forget that in all cases, even if a duty of care is proved, to win the case C will still have to prove that the duty was breached, and that the breach caused the loss suffered.

Links to the non-substantive law

ELS: For links to the English legal system, look back at the diagram and examples in the introduction to Part 1. In particular, where a principle of law has been established the system of appeals is relevant, as these principles are established in the higher appeal courts, i.e., the CA and SC. ADR is always relevant to tort cases too, as is access to justice, because cases can be expensive to take to court so alternatives or help with expenses may be needed.

The nature of law: The role of law is to mediate between the parties in a case and provide a fair remedy where appropriate. The remedy will be based on the level of fault, or blameworthiness. If someone is found to be at fault then this justifies the court imposing a penalty. In civil law, this is done by way of compensation (or sometimes an injunction as you will see with remedies). In cases of economic loss, the law is less strict (for D) than where physical harm has been caused, so the rules on imposing a duty of care are more severe. However, if a professional has taken on an assumption of responsibility the law is more likely to impose a duty as the level of fault is higher in such situations. In case like **White v Jones** there also seems to be a moral element to the decision. It would be wrong (and arguably immoral) to allow a potential beneficiary not to be compensated for losses which have occurred due to the solicitor's negligence as it would mean the wishes of the person who made the will were not met. As with most of tort Mill's 'harm principle' can be discussed. Where harm has been caused it is right for the law to be involved, and this would include economic harm. However, as this type of harm can be widespread the law imposes stricter rules, thus achieving a balance. The rules for proving a duty are stricter than for physical harm for policy reasons. It is not in the public interest for the courts to be flooded by claims. Where people have acted on negligent advice and lost money, the number of potential claimants could be huge in such a connected multi-media world.

Self-test questions

1. What constitutes a special relationship?
2. Why did the claim fail in the Mutual Life case?

3. ***Smith v Bush*** *shows a surveyor for a building society can owe a duty to a buyer. When might there not be such a duty?*

4. *Can you give a case example where **Smith v Bush** was distinguished for this reason?*

5. *On what was the emphasis in **White v Jones**?*

6. *How did Longmore LJ summarise the position in **Customs and Excise Commissioners v Barclays Bank**?*

Answers to the tasks and self-test questions are on my website at www.drsr.org. Please click on 'Answers to tasks'. For a range of free interactive exercises, click on 'Free Exercises'.

Chapter 9 Duty of Care for psychiatric harm)

"In cases involving nervous shock, it is essential to distinguish between the primary victim and secondary victims. In claims by secondary victims the law insists on certain control mechanisms, in order, as a matter of policy, to limit the number of potential claimants" – Lord Lloyd

By the end of this chapter you should be able to:

- **Explain the rules for proving a duty of care in cases of psychiatric harm**
- **Show how the law applies by reference to cases**
- **Identify problems with the law and/or discuss its development in order to evaluate it**

What is meant by psychiatric harm?

Psychiatric harm (sometimes referred to as 'nervous shock'), covers a wide range of mental disorders including such things as post-traumatic stress, clinical depression and personality change. When someone has suffered harm due to another's negligence, but that harm is psychiatric rather than physical, the courts tend to limit liability, mainly because of what is called the 'floodgates' argument. This means that because the number of potential Cs could be vast it could open the 'floodgates' to claims. The opening quote relates to this, it is from **Page v Smith 1995,** discussed below. As with economic loss the limits only apply where the harm is *purely* psychiatric, if psychiatric harm is suffered along with a physical injury the claim will come within the **Caparo v Dickman 1990** rules as normal.

Example

A drunk driver ploughs into a queue of people at a bus stop. Many are killed or injured. Any of these people (who are called primary victims) can claim in the normal way. If anyone who was injured also suffered a psychiatric illness of some sort, they can also claim as normal, for both the physical and the psychiatric harm. The driver will owe them a duty based on foreseeability, proximity, and whether it is fair, just and reasonable to impose a duty (**Caparo**). However, hundreds of other people may have seen the accident and been traumatised by it. For these people, called secondary victims, the rules are stricter.

A claim in negligence for psychiatric harm requires the usual proof of duty, breach and causation. It is only the rules on duty that change where harm is not physical. Foreseeability and proximity (**Caparo**) are still required but subject to a stricter test.

The current law will be better understood in the light of its development, so we'll look at that first.

Development

A claim in negligence for psychiatric harm requires the usual proof of duty, breach and causation. It is only the rules on duty that change, depending on the type of harm. Foreseeability and proximity (**Caparo v Dickman 1990**) are still required (see **King** and **Bourhill** below), but subject to a stricter test.

The first successful claim was **Dulieu v White 1901**. Here a person suffered shock when a van and horses drove into the pub where she was working (yes, horses – but note the date). It was held that the driver owed her a duty of care. The principle was established that in order to succeed C must be in fear for his or her own safety.

In **Hambrook v Stokes 1925**, a mother was successful in her claim when she suffered shock after seeing a runaway lorry careering towards her children. Although they were not harmed and she was not in danger herself the court recognised that the close relationship could bring her within the class of people to whom a duty was owed. She had also seen the incident herself. The principle here is that even if you are not in danger yourself, a particularly close relationship to someone who is may be enough *if* you see the incident with your own eyes.

In **Bourhill v Young 1943**, a pregnant woman heard a crash and was so traumatised that she later gave birth to a stillborn baby. Although drivers usually owe pedestrians a duty of care the court rejected her claim because she was some distance away and safe herself. The court held that no duty is owed unless C is in proximity to a foreseeable danger.

In **King v Phillips 1952**, a mother suffered shock when she (wrongly) believed that her son had been run over by a taxi. She failed in her claim against the driver. The court held that injury *by shock* had to be foreseeable.

Examination Pointer

The development is useful for essay questions where you may need to discuss how the law has changed over the years. For problem questions only the current law and a few example cases will be needed. Make sure you learn the key cases as these establish the legal principles. Which other cases you need will depend on the scenario you are given so learn a few involving different circumstances.

The current rules on proving a duty in respect of psychiatric harm were established in **McLoughlin v O'Brien 1982** by the HL and confirmed in **Alcock v CC of South Yorkshire 1991**, where the HL referred to them as 'control mechanisms'. This is because they are used to control the number of claims.

Key cases

In **McLoughlin v O'Brien 1982**, the first case to reach the HL since **Bourhill,** a test for dealing with claims by secondary victims was established. Mrs McLoughlin was told about an accident in which her husband and children had been seriously injured; one child had, in fact, died. She went straight to the hospital where she saw them before they had been attended to. She suffered psychiatric harm as a result. She sued the person who negligently caused the accident. In allowing her claim the HL held that there were three matters to consider in claims where the harm caused was psychiatric rather than physical:

the relationship between C and the primary victim

the proximity of C to the accident

the means by which the shock was caused.

In **Alcock v CC of South Yorkshire 1991**, many people had been injured or killed in the Hillsborough football stadium disaster, caused by police negligence. These people could claim against the police using the normal **Caparo** rules. There were also many claims for psychiatric harm from people who were not physically hurt but who had been at the ground or had watched the news on television and knew that their loved ones were at the stadium. The HL confirmed that the above test applied to these people, but said the first point extended to those with 'close ties of love and affection'. There must also be a *sudden shock* and the shock must cause a *recognisable psychiatric illness* (mere grief is not enough). It was also said that those watching the events on television could not succeed. There were, however, *obiter dicta* to the effect that a live broadcast may be different. A hypothetical example was given of seeing live television pictures of a hot-air balloon catching fire knowing that your children were in it.

Key principles: McLoughlin 1982 established the need for there to be closer proximity both in time and space (to the event and to the victim) and set out the control mechanisms. **Alcock** confirms these and added that there must also be a sudden shock and a recognisable psychiatric illness.

Task 27

Look at the rules from **Mcloughlin** and **Alcock**. Briefly apply these to the situations in **Bourhill** and **McLoughlin** to show why one failed and the other succeeded. This will give you a taste of how the rules will be applied when we look at them in more detail.

Before looking at *how* the test applies, we need to consider to *whom* it applies. An important distinction is made in **Page v Smith 1995** between primary and secondary victims.

Primary and secondary victims

Key case

In **Page v Smith**, C was a passenger involved in a car accident and, although he was not physically hurt, his ME condition, which had been in remission, recurred. The HL drew a distinction between primary and secondary victims. A primary victim is someone who is directly affected and in danger of harm. A secondary victim is not directly affected, but a passive witness to the events. In all cases, *some* harm must be foreseeable, whether physical or psychiatric. However, in the case of secondary victims, only foreseeability of *psychiatric* harm, in a *'person of normal fortitude'*, will suffice. The HL held that here the C was a primary victim as he was directly involved in the accident, so there was no need to prove that psychiatric harm was foreseeable. In the opening quote Lord Lloyd refers to secondary victims. He then goes on to say that the control mechanisms have no place where C is a primary victim.

Key principle: it is important to distinguish between primary and secondary victims, and the control mechanisms only apply to the latter.

This case is also an example of the 'thin-skull rule' – that you must take your victim as you find them. Under the thin-skull rule some harm must be foreseeable, but if it is, then the fact that the C suffered greater harm due to a pre-existing weakness will not cause the claim to fail.

Task 28

Compare this case to the next one. Can you identify the difference between the passenger in **Page** and the police in **White** and explain why the police claims failed?

In a further case involving the Hillsborough disaster, **White v CC of South Yorkshire 1999**, the HL clarified the position on rescuers and restated the test for secondary victims. Police assisting at the scene had claimed compensation and, in what was then called **Frost v CC of South Yorkshire 1998**, the CA accepted that their claim should succeed on the basis that they were rescuers. In **White** the HL reversed the decision of the CA.

Key case

In **White**, the CA had suggested that as the police were rescuers there was no need to prove close ties to the victims. The HL reversed the decision, and held that they could only succeed if their own safety was at risk. This made it clear that rescuers are treated as secondary victims if not in any danger, so the control mechanisms must be applied. Lord Hoffmann restated these as follows:

C must have close ties of love and affection with the victim. Such ties may be presumed in some cases (e.g., spouses, parent and child) but must otherwise be established by evidence

C must have been present at the accident or its immediate aftermath

The psychiatric harm must have been caused by direct perception of the accident or its immediate aftermath, and not upon hearing about it from someone else

Key principle: rescuers are treated as secondary victims if not in any danger, so the control mechanisms must be applied

In **Donachie v Chief Constable of Greater Manchester 2004**, the issue of primary and secondary victims arose again. A policeman was instructed to attach a tag to the car of suspected criminals. It was parked near a pub where the suspects were drinking. His colleagues kept watch from the tracker van in case they left the pub. He attached the device but it did not work. He made several trips to retrieve and then reattach it until it finally gave a signal. He became increasingly frightened of being caught by the suspects. Unknown to his employers, he had hypertension and suffered psychiatric harm that led to a stroke. The judge found they had been negligent as there was a history of problems with the tagging devices. The issue was which type of victim C was. The judge classed him as a secondary victim. He therefore had to prove *psychiatric* harm was foreseeable. As his employers did not know of his existing condition the psychiatric harm that led to the stroke was not foreseeable and they were not liable. On appeal C argued that he was a primary victim because there was a danger of being assaulted by the suspects. The CA agreed he had been in danger of harm and so a primary victim and allowed the appeal.

In **Monk v Harrington 2008**, C had supervised the construction of a platform that collapsed, causing one death and several injuries. He went to the scene and offered assistance as a first-aider. He then suffered psychiatric harm and claimed damages from the employers of the crane driver, whose actions had actually caused the platform to fall. He said he was a rescuer and a primary victim because he believed he was in danger himself. He also argued that he believed he had been partly to blame for the accident and so was a participant. The court agreed that he was a rescuer, but held he was not in danger himself and that any belief he had as to the danger he might be in had to be reasonable. On the evidence his belief that he was in danger was not reasonable. He was therefore a secondary victim and so subject to the usual rules.

Although the primary/secondary distinction was explicitly made in **Page**, examples of it can be seen in earlier cases involving rescuers at the scene of an accident. It is worth knowing this as a comparison will help show how the rules apply.

Rescuers

In **Chadwick v BTC 1967**, a rescuer at a train crash was successful in a claim for psychiatric harm after assisting for several hours. He can be seen as a 'primary' victim because he was in danger at the time. Compare this case to **McFarlane v Caledonia Ltd 1993.** A person on a support ship which rescued people from a fire on an oil rig was classed as a 'bystander' not a 'rescuer', because he was not in danger. He therefore had to satisfy the test for secondary victims. As the ship had not got into close proximity to the disaster, and he had no close relationship with the victims, his claim failed. The court also repeated the point that C must be compared to a *"person of ordinary fortitude and phlegm"*.

In **Greatorex v Greatorex 2000**, the slightly unusual question that arose was whether D owed a duty to a rescuer who was also his father. D was injured in a road accident as a result of his own negligence. His father was a fireman who assisted in the rescue and as a result suffered psychiatric harm. He brought an action against his son. It was held that D did not owe his father a duty of care for policy reasons. It would be *"undesirable and detrimental to family life and relationships"* for members of a family to sue each other. It was also made clear that, following **White**, where there is no personal risk, a rescuer is a secondary victim and so has to satisfy the **McLoughlin/Alcock** control mechanisms.

Examination pointer

The **McLoughlin/Alcock** control mechanisms confirmed in **White** will be needed for establishing a duty for secondary victims. Reference to the primary/secondary distinction in

Page will also be needed. Watch carefully for the type of harm suffered and whether C is in any danger. For primary victims the usual rules (**Caparo v Dickman 1990**) apply. For secondary victims apply the mechanisms. You may also need to refer to the role of rescuers.

Task 29

Compare the cases of **Chadwick** and **McFarlane** and explain why a duty was/was not owed in each case. What did the HL make clear in **White** and which of the above two cases would be most appropriate to support this?

The control mechanisms

Let's run through the control mechanisms in a little more detail.

Close ties of love and affection

C must have close ties of love and affection with the victim. Such ties may be presumed in the case of spouses, or parent and child (**McLoughlin**) but must otherwise be established by evidence (**Alcock**). As regards rescuers, if in danger themselves they would be primary victims and so the normal rules on duty would apply (compare **Chadwick** and **White**). If not, they will be secondary victims and have to prove 'close ties' to the victim (so the claims failed in **McFarlane** and **White**).

Evaluation pointer

Extending the relationship from the immediate family to those with close ties seems fair. A loving relationship with a partner may be much closer than one between a husband and wife who have grown apart. The problem is how you prove 'close ties'. It is presumed in cases of spouse and parents but what about brothers, uncles, grandparents and friends – all of whom failed in **Alcock**? The Law Commission proposes that the 'close ties' requirement should be kept, albeit with some extension of the presumptions.

Immediate aftermath

This is also a question of proximity, but this time to the event or its 'immediate aftermath' rather than the victim. What amounts to the immediate aftermath is not clear-cut. In **McLoughlin**, the mother heard about the accident an hour or so after it happened and went straight to the hospital, which brought her within the immediate aftermath. In **Alcock,** a lapse of 8 or 9 hours before going to the mortuary caused several claims to fail. In **Atkinson v Seghal 2003**, a mother arrived at the scene of a road accident to be told her daughter had been killed. The body had already been removed and she went to the mortuary. She then suffered a psychiatric illness. The trial court held that the visit to the mortuary was not within the immediate aftermath. The CA reversed this decision and held that the aftermath extended to the mortuary visit.

In **Taylor v A Novo (UK) Ltd 2013**, C suffered psychiatric harm after witnessing the sudden collapse and death of her mother who had been injured at work by D's negligence a few weeks earlier. The CA held that she was a secondary victim and referred to the 'control mechanisms' from **Alcock**. In the case of secondary victims the starting point was whether psychiatric injury was a reasonably foreseeable consequence of D's negligence. Secondly, there had to be a relationship of proximity between C and the victim. There was clearly a relationship of proximity between her and her mother, and if she had been in physical proximity to her mother at the time of the original injury she would have satisfied the tests. However, the event which caused the harm (her mother's death) was some weeks after the original injury. Cases such as **Atkinson v Seghal** could be distinguished. Her claim failed. This case shows that although not clear-cut, the immediate aftermath cannot be extended indefinitely.

Evaluation pointer

So, what is the 'immediate aftermath'? Do we measure this in minutes, hours or days? These decisions raise some serious questions about the state of the law. Reporting in the **New Law Journal** in 1995 Andrew Ritchie says: *"It would appear that unless the victim is seen in hospital, covered in blood, success may be tricky. In my opinion this is not an admirable distinction to make"*.

Examination pointer

As you can see, the cases are not fully consistent so it is a good idea to use more than one to support your answer in respect of this part of the test. If there has been a gap between the event and the psychiatric harm you could use **Taylor** to suggest the claim might fail, but if the time lapse is short you could use **McLoughlin** to suggest it will succeed.

How the shock was caused

As explained in **White**, the psychiatric harm must have been caused by direct perception of the accident or its immediate aftermath, and not upon hearing about it from someone else. This usually requires first-hand knowledge so would not include being told by a third party, nor to seeing events on television (as discussed in **Alcock**). **Atkinson v Seghal** helps explain this. The trial court had held that the shock was caused by the news of the death, not the visit to the mortuary. This meant the claim failed as the news of the death was not first-hand knowledge but came from a third party, the police. When the CA held that the illness was caused in part by the visit to the mortuary this brought her within the rule. The visit to the mortuary was a direct perception of the immediate aftermath of the accident.

Evaluation pointer

Arguably, this has not been entirely consistent. In **McLoughlin**, she was told by a third party (although she then did see the resulting injuries). Also there were *obiter dicta* in **Alcock** to the effect that there could be occasions where seeing events on television would be enough – such as a live broadcast.

Sudden shock

The HL in **Alcock** also made clear that there must be a ***sudden shock*** and that the shock must cause a ***recognisable psychiatric illness***. Medical evidence will be needed. The HL also said that ***mere grief is not enough***.

In **Sion v Hampstead AHA 1994**, a father suffered psychiatric harm after watching his son deteriorate and die over a period of two weeks. Although the hospital had been negligent there was no liability to the father for the psychiatric harm because it was not caused by a sudden shock.

However, in **North Glamorgan NHST v Walters 2003**, a mother suffered psychiatric illness after sitting with her 10-month old baby as his condition deteriorated following the (admitted) negligence of the hospital. After 36 hours, his life support system was turned off. There were various reasons behind the CA's decision, but one issue was whether the 'sudden shock' requirement in **Alcock** was satisfied. The CA decided it was and allowed her claim for psychiatric harm caused by the hospital's negligence.

The meanings of both 'sudden' and 'shocking' in the context of a sudden shock were discussed in several more recent cases which have perhaps narrowed the principle.

In **Wells v University Hospital 2015** a man claimed psychiatric harm after his child died in hospital. The court followed **Alcock** and held that although he satisfied most parts of the test and had suffered profound distress there was no "assault on the senses" or horrifying event which caused a sudden shock.

In **Shorter v Surrey & East Sussex NHS Trust 2014** it was made clear it was an objective test – an event that a person of ordinary susceptibility (fortitude) would regard as horrifying. This case made clear a series of events would not suffice, there must be a 'horrifying event' that was 'sudden and unexpected'.

Shorter was followed in **Liverpool Women's Hospital NHS Trust v Ronayne 2015** where the CA also held there must be clear reference to exactly what psychiatric harm was suffered to help decide on "complex causation issues". Here a man claimed psychiatric harm after witnessing his wife's reaction to a negligent hysterectomy over a period of 10 days. The CA rejected his claim and said to succeed there must be something "exceptional in nature".

Finally, in **Owers v Medway NHS Trust 2015** a man suffered post-traumatic stress disorder after seeing the negligent treatment of his wife's stroke. The court accepted he had suffered PTSD as a result but that this was not enough "to satisfy the common law test from **Alcock**" of suffering a sudden shock. All four of these cases failed on this point.

Evaluation pointer

The implication in **Alcock** was that 'sudden shock' would not include any illness caused by, for example, long-term caring for a terminally ill relative. **Walters** showed that this requirement may have been relaxed. However, the four cases above indicate a tightening of the rules. It remains to be seen how far the **Alcock** rules will be strictly adhered to. In several cases the higher courts have suggested this should be decided on a case-by-case basis, depending on the circumstances, but although that may achieve justice in a particular case it does not satisfy the requirement of clarity and certainty in the law.

This brings us on to a general criticism, which is that if the law is unclear it is impossible for people to know what it is. It is also hard for a lawyer to advise a client as to how a case is likely to be decided. This means fewer cases can be settled out of court by negotiation.

Law Commission proposals for reform

The Law Commission has examined the law on this area. A consultation paper was issued in 1995 followed by a report in 1998 (*Report No 249*), which recommended the removal of the requirements of proximity to the accident and the limits on the means of hearing about it. However, the Commission suggested that the 'close ties' aspect should be retained, but extended to other relationships regarding the presumptions (currently only parents, children, spouses). The courts have shown a reluctance to expand the law any further and have indicated that it is up to Parliament to address the matter. However, the project is now complete and the Government decided not to proceed with the recommendations.

Examination pointer

Note that proving a duty is just the first step in a negligence case. To win, C will still have to prove that the duty was breached, *and* that the breach caused the loss suffered. This applies whatever the type of harm.

Example

In **Brown v Richmond upon Thames LBC 2012**, C suffered a mental breakdown caused by stress at work. The council knew he had work-related problems and had drawn up an action plan some time before. They were at fault in failing to implement this plan. As decided in **Page**, a primary victim is someone who is directly affected and in danger of harm, this was the case here so the normal rules applied. The risk of harm was foreseeable. Proximity was satisfied because there is a clear relationship between an employer and employee. On the facts it was fair to impose a duty. The duty was breached by the council's failure to implement the plan, which a reasonable employer would have done. The psychiatric harm would not have occurred 'but for' their failure, and as the harm was foreseeable it was not too remote from the breach of duty.

Summary of the rules

no duty is owed unless C is in foreseeable danger and in proximity to the accident	Bourhill v Young 1943
established the 3 matters to consider in nervous shock claims	McLoughlin v O'Brien 1982
confirmed the McLoughlin test but added 'close ties of love & affection' and that there must be a 'sudden shock' which caused a recognisable psychiatric illness	Alcock v CC of South Yorkshire 1991
distinction between primary and secondary victims drawn	Page v Smith 1995
reconfirmed the test but said that rescuers had to meet the test for secondary victims unless in danger themselves	White v CC of South Yorkshire 1999
Made clear the immediate aftermath could not be extended indefinitely	Taylor v A Novo (UK) Ltd 2013

Summary of the application of the rules

Has C suffered a recognisable psychiatric illness?

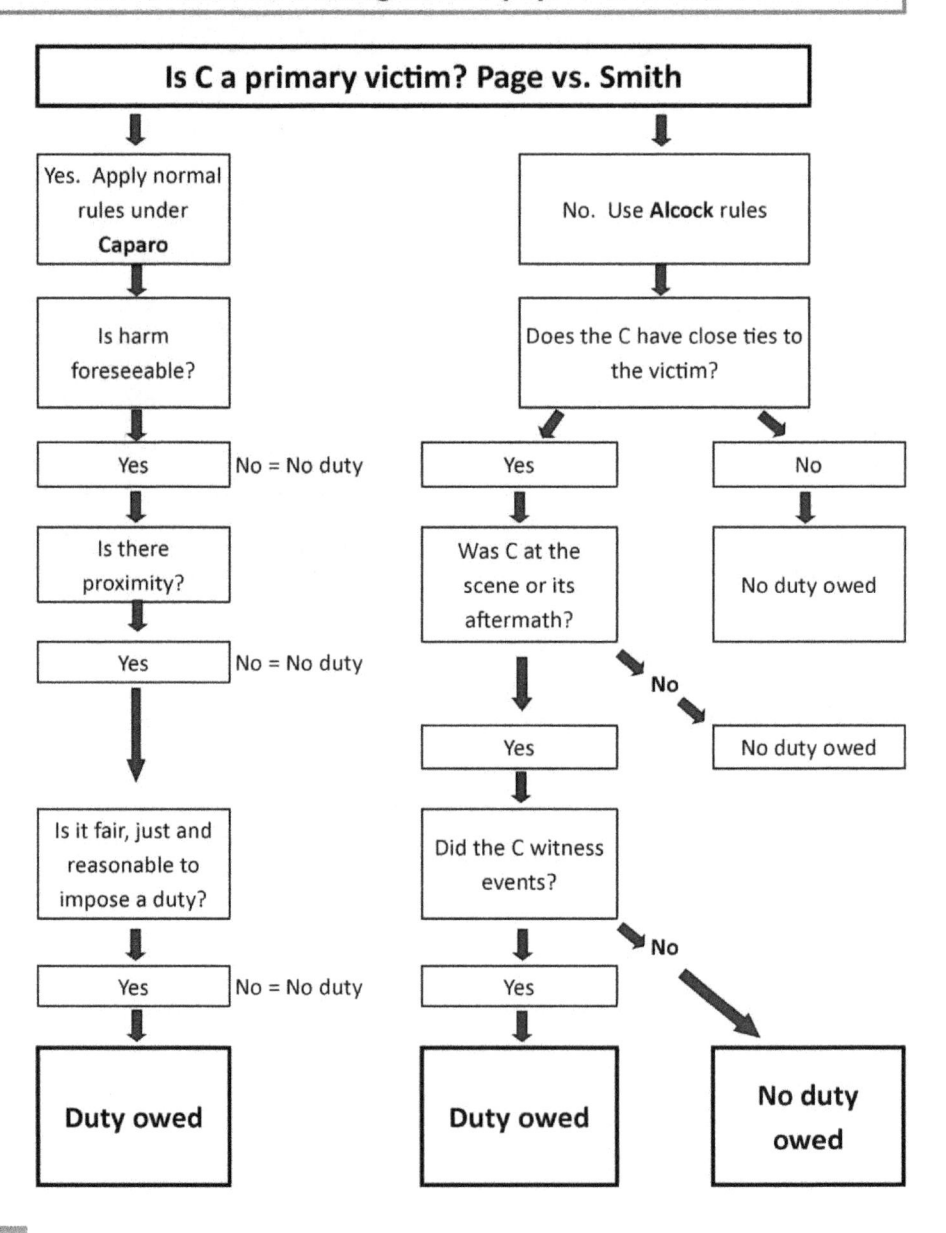

Is C a primary victim? Page vs. Smith

Left branch: Yes. Apply normal rules under **Caparo**
- Is harm foreseeable?
  - Yes → Is there proximity?
    - No = No duty
  - No = No duty
- Is there proximity?
  - Yes → Is it fair, just and reasonable to impose a duty?
  - No = No duty
- Is it fair, just and reasonable to impose a duty?
  - Yes → **Duty owed**
  - No = No duty

Right branch: No. Use **Alcock** rules
- Does the C have close ties to the victim?
  - Yes → Was C at the scene or its aftermath?
  - No → No duty owed
- Was C at the scene or its aftermath?
  - Yes → Did the C witness events?
  - No → No duty owed
- Did the C witness events?
  - Yes → **Duty owed**
  - No → **No duty owed**

Links to the non-substantive law

ELS: For links to the English legal system, look back at the diagram and examples in the introduction to Part 1. In particular, where a principle of law has been established the system of appeals is relevant, as these principles are established in the higher appeal courts, i.e., the CA and SC. ADR is always relevant to tort cases too, as is access to justice, because cases can be expensive to take to court so alternatives or help with expenses may be needed. However, it can be said that in case of psychiatric harm the rules are rather too complex for mediation by non-lawyers. Some of the control mechanisms lack certainty, especially as regards what is an immediate aftermath and what is a sudden shock. A judge is better able to apply the law in difficult cases. The appeals system is also important, to help correct any inadequacies in the lower courts.

The nature of law: The role of law is to mediate between the parties in a case and provide a fair remedy where appropriate. The remedy will be based on the level of fault, or blameworthiness. If someone is found to be at fault then this justifies the court imposing a penalty. In civil law, this is done by way of compensation (or sometimes an injunction as you will see when we look at remedies). In cases of psychiatric harm, the law is less strict (for D) than where physical harm has been caused, so the rules on imposing a duty of care are more severe. As Lord Lloyd said in **Page v Smith 1995**, the law insists on the control mechanisms as a matter of policy when imposing a duty of care. This is in order to limit the number of claimants (the floodgates argument). In **White** the decision was partly based on morality, in that it would not be right to refuse so many relatives but allow the police to claim. Similarly, in **Greatorex**, it was seen as immoral to allow claims between family members in such circumstances.

As noted in the last chapter, with most of tort Mill's 'harm principle' can be discussed. Where harm has been caused it is right for the law to be involved, and this would include psychiatric harm. However, as this type of harm can be widespread the law imposes stricter rules, thus achieving a balance. The rules for proving a duty are stricter than for physical harm for policy reasons. It is not in the public interest for the courts to be flooded by claims and hundreds or even thousands of people could witness a shocking event.

Self-test Questions

1. Which case highlighted the distinction between primary and secondary victims?
2. Explain these two terms and why the distinction is important
3. In which case (in the HL) was the first successful claim for psychiatric harm by a secondary victim?
4. In that case what did the Lords say needed to be looked at in such claims?
5. What was added in **Alcock**?

Answers to the tasks and self-test questions are on my website at www.drsr.org. Please click on 'Answers to tasks'. For a range of free interactive exercises, click on 'Free Exercises'.

Summary 2: Economic loss and psychiatric harm,

The rules on duty in relation to harm caused by another's negligence are different depending on the type of harm.

- *Physical harm: Damage to a person or property*
- *Economic harm: Financial loss*
- *Psychiatric harm: Mental rather than physical harm*

Example

In **Donoghue v Stevenson 1932**, a woman suffered **physical** harm after consuming a drink containing a decomposed snail.

In **Caparo v Dickman 1990**, a purchaser of shares suffered **economic** loss having relied on the information provided by auditors who had negligently prepared a company's accounts. Liability for economic loss is based on whether D has made a negligent misstatement.

In **Bourhill v Young 1943**, a pregnant woman suffered **psychiatric** harm having heard a crash and gone to the scene.

Each type of loss, or harm, has special rules for proving a duty of care.

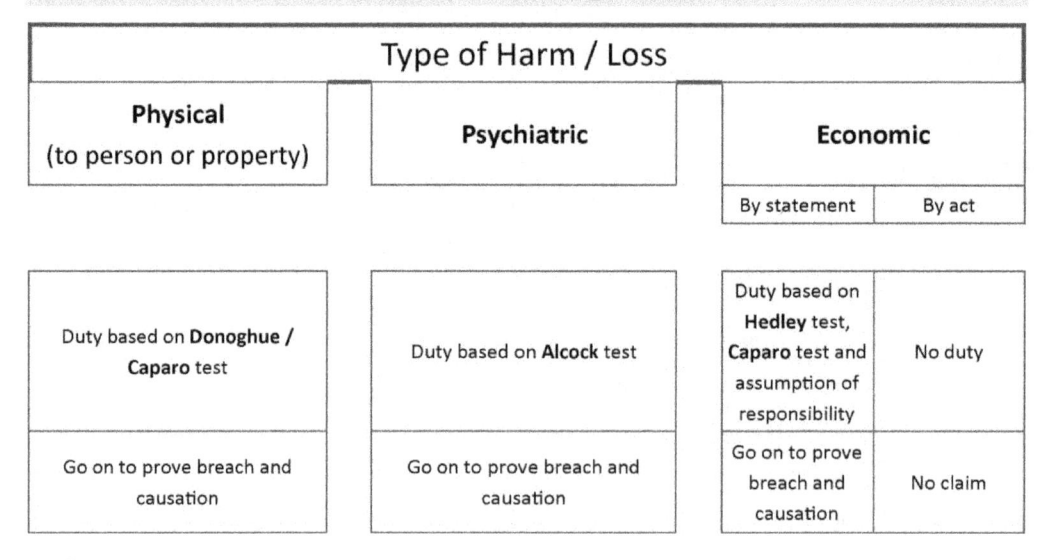

Type of Harm / Loss				
Physical (to person or property)	**Psychiatric**	**Economic**	
		By statement	By act
Duty based on **Donoghue / Caparo** test	Duty based on **Alcock** test	Duty based on **Hedley** test, **Caparo** test and assumption of responsibility	No duty
Go on to prove breach and causation	Go on to prove breach and causation	Go on to prove breach and causation	No claim

Task 30

Look up the tests mentioned above. Draw a diagram adding the tests for each type of harm or damage. Keep this for revision.

Breach of duty

The standard expected of D is that of the reasonable person, an objective test. This is shown in **Nettleship v Weston 1971** – a learner driver should reach the standard of a competent driver

Note, though the subjective element:

Bolitho v City & Hackney HA 1998 – professionals

Mullin v Richards 1998 – children

Here is the diagram from Part 1 as a reminder.

Breach of duty

The courts will consider:
- The degree of risk
- The seriousness of potential harm
- Whether the risk was justifiable
- The expense and practicality of taking precautions

These factors are balanced against each other when the courts are deciding whether D breached the standard of care to be expected

Where D acts in a professional capacity, the skill expected is that of the profession – **Bolam / Bolitho**

Damage caused by the breach

- *Would the harm have occurred 'but for' D's act or omission? Barnett v Chelsea & Kensington HMC but note also Fairchild v Glenhaven Funeral Services Ltd 2002*
- *Was the harm foreseeable or was it too remote? The Wagon Mound 1966*
- *Was this type of harm foreseeable? Hughes v Lord Advocate*
- *Does the thin-skull rule apply? Smith v Leech Brain*

Note that foreseeability comes into all 3 areas, but becomes more specific at each stage.

Task 31

Add the rules on breach and causation to your diagram on the duty rules and keep this for revision.

Key criticisms

- *It is questionable whether there should be a distinction be made between economic loss by actions and by statements if D has been negligent*

- *There are arguments for and against cases such as children being able to sue the council for failing to, e.g., diagnose dyslexia. The money could arguably be better used in employing more (and better) psychologists*
- *It may be difficult to prove 'close ties' in psychiatric harm cases outside the presumed relationships*
- *The 'immediate aftermath' is hard to measure*
- *What amounts to a sudden shock is also somewhat unclear*
- *The law has not been entirely consistent on these issues*
- *Psychiatric harm has many problems, look back at the evaluation pointers for more*
- *The LC proposals for reform were rejected by the Government in 1998 and have not been revised*

You have now covered liability in negligence at common law and under the OLAs. Now we can look at other torts and then at the two defences which apply to all the torts in this book.

Chapter 10 nuisance

"the answer to the issue falls to be found by applying the concepts of reasonableness between neighbours and reasonable foreseeability" – Lord Cooke on how to prove nuisance

By the end of this chapter you should be able to:

- **Explain the rules relating to both public and private nuisance**
- **Show how the law applies by reference to cases**
- **Identify problems with the law and/or discuss its development in order to evaluate it**

What is nuisance?

Nuisance relates to quality of life. Examples include noise, smells, pollution and overhanging tree branches. Nuisance cases usually involve inconvenience rather than physical harm, but can include physical damage to property. There are three types: statutory, public and private. Private nuisance overlaps with negligence and an action may be brought in both torts, as Mrs Stone did in **Bolton v Stone 1951**.

There are now many statutes dealing with pollution and other matters which affect the environment and public health. Some deal with specific problems which occur between neighbours, such as noise and high hedges (the **Anti-Social Behaviour Act 2003** covers both of these) and many others cover public nuisance, which is a crime. Neither statutory nuisance nor public nuisance is likely to be examined. However, public nuisance is a tort as well as a crime and it may help you to understand private nuisance if you know just a little about this.

Public nuisance

Public nuisance was defined by Romer LJ in **AG v PYA Quarries 1957**, as one which *"materially affects the reasonable comfort and convenience of life of a class of Her Majesty's subjects"*.

It is thus a nuisance which affects the public or a section (class) of the public. Public nuisance is a crime, prosecuted by the Attorney General. However, if an individual suffers 'special damage' there is a remedy in tort.

In **Wandsworth LBC v Railtrack 2001**, droppings from pigeons roosting under a railway bridge fouled the pavements and sometimes landed on passers-by (*a class* of people). The local council suffered *'special damage'* because it had to pay to remedy the problem. The court held that the council could sue in public nuisance to recover the cost of doing so. Even though Railtrack had no general control over wild pigeons, it had the necessary knowledge, opportunity and resources to have taken steps to prevent this particular nuisance, and had not done so. The CA rejected Railtrack's appeal.

In **Castle v St Augustine's Links 1922**, golf balls were frequently hit onto a nearby road. The siting of the hole so near to the road was a public nuisance. It affected road users who are a *'class'* of people. A taxi driver who was injured when a golf ball broke his windscreen was able to sue in tort as he suffered *'special damage'*. Nuisance is similar to negligence but something must usually happen often to be deemed a nuisance, thus the claim failed in **Bolton v Stone 1951**.

Task 32

Compare **Bolton v Stone** to **Castle v St Augustine's Links**. Make a note of the differences and why the latter claim succeeded whereas the first failed.

The definition of private nuisance

As nuisance is a tort, and so defined in common law and not a statute, the definition is not set in stone. Traditionally, private nuisance was defined as *'unreasonable interference with a person's use or enjoyment of land'*. In recent times, the CA and SC have described it slightly differently, but still in terms of reasonableness. Here are the definitions; the cases are discussed further below.

In **Hirose Electrical UK Ltd v Peak Ingredients Ltd 2011**, the CA held that C must prove that D had *'unreasonably interfered with the claimant's enjoyment of the premises'*. It is sometimes referred to as *unlawful* interference, but essentially it only becomes unlawful if it is found to be unreasonable.

In **Coventry Promotions v Lawrence 2014**, the SC defined nuisance as an act or omission which causes *'an interference with the claimant's reasonable enjoyment of his land'*. This is not really different except that reasonableness has moved from the interference by D to the enjoyment by C. The effect is much the same.

Example

It is your birthday and you have a very noisy party which goes on all night. The neighbours complain that they cannot sleep. They may call this a 'nuisance', but it is unlikely to be found unreasonable, as it is only a one-off. It is therefore not unlawful and they cannot sue. However, if you have a party every night this becomes unreasonable. The neighbours can sue and ask the court to stop you doing this and/or claim compensation for their sleepless nights because it affects their reasonable enjoyment of their property.

Note that although compensation (a monetary award, called damages) is a remedy for all torts another remedy is an injunction. This is a court order used to prevent an action, so is particularly appropriate in nuisance cases. As in my example, the neighbours can ask the court for an injunction to prevent the nuisance continuing. There is more on this under remedies.

Although traditionally nuisance dealt with indirect interference and usually related to a person's use or enjoyment of land, three types of interference were noted in the next case.

Key case

In **Hunter v Canary Wharf 1997**, C complained about interference with television reception caused by a tower block. The claim was rejected because C did not have a proprietary interest in land (see under 'who can sue'). However, the HL also held that this *type* of interference was not actionable. Lord Lloyd said that private nuisance was of three kinds:

> **encroachment onto land**
>
> **direct physical injury to a neighbour's land and**
>
> **interference with a neighbour's quiet enjoyment of land**

Key principles: C must have an interest in land. Television interference did not come within nuisance (interference in each of the three types identified refers to land)

The 3 forms of interference discussed in **Hunter** overlap.

Example

I have a big tree in my garden. Some branches overhang my neighbour's garden. The roots also grow under my fence onto her land. The branches and the roots *encroach* on her land. If the roots also cause damage to her lawn this is *direct physical injury* to the land. If the shade from the branches prevents her sunbathing, this *interferes with her enjoyment* of the land.

Examination pointer

Watch for the overlap between nuisance and other torts. Not only is there an overlap with negligence, as in **Bolton v Stone 1951**, but also with occupier's liability and **Rylands v Fletcher**. You may need to discuss more than one possible claim. In Summary 3 there is a comparison chart for nuisance and **Rylands v Fletcher**.

There is also an overlap between public and private nuisance. In **Halsey v Esso Petroleum Co 1961**, dirt and noise from D's depot affected the neighbourhood (public nuisance), damaged C's car (public nuisance, but he could bring a case in tort as he suffered 'special damage') and damaged washing hanging in his garden (private nuisance).

What is unreasonable interference?

Some types of interference are unlikely to amount to nuisance. In **Hunter**, it was held that interference with television reception caused by a tower block was not actionable. This was based on the fact that it was similar to the blocking of a view, which had long been held not to give rise to such an action. In **Network Rail v Morris 2004**, a rail company had installed a new signalling system. C owned a recording studio nearby and complained of electromagnetic interference. His nuisance claim succeeded at first instance, but the CA did not consider that such interference should amount to nuisance and allowed the rail company's appeal. This was partly based on the fact that such interference was not foreseeable as it was rare.

Evaluation pointer

It seems strange that interference with television reception is not actionable. This is something that affects people's everyday lives. It certainly affects the 'use and enjoyment' of a property. For many people not being able to watch television would be a major problem. The **Network Rail** case seems to confirm the view in **Hunter** that the law of nuisance does not protect such amenities, although this case was partly based on lack of foreseeability and sensitivity of the claimant.

The courts will look at, and balance, several factors in deciding if any interference is unreasonable. I have not made any of these key cases as they illustrate different points and are equally important. Make sure you know at least one for each point.

Frequency and duration

A 'one-off' or temporary act is not generally enough. A claim is only likely to succeed where something happens frequently. Thus in **Bolton v Stone 1951**, where the cricket ball went over only 6 times in 35 years, it was not deemed to be a nuisance. In **Miller v Jackson 1977**, a cricket club had played cricket on a site near C's house for some 70 years before she moved in. Balls from the ground landed in her garden several times a year and she succeeded in an action in nuisance.

Building works could be a nuisance but this is unlikely as they are only temporary. However, if they went on for a long time or if they occurred at night an action in nuisance might succeed. In **De Keyser's Hotel v Spicer 1914**, pile-driving at night was deemed a nuisance although it was only temporary. An injunction was granted to limit the activity to the daytime.

In **Peires v Bickerton's Aerodromes Ltd 2017**, C had complained about noise from helicopters doing training exercises on neighbouring land. The complaint related to frequency and duration and the court held that Ds activities amounted to an unreasonable interference with Cs enjoyment of her property (although D's appeal was allowed on the basis of statutory authority – see defences below).

State of affairs

An apparent exception to the need for frequency is where something constitutes a continuing 'state of affairs'. An illustration is **Spicer v Smee 1946**. Here D's faulty wiring led to a fire which damaged C's property. Although this seemed to be a one-off, the claim in nuisance succeeded on the basis that the faulty wiring amounted to a continuing 'state of affairs'. In **Castle v St Augustine's Links** above, the siting of the hole on the golf course was considered to be a 'state of affairs'. Although in that case the golf balls were quite frequently hit into the road, the fact that the siting of the hole was deemed to be a state of affairs means a claim could have succeeded even if they had been less frequent.

Locality

Where the nuisance happens will be a relevant factor in assessing reasonableness. In **Sturges v Bridgman 1879**, Thesiger LJ said, "*what may be a nuisance in Belgrave Square may not be so in*

Bermondsey." This means that much will depend on the type of area. The remark is hardly politically correct, but the point is valid. Noise or smells in a quiet garden suburb may constitute a nuisance, whereas the same noise or smells elsewhere may not. It is perhaps better to say that what may be a nuisance in a residential area may not be in an industrial estate.

In **Hirose Electrical UK Ltd v Peak Ingredients Ltd 2011**, the owner of a manufacturing business brought a claim in nuisance against a food manufacture because of the smells which entered his adjoining premises. At trial the judge rejected the claim. One reason was that the character of the neighbourhood was that of a light industrial estate and not a residential area. The CA agreed that the central issue was whether or not the smells amounted to private nuisance given the character of the neighbourhood, and dismissed C's appeal.

However, in **Laws v Florinplace 1981**, a company took over a dress shop and turned it into a sex shop. The area was mostly commercial with a few residential homes, but when several residents complained the court held it amounted to a nuisance.

An important distinction between physical damage and discomfort was made in **St Helen's Smelting Co v Tipping 1865**. Here C lived in a manufacturing area, and fumes from D's copper works caused damage to his garden plants. The action for an injunction succeeded. The HL held that where material damage had been suffered, *the locality was not relevant.* D could not say that the locality abounded in similar manufactures so they should not be liable; no-one could carry on an activity which caused actual harm whatever type of area it was in.

Social benefit or usefulness

If something is for the public benefit it is less likely to be a nuisance – this is often called the 'utility' argument. However, it is unlikely to suffice alone and the other factors, in particular the locality, will be balanced against the usefulness. Thus in **Adams v Ursell 1913**, smells from a fish and chip shop amounted to a nuisance. Although providing a service, it was opened in a residential area. Even if an activity amounts to a nuisance, if it has a social benefit the court may allow it to continue. In **Miller**, although she won her case, no injunction was granted because cricket has a social benefit.

In **Barr v Biffa Waste Services Ltd 2011**, residents claimed in nuisance because of smells from D's landfill site. The CA restated that the relevant control mechanism, applicable in all nuisance cases, is whether or not there is reasonable use of the land in all the circumstances. The court also noted that **Miller v Jackson** had shown that the fact that the nuisance is caused by activities which are beneficial will not in itself provide a defence to a nuisance claim, although it may be a relevant factor to be taken into account when assessing reasonable use or the appropriate remedy. On the facts, especially considering the residential character of the area, there was a case in nuisance.

Task 33

Compare **Bolton v Stone 1951** to **Miller v Jackson 1977** and consider why the latter claim succeeded and the first failed.

Seriousness of the interference

The more serious the interference the more likely it will amount to a nuisance. Where actual damage (rather than mere discomfort) is caused, this is likely to be deemed serious. An example is **Halsey** where damage was caused to his washing. Another is **St Helen's** where the HL held damage was an important factor and that the locality was not relevant where physical harm was caused. So, although seriousness is only one factor to be taken into the balance it seems to carry more weight than some.

Sensitivity

If C (or what is harmed) is particularly sensitive, then an action is unlikely to succeed. In **Robinson v Kilvert 1889**, heat from a neighbour's boiler damaged special paper stored above. Normal paper would not have been affected and so the claim failed. However, if normal paper *would* have been affected then the claim could succeed and include sensitive items. In **McKinnon Industries v Walker 1951**, C was able to obtain compensation in respect of damage to some delicate orchids because it could be shown that normal plants would have been damaged. In **Network Rail v Morris 2004**, above, the CA noted that no one else had complained of interference. The claim would therefore probably have failed on the sensitivity issue even if it had been accepted that electronic interference was actionable.

Malice

Malice and motive are rarely relevant in law. *Why* you do something is usually unimportant; it is whether what you do amounts to an illegal act that matters. However, if one person acts out of spite it could tip the balance when considering 'unreasonableness'. In **Christie v Davey 1893**, two neighbours caused a nuisance to each other, one by giving piano lessons, the other by retaliating during these lessons by banging tin trays together and whistling. The latter was found liable in nuisance because his behaviour was malicious and unreasonable. Similarly, in **Hollywood Silver Fox Farm v Emmett 1936**, D was liable in nuisance when he told his son to fire a shotgun near his neighbour's silver fox farm at breeding time. He knew this would cause problems with the breeding programme (silver foxes are nervous animals) and he had acted out of spite. His malice made it an actionable nuisance.

Examination pointer

For any problem question you will need to define nuisance and refer to the factors which the courts take into the balance. Make sure that you know at least one case on each factor.

Task 34 (there is no answer to this as it depends what you found)

Look – and listen – around your neighbourhood. Is there something happening that you think might be a nuisance? Apply the above tests and see if, on balance, it would amount to a nuisance in law. Don't rush off and sue anyone though!

Claimants: who can sue?

A nuisance is an interference with the use of land. It has long been accepted that this tort is there to protect such interests. It is therefore not available to those who have no proprietary interest in land. This was established in **Malone v Laskey 1907**.

Proprietary means a legal interest in the land or property. This would include an owner or tenant, but not a lodger or members of a household who do not have a legal interest in the property. One claim by the daughter of a household, for an injunction to prevent nuisance telephone calls from her ex-boyfriend, succeeded. This was in **Khorasandjan v Bush 1993**, where the HL allowed her claim even though she had no legal interest in the property. However, this situation has now been dealt with by the **Protection from Harassment Act 1997**, so there is no longer a need for a common law remedy. The case has since been overruled by **Hunter v Canary Wharf 1997** (discussed above), which re-established **Malone** and confirmed that someone without a proprietary interest cannot claim in nuisance.

Defendants: who can be sued?

In most cases D is the 'creator' of the nuisance. This usually means the owner or occupier of the property from which the nuisance comes (i.e., the landlord or the tenant), but can include someone who created the nuisance even if no longer in occupation. There may also be liability if you *know* about a nuisance you did not personally create, but you continue, or 'adopt' it. This can include acts of a third party or natural hazards. The following three cases illustrate the courts' approach to this issue. Again, none is a key case as they are equally important, but make sure you understand **Coventry Promotions v Lawrence 2014** as it involved several issues and is discussed further under remedies.

In **Sedleigh Denfield v O'Callaghan 1940**, D was liable for the flooding of C's land. A blocked pipe laid along his property by the local authority, caused the flooding. However, he *knew* of its existence and had *used* it, thus he had 'adopted' the nuisance.

In **Tetley v Chitty 1986**, C brought an action against the council in relation to disturbance from a go-kart track. A club, who leased the land from the council, ran the track. The council were found liable on the basis that the 'interference' was a necessary consequence of operating this activity on the council's land. In effect, they had implied *knowledge* of it. An injunction was granted to stop the activity. This can be compared to:

Key case

Coventry Promotions v Lawrence 2014.

This case had similar facts to **Tetley** but here the SC held that it was not possible to hold the landlords liable for noise from a motor sports track because the nuisance was not a 'necessary' or 'highly probable' consequence of the lettings, and nor had the landlord either authorised or participated in the activity. One of these had to be shown for a landlord to be liable for the nuisance of a tenant. (Note though, that the tenants/operators of the track were liable as the people who actually caused the nuisance.)

Key principle: a landlord will not be liable for a tenant's nuisance unless the nuisance was a necessary consequence (as in **Tetley**) or the landlord had authorised or participated in the activity.

In **Goldman v Hargrave 1967**, lightning struck a tree on D's land and it caught fire. He cut it down and left it to burn. Fire spread to C's land when a strong wind rekindled it a few days later. He was found liable for the damage caused as he *knew* about the risk and so had a duty to do something about it. The decision was much influenced by the case of **Sedleigh** above.

Both cases were referred to in **Coope v Ward 2015**. D's wall collapsed into C's garden after a heavy fall of snow. C claimed that the collapse was due to the build-up of earth on C's property over a number of years and that this amounted to a nuisance. The CA held that there was no liability in nuisance for the collapse as D had neither created any nuisance nor continued it with knowledge of the danger. It was not possible to see that the wall was under stress from the amount of earth and the collapse was due to the addition of the snow, which was not under D's control.

In cases where D has 'adopted', rather than 'created', the nuisance the test for what is reasonable is subjective rather than objective, i.e., it is what *this particular* D should have done, not what *the average* person would do. In **Leakey v National Trust 1980**, due to natural causes, part of a mound on the Trust's property slid down a hill onto neighbouring land. It was held that they were liable for the damage caused because they knew of the risk. Megaw LJ said that when deciding if D was acting reasonably regard should be had how much it would cost to eliminate the danger and to D's means, or resources. As we saw in **Wandsworth LBC v Railtrack 2001**, the court held that although Railtrack had no general control over wild pigeons, it had the necessary knowledge, opportunity and resources to have taken steps to prevent this particular nuisance, and had not done so.

As well as financial considerations, foreseeability is also a factor. In **Holbeck Hall Hotel v Scarborough Borough Council 2001**, a hotel collapsed due to erosion on neighbouring land owned by the council. The court held that liability would partly depend on the resources of the council and the expense of any remedial work, as above, but another point was whether the damage was foreseeable. As the destruction of the hotel was not foreseeable the claim failed. In **Rees v Skerrett 2001**, D knocked down his own property, thus exposing his neighbour's wall to the elements. Here the damage to the neighbour's wall was foreseeable, and failure to take reasonable remedial action was actionable.

Evaluation pointer

Consider the following questions.

Should C have an interest in land or should it be enough that they live in the affected property? Compare **Khorasandjan v Bush** with **Hunter v Canary Wharf**.

Should a person be liable for natural dangers? Compare **Holbeck Hall Hotel v Scarborough BC** with **Rees v Skerrett**.

Should a person be liable for the actions of a third party as in **Sedleigh Denfield** and **Tetley v Chitty**?

Should D's resources be taken into account as suggested in **Leakey v National Trust** and **Wandsworth LBC v Railtrack**? It seems fair in certain cases that you should only be expected to do what you can reasonably afford to do, but is this fair to C? Should a claimant living next to a pop star have a different right to one living next to a person with limited means? As always there is no right answer to these questions so feel free to explore your own ideas. Don't forget, though, to use cases to support any argument you make.

Examination pointer

For any problem question you will need to define nuisance and refer to the factors which the courts take into the balance. You should expand on any of the particularly relevant factors to decide whether the use of land is unreasonable in the particular circumstances given. In **Bolton v Stone 1951**, the most relevant factor was 'frequency'. The fact that the balls did not go over the fence frequently excluded an action in nuisance. An infrequent act like this could amount to negligence so you may need to discuss that as an alternative. In **Bolton**, it wasn't negligent on the facts as the club had taken sufficient care, so there was no breach of duty.

Causation

As with negligence, it must be proved that D's nuisance caused the harm suffered. This means applying **The Wagon Mound 1966** test for remoteness of damage. This was confirmed in **Cambridge Water Co Ltd v Eastern Counties Leather plc 1994**. A claim was brought in three different torts: negligence, nuisance and **Rylands v Fletcher** (see next chapter). The HL held that for all three torts **The Wagon Mound** test applies. D is not liable for unforeseeable damage.

Key case

In **Cambridge,** D used chemicals in the process of manufacturing leather. Some spillages leaked into the soil and eventually found their way into C's waterworks where water was extracted for public consumption. Due to a European Directive, issued after the spillages occurred, the water could not be used for drinking, so the company sued for their loss. The HL held that **The Wagon Mound** test of foreseeability also applied to both nuisance and **Rylands** (see next chapter). This meant D was not liable if damage could not have been foreseen, as was the case here.

Key principle: **The Wagon Mound** test also applies to both nuisance and **Rylands** so the damage must be foreseeable.

Task 35

Explain which of the factors that the court will consider are most relevant in the following cases. There may be more than one factor in a case.

Bolton v Stone 1951

Miller v Jackson 1977

Sturges v Bridgman 1879

Hirose Electrical UK Ltd v Peak Ingredients Ltd 2011

St Helen's Smelting Co v Tipping 1865

Adams v Ursell 1913

Barr v Biffa Waste Services Ltd 2011

Robinson v Kilvert 1889

McKinnon Industries v Walker 1951

Christie v Davey 1893

Defences

There are two special defences to an action in nuisance.

Statutory authority

This means authorised by an Act of Parliament. In **Allen v Gulf Oil 1981**, an Act of Parliament authorised the building of an oil refinery. The court held that it would be inconceivable that it would authorise the building but not the running of it. There was therefore implied authorisation for the latter so Gulf Oil could not be liable in nuisance for noise from the refinery. The defence succeeded.

In **Peires v Bickerton's Aerodromes Ltd 2017**, C had complained about noise from helicopters doing training exercises on neighbouring land and claimed both damages and an injunction. The court held that Ds activities amounted to an unreasonable interference with Cs enjoyment of her property and issued an injunction to restrain the activity to certain areas and times per week. D argued the defence of statutory authority under the **Civil Aviation Act 1982** which authorised flights over other property. The trial judge rejected the defence on the basis that the statute covered noise from flight, which could include take-off and landing but not exercises. D appealed. The CA accepted that there was no reason to differentiate between flying and training. Flying was authorised so the CA allowed the appeal.

Planning permission is unlikely to amount to statutory authority as it does not come from an Act of Parliament, but it may have an effect. If it changes the character of the neighbourhood, the courts look at the locality factor *after* it has changed. In **Gillingham Borough Council v Medway Docks 1993**, planning permission was granted to turn the docks into a commercial port. This meant increased noise and traffic, which local residents complained about. Although the court held that planning permission did not equate to statutory authority, it had meant that the area had become a busy commercial dock. The commercial nature of the locality meant there was no nuisance. If the permission does not have the effect of altering the character of the neighbourhood it is unlikely to be accepted as a defence, however. In **Wheeler v Saunders 1995**, planning permission was granted to erect pig houses but it was held that the smells from the pigs could constitute a nuisance. Similarly, in **Barr v Biffa** above, the defence of statutory authority failed even though D was operating under a permit granted by the Environment Agency.

A statutory scheme may also exclude an action in nuisance. In **Marcic v Thames Water Utilities Ltd 2003**, D's garden was subject to flooding after heavy rain, due to water overflowing from the sewerage system. The CA had relied on **Goldman v Hargrave 1967** and **Leakey v National Trust 1980** and found the sewerage company liable. However, the HL allowed the appeal on the basis that the **Water Industry Act 1991** made provision for enforcement by an independent regulator whose decisions were subject to judicial review by the courts. To allow a common law right would effectively supplant this regulatory role, which D had chosen not to use. Although not strictly used as a defence the effect was similar. As there was a statutory scheme C could not rely on the common law to claim.

Prescription

The defence of prescription applies where a nuisance has continued for 20 years without complaint. Once 20 years has passed D has a right to continue the activity. It is important to note that time starts from when the nuisance starts. In **Sturges v Bridgeman 1879**, a doctor built consulting rooms near to D's workshop and then claimed the noise from the workshop was a nuisance. D could not use the defence of prescription because the *nuisance* had not been going on for 20 years. It didn't become a nuisance until the doctor built his consulting rooms. The effect is that D cannot argue that C 'came to the nuisance'.

A case which illustrates both defences is **Watson & Ors v Croft Promo-Sport Ltd 2009**. Permission had been granted by a local authority for racing events to be staged in the area. These later increased, and as well as the races on several days the public was allowed to use the track all day. C claimed this amounted to a nuisance. The CA considered the defences.

- **Defence of statutory authority**: The CA confirmed that it was not possible for a local authority to authorise a nuisance through planning permission unless such permission changed the character of the neighbourhood, thus making the use of the land reasonable (**Gillingham**). On the facts, the CA held that the use of the circuit was unreasonable in the circumstances, so the defence failed.

- **Defence of prescription**: Another point which arose was whether there was any defence of 'coming to the nuisance', as the track had been operating for several years before C moved to the area. Relying on **Sturges v Bridgman**, the CA held that this was no defence.

Other defences that may apply are act of a stranger and act of God. These are more commonly seen in **Rylands v Fletcher** and are discussed in the next chapter. Briefly they mean D has a defence because a third party caused the nuisance or because it was an act of nature. In nuisance cases they are not likely to apply where D has knowledge of the nuisance. In **Sedleigh Denfield**, the defence of act of a stranger did not apply because D knew of the pipe so had adopted the nuisance. Similarly, in **Goldman v Hargrave,** act of god did not apply because D knew of the danger. Consent and contributory negligence also apply, as to all torts covered in this book (see Chapter 13 and Chapter 14).

Evaluation pointer

The effect of **Sturges** is that C can effectively 'self-inflict' the nuisance. This can seem unfair. For example, I build a nice Gazebo at the end of my (very long) garden. Should I be able to sue my neighbour if I am now disturbed by the noise he makes with his car repair workshop, which he has been running for generations?

Remedies

A monetary award of damages may be appropriate if actual harm has occurred. Another remedy is an injunction. This is a court order used to prevent D carrying out some type of act. It is most commonly used in nuisance cases.

Example

Tim has started a pop group and they practise at home every night. Alan is a neighbour who cannot sleep. Alan doesn't really want compensation; that won't help him to sleep. He could sue Tim in nuisance and if he wins he should apply to the court for an injunction.

There are two other remedies which are particularly relevant to nuisance, the other is abatement. We'll look at each in turn.

Injunction

The most effective remedy for a claim in nuisance is an injunction. This is a court order to stop the nuisance happening. In **Shelfer v City of London Electric Lighting Co 1895**, the court held that an injunction should be the remedy unless there are exceptional circumstances. The principle is that D should not be able to 'buy' the right to commit a nuisance by paying money to C. The exceptional circumstances referred to in **Shelfer** were that an injunction would be oppressive or that the injury to C's rights was small and capable of being compensated by an award of money. This happened in **Miller v Jackson 1977**. No injunction was granted but damages were awarded instead. In **Regan v Paul Properties Ltd 2006**, the CA confirmed the rule in **Shelfer**. C had complained about D's building blocking his light within a month of him starting to build. He had lost several thousands of pounds in the reduction of value of his property and wanted the building stopped rather than an award of money. The CA confirmed that the court had the discretion to award damages rather than an injunction but that this should only be exercised in exceptional circumstances. Here, an injunction would not be oppressive and it would be unfair to C not to grant one as this would effectively force him, against his wishes, to accept money instead of solving his problem.

However, there has been a retreat from **Shelfer** and **Regan**.

Key case

In **Lawrence v Fen Tigers Ltd (No 2) 2014**, the SC suggested that in a modern world the principle was out of date. Lord Neuberger said, "it is unfortunate that it has been followed so recently and so slavishly" and noted that it had been devised at a time when there was less property and fewer statutory controls. He also indicated that the whole area should be reviewed because so few cases had reached the highest court that "for authoritative statements at the highest level on this area of the law one has to go back almost 150 years, to the landmark case of St Helen's Smelting Co v Tipping (1865)".

Key principle: an injunction may not always be appropriate and damages should be considered as an alternative (rather than slavishly following traditional principles).

Note that the facts of this case are the same as **Coventry Promotions v Lawrence 2014**. The case name changed because there were several trials. Lawrence was the C, and there were originally six defendants, including the operators (Fen Tigers), the landlord/owner of the stadium (Coventry) and others. The trial court held the operators liable but not the landlord. The CA held the operators were not liable and didn't therefore consider the landlord. The SC reversed the CA judgment but as the landlord was not part of that another hearing took place, where the landlord was held not liable.

Sometimes a partial injunction may be granted to limit the activity in some way, rather than stop it altogether. This seems to be a fair compromise and a good way to balance the competing interests involved.

Example

Using my earlier example, an injunction would stop Tim practising at home. A partial injunction could stop him doing so at certain times, after midnight for example.

As we saw earlier, in **De Keyser's Hotel v Spicer 1914**, a partial injunction was granted to limit the pile-driving to the daytime. In **Kennaway v Thompson 1981**, an injunction was granted to stop the noise on a lake caused by speedboat racing, which limited the activity to particular times.

Evaluation pointer

In **Miller v Jackson 1977**, no injunction was granted. In **Kennaway v Thompson 1981**, a partial injunction was granted and in **Tetley v Chitty 1986**, a full injunction was granted. This not only makes the law uncertain it seems the courts are deciding the issue to some extent on policy considerations. It was not felt appropriate to grant an injunction in **Miller** because cricket is a social activity. It could be argued that plenty of people like go-karting too but this activity was stopped by the court. The **Kennaway** decision is perhaps the most acceptable as it is a compromise and much more in line with the 'give and take' idea of nuisance. Granting a partial injunction meant the activity could continue to some extent but the nuisance was reduced.

We saw above in **Watson & Ors v Croft Promo-Sport Ltd 2009**, that the defences of statutory authority and prescription both failed. Finally, the issue of whether to grant damages or an injunction arose. The judge had awarded damages but not granted an injunction. The CA held that only in exceptional circumstances (as stated in **Shelfer**) should damages be awarded and awarded an injunction to limit the activities to the racing events.

As an injunction is the most likely remedy you will need to discuss in a nuisance case, here is a quick summary.

Shelfer	the principle was established that an injunction should be the remedy unless there are exceptional circumstance e.g., an injunction would be oppressive
Tetley v Chitty	a total injunction was granted to prevent the activity
Kennaway v Thompson	a partial injunction was granted to restrict the activity to particular times
De Keyser's Hotel	a partial injunction was granted to limit the pile-driving to the daytime
Miller v Jackson	no injunction was granted because cricket has a social benefit
Regan v Paul Properties Ltd	an injunction was granted because it would not be oppressive (confirming **Shelfer**)
Lawrence v Fen Tigers Ltd (No 2)	an injunction may not always be appropriate and damages should be considered as an alternative

Abatement

Another remedy, which is specific to nuisance, is abatement. This is a 'self-help' remedy to stop the nuisance. An example would be chopping off overhanging branches from your neighbour's tree. However, this can only apply if it can be done without trespass. This means you should either do it from you own side of the fence or ask permission to enter your neighbour's garden.

In **Perrin and Another v Northampton BC 2007**, the CA held that the remedy of abatement only extended to cutting roots and branches encroaching C's land. It did not include cutting down the tree itself. If cutting the roots and branches did not remedy the situation, then C should seek damages or an injunction.

C may also be able to claim damages to cover the cost of remedying the situation.

In **Delaware Mansions Ltd v Westminster City Council 2001**, a local authority owned a tree and the roots caused damage to nearby flats. C undertook some work to remedy the problem and then claimed against the authority to recover the costs. The HL held that where there is a continuing nuisance of which D knew, or ought to have known, an owner who had spent money in an attempt to remedy the problem may recover reasonable expenditure. The tree was close to the property, so a real risk of damage was foreseeable. The authority had plenty of notice before the work was done and was therefore liable to pay the costs.

As mentioned earlier, there is a clear overlap between negligence and nuisance cases. In **Delaware Mansions**, the HL treated the labels 'nuisance' or 'negligence' as of no real significance. They looked at the concepts of reasonableness between 'neighbours' and reasonable foreseeability. The opening quote came from this case. Reference was made to the **Wagon Mound 1966**, where the judgments were based on what a reasonable person would have done in the circumstances. Many cases involve a claim in both torts.

Evaluation pointer

It is arguable that the law on private nuisance should rely on fault in the same way as negligence. The two torts clearly overlap and the test for reasonableness takes into account so many different issues that it is unnecessarily complicated. On the other hand, this does allow for flexibility so the courts can compromise between the parties. Nuisance has long been said to rely on give and take between neighbours so this may be preferable.

Examination pointer

Remember to consider causation and defences where relevant. You may also need to consider who can sue and who can be sued. Look for references to whether C owns land, whether D 'adopted' a nuisance, and/or to D's resources. As always, any such 'clues' are in the examination scenario for a reason.

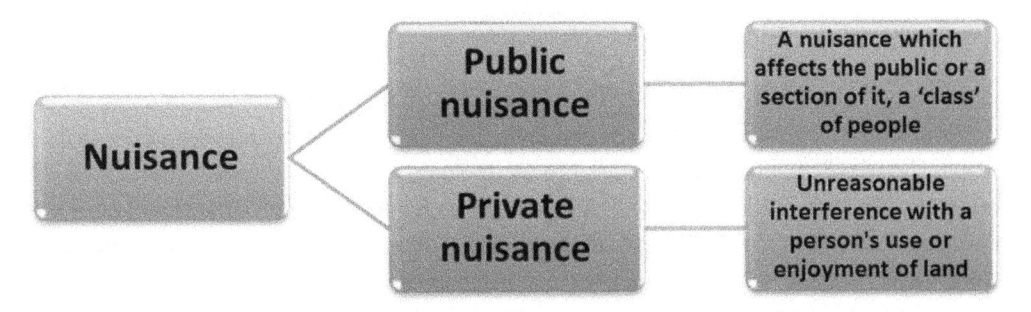

Nuisance
- **Public nuisance** — A nuisance which affects the public or a section of it, a 'class' of people
- **Private nuisance** — Unreasonable interference with a person's use or enjoyment of land

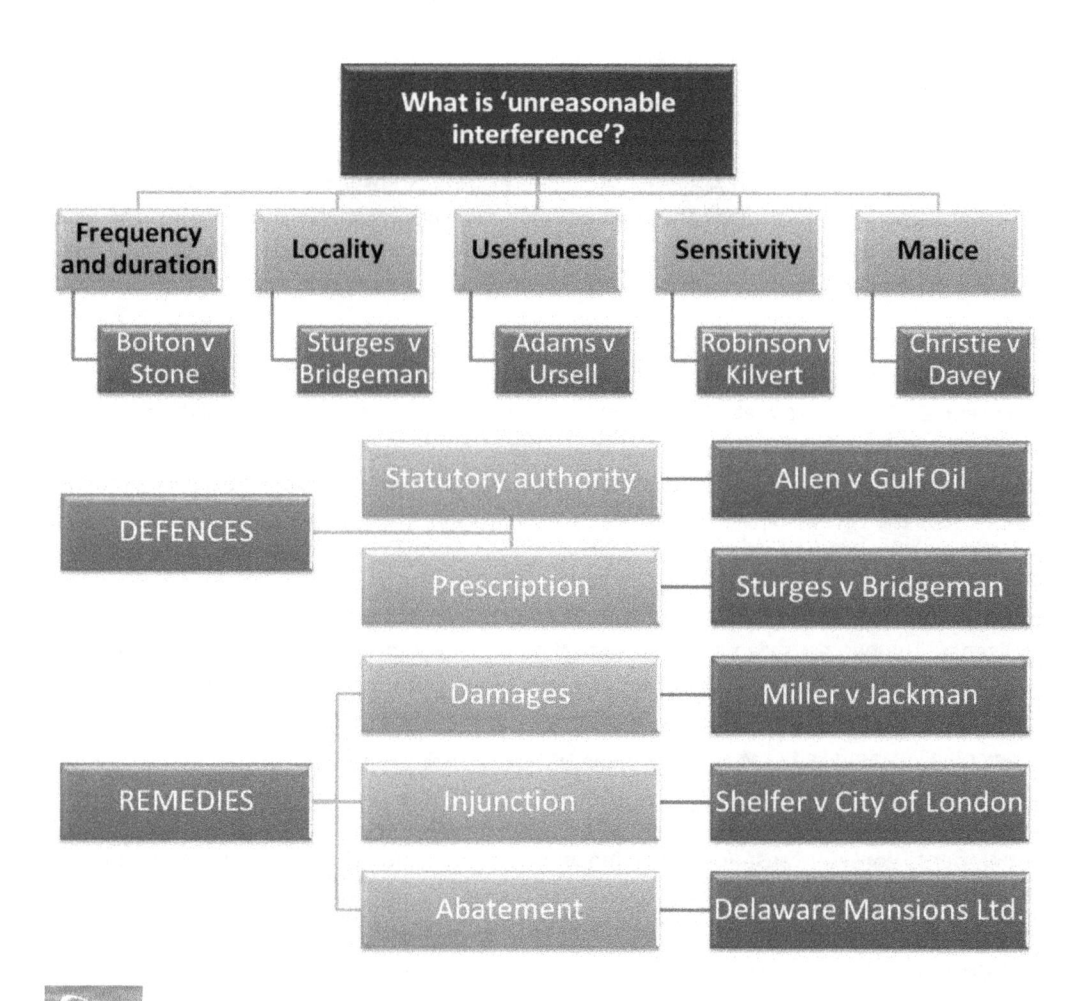

```
                    What is 'unreasonable
                         interference'?
    ┌──────────┬──────────┬──────────┬──────────┬──────────┐
 Frequency   Locality   Usefulness  Sensitivity   Malice
 and duration
    │            │           │           │           │
  Bolton v   Sturges v   Adams v    Robinson v   Christie v
   Stone     Bridgeman    Ursell     Kilvert       Davey
```

```
                 Statutory authority ── Allen v Gulf Oil
   DEFENCES ──┤
                 Prescription ── Sturges v Bridgeman

                 Damages ── Miller v Jackman
   REMEDIES ──┤ Injunction ── Shelfer v City of London
                 Abatement ── Delaware Mansions Ltd.
```

Links to the non-substantive law

ELS: For links to the English legal system, look back at the diagram and examples in the introduction to Part 1. In particular, where a principle of law has been established the system of appeals is relevant, as these principles are established in the higher appeal courts, i.e., the CA and SC. ADR is always relevant to tort cases too, as is access to justice, because cases can be expensive to take to court so alternatives or help with expenses may be needed. Nuisance is particularly relevant to ADR as the dispute is often between neighbours and going to court can make the relationship worse. Much the same applies to **Rylands**.

The nature of law: The role of law is to mediate between the parties in a case and provide a fair remedy where appropriate. The remedy will be based on the level of fault, or blameworthiness. If someone is found to be at fault then this justifies the court imposing a penalty. In civil law, this is done by way of compensation but more often in a nuisance case an injunction. Nuisance cases can be seen as extending the moral principle of do not harm your neighbour to do not interfere with your neighbour's enjoyment. Look back at the evaluation pointers for more ideas especially regarding taking D's resources into account. This can be related to fault as unreasonableness is the normal criterion, not money. The defence of prescription can also be related to fault as it seems wrong to make D pay compensation in a case like **Sturges** where there was no nuisance until C moved his surgery. Fault may tip the balance in nuisance cases where one person has acted maliciously, as in **Christie v Davey** and **Hollywood Silver Fox Farm v Emmett**.

Balancing competing interests is connected to all nuisance cases as they are based on disputes between two or more people, often neighbours. The courts will need to balance the interests to decide on whether to grant an injunction. See how they have done this by looking at some case and note there is more on injunctions in Chapter 14 on remedies.

Miller is one case example. The public interest was balanced against Mrs Miller's interests and prevailed, as it often will where there is a public benefit involved.

Self-test questions

1. State three factors which help the court to decide on whether something is unreasonable?
2. When might a one-off occurrence amount to a nuisance?
3. Who can sue and which case re-established this?
4. When are D's own resources, or means, relevant?

Answers to the tasks and self-test questions are on my website at www.drsr.org. **Please click on 'Answers to tasks'. For a range of free interactive exercises, click on 'Free Exercises'.**

Chapter 11 Rylands v Fletcher (the escape of dangerous things)

"the person who, for his own purposes, brings on his land and collects and keeps there anything likely to do mischief if it escapes, must keep it in at his peril" – Blackburn J

By the end of this chapter you should be able to:

- **Explain how the constituent parts of the 'rule in Rylands v Fletcher' apply**
- **Show how the law applies by reference to cases**
- **Identify problems with the law and/or discuss its development in order to evaluate it**

The rule in Rylands v Fletcher

This is a tort in its own right, named after the case in which it was first established, **Rylands v Fletcher 1868**. The facts of the case were that a land owner employed a contractor to build a reservoir on his land. The contractors discovered some disused mine shafts but they appeared to be filled in so they didn't seal them. When the reservoir was filled water flooded through these shafts and caused damage to C's mine. He sued for compensation but the court held that there was no case. He then took the matter to the Court of Exchequer Chamber, where Blackburn J said:

"...the person who, for his own purposes, brings on his land and collects and keeps there anything likely to do mischief if it escapes, must keep it in at his peril; and if he does not do so, is prima facie *answerable for all the damage which is the natural consequence of its escape"*

He added that to be liable D must have brought on to the property something that was *"not naturally there"*. The case then went to the HL where Lord Cairns LC quoted the words of Blackburn J with approval and developed "not naturally there" to *"putting the land to a non-natural use"*.

Evaluation pointer

In its report on *Civil Liability for Dangerous Things and Activities* 1970 (No 32), the Law Commission described the state of the law in this area as *"complex, uncertain and inconsistent in principle"*. As you read the cases try to form your own opinion on this.

Examination pointer

Note carefully the various constituent parts ('brings onto land', 'do mischief', 'escapes' and so on). All of the parts to the rule must be satisfied, so you will need to apply each of them to a given scenario in a problem question on this area, using case examples as appropriate.

Brings onto land

This requires that whatever causes the harm was not *naturally* on the land. In **Rylands** the water was not naturally on the land but *brought onto it* to fill the reservoir (compare this to, for example, a heavy rainfall or a river). In **Giles v Walker 1890**, D ploughed up a field and thistles grew on it, thistledown escaped onto a neighbour's land and seeded itself. D was not liable as he did not *bring on* the thistles, they were *naturally* there. The **Rylands** requirement that D must have brought on something 'not naturally there', was referred to in the HL as 'non-natural user', this suggest an unusual activity on the land or a special use of it. Many cases fail on this point.

Non-natural user

This is interpreted narrowly. In **Rickards v Lothian 1913**, C claimed for damage caused by flooding from D's basin on a higher floor in the office block. The 'non-natural' requirement was interpreted to mean *abnormal*. Water in the wash-basin was found to be natural, even though it was arguably 'brought on', and not there by nature but by plumbing. In **Read v Lyons 1947**, the HL held that the manufacture of high-explosive shells in wartime was *natural* use (although on the facts the case was decided on the issue of 'escape', discussed below). They said one must look at all the circumstances, and these will include time, place and normal practice.

This was confirmed in **Mason v Levy Autoparts 1967.** Here, D kept large quantities of petrol, paint and other combustible materials. They ignited and the fire spread to C's premises. In deciding that this was *non-natural user* the court held that the relevant matters to consider were:

- *the quantities of combustible material*
- *the way in which it was stored*
- *the character of the neighbourhood*

Examination pointer

There is an overlap between *non-natural* use and *negligent* use. The factors looked at in **Mason** would, as the judge recognised, also be relevant to a finding of negligence. Be prepared to consider alternatives.

The HL had a chance to reconsider the rule in the following case.

Key case

Transco Plc v Stockport BC 2004 involved an accumulation of water which escaped from D's property, as in **Rylands** itself. This caused subsidence, which threatened C's property. On the facts, the HL decided that the use was natural and D was not liable. The HL did, however, attempt to clarify the rule, and restated that there must be **an escape** and a **non-natural use of land**. Lord Bingham said that non-natural use was one that was 'extraordinary and unusual'. This suggests that, as in **Mason** and **LMS** (below), the quantity of the material and the way in which it is stored will be relevant. The HL also suggested that a claim for death or personal injury was outside the rule, because it does not relate to any right in land and this was confirmed in **Corby Group Litigation v Corby Borough Council 2008**.

Key principle: There must be an escape from land and a non-natural use of land which was 'extraordinary and unusual'.

Lord Hoffman said, *"there is a broad and ill-defined exception for 'natural' uses of land. It is perhaps not surprising that counsel could not find a reported case since the second world war in which anyone had succeeded in a claim under the rule. It is hard to escape the conclusion that the intellectual effort devoted to the rule by judges and writers over many years has brought forth a mouse"*. Lord Bingham felt that it should be restated *"so as to achieve as much certainty and clarity as is attainable, recognising that new factual situations are bound to arise posing difficult questions on the boundary of the rule, wherever that is drawn"*.

Evaluation pointer

In **Transco**, Lord Hoffman recognised that what was natural was "ill-defined" the HL did not agree on what it *did* amount to, so this remains a difficulty. Do you think the law should be more clear-cut? Lord Bingham recognised the need to be able to apply it to new situations, so perhaps if it were *too* clearly defined it would be inflexible.

On the plus side, the HL did restate the rule in somewhat clearer terms and noted that most of the confusion had come from later cases rather than **Rylands** itself. Perhaps the mouse will roar yet!

In **LMS International Ltd v Styrene Packaging & Insulation Ltd 2005**, the court approved **Transco** and restated the criteria:

- *D must have brought on something likely to do mischief*
- *D's actions must arise from a non-natural use of land*
- *damage must be foreseeable*

In applying these to a case of a fire spreading from a factory to neighbouring land, the court found D liable. Flammable material was stored near to machinery which got very hot. Storage was therefore *non-natural* and it was *foreseeable* it could catch fire.

Task 36

Look at the cases of **Transco** and **LMS** and answer the following questions

In which 1913 case did the court decide that the water which escaped from the premises was natural use?

LMS was concerned in part with how the materials were stored. In which 1967 case did the court say that circumstances such as this were relevant in deciding on non-natural use?

In relation to whether the thing that escaped was likely to cause mischief, in which 1938 case did the court say the risk of harm was foreseeable (so likely to cause mischief)?

What particular circumstances led to the storage of material in LMS being held to be non-natural?

Examination pointer

If D did not bring on the thing that escaped, or it is found to be natural, there may still be an action in nuisance, so you should be prepared to discuss this as an alternative. Nuisance may be easier to prove because it only requires use to be 'unreasonable' rather than 'unnatural'. Also, if physical damage occurs the locality will not be a relevant factor (**St Helen's**), although the other 'nuisance' factors will be taken into account. Negligence is another alternative but here C will need to prove breach of duty.

Likely to cause mischief – must it be dangerous?

The 'mischief' requirement would indicate that whatever is brought onto the land must be dangerous in some way. However, it need only be dangerous ('likely to cause mischief') *if it escapes*. This means quite ordinary things could be included, such as water, gas, fire, animals, etc. In **Shiffman v Grand Priory of St John 1936**, a flagpole came within the law when it fell over and hit someone.

Example

Mary has a little lamb. She lives in a house next to a garden centre. The lamb is not 'dangerous', but if it gets into the garden centre it could *cause mischief*. Mary could be sued under the rule in **Rylands** if it escapes and causes damage.

If it escapes

The thing that is brought onto the land must escape and cause damage *off* the land. Thus the claim failed in **Read v Lyons**. The explosion which injured C occurred at the factory making the shells, so there was no 'escape'.

Examination pointer

In an examination question involving someone's land look at whether there is an 'escape'. If not consider occupier's liability as an alternative.

In **Crown River Cruises Ltd v Kimbolton Fireworks Ltd 1996**, the court held that it was possible to include 'accumulations' on a boat. Here fireworks from a display on a boat had caused damage to a nearby barge. An action was brought in negligence, nuisance and under the rule in **Rylands**. The decision was based on liability in nuisance, but the point was made that the escape does not need to be from *land*.

Earlier cases had conflicted on whether a person without an interest in land could sue, and whether personal injury could be claimed. In **Crown**, the owners of a barge were able to sue (although possibly on the basis that the boats were permanently moored and so *equated* to land) and a claim for personal injury was allowed in **Hale v Jennings 1938**, where a stallholder at a fair suffered injury when a 'chair-o-plane' *escaped* from D's ride. However, according to the HL in **Transco** the answer is 'no' to both these questions and this was confirmed in the next case.

In **Gore v Stannard 2012**, D was a tyre fitter and had a large accumulation of tyres on his land. A fire started and the tyres ignited. The fire 'escaped' and caused damage to C's land. The trial judge decided that the number of tyres and the way they were stored was 'non-natural' and so the rule in **Rylands** applied. The CA allowed D's appeal against liability since the thing brought on to D's land was the tyres, not the fire. Following **Transco**, the CA said that the thing which was brought onto the land must be the thing that escapes and causes damage, and this was not the case. It was the fire which escaped and caused the damage and D did not bring this onto the land. Therefore, the rule in **Rylands** could not apply.

The CA provided a useful summing up of the rules in **Gore**:

- *D has to be the owner or occupier of land*
- *D must bring or collect a dangerous or mischievous thing on the land*
- *D must realise there was a high risk of danger or mischief if that thing should escape*
- *D's use of land had to be extraordinary and unusual, having regard to all the circumstances*
- *The thing had to escape from D's property to the property of another*
- *The escape had to cause damage to C's land*
- *Damages for death and personal injury were not recoverable*

This case casts doubt on whether situations like that in **Mason** and **LMS**, where what escaped (fire) was not what was brought on to the land (flammable material), will still come within the rule. However, it is possible the rule will still apply where the material accumulated is itself likely to catch fire, as was the case in **Mason** and **LMS** but not **Gore**.

Task 37

Note the appropriate case to the following points raised in court.

- *D was not liable as he did not bring on the thistles, they were naturally there*
- *D was not liable as water is natural in a basin*
- *D was not liable as high-explosive shells were natural in war-time*
- *D was liable because combustible materials were not natural because of the quantity and the way in which they were stored*
- *D was not liable as there was no escape because C was on D's land at the time*

- **D was not liable as the thing that escaped was fire not something that D had brought on to the land**
- **The Wagon Mound test of foreseeability applies so D is not liable if damage could not have been foreseen**

Another case brought in negligence, nuisance and under the rule in **Rylands** is **Cambridge Water Co. v Eastern Counties Leather plc 1994**. It is important in relation to causation so I have repeated it here.

Key case

In **Cambridge,** D used chemicals in the process of manufacturing leather. Some spillages leaked into the soil and eventually found their way into C's waterworks where water was extracted for public consumption. Due to a European Directive, issued after the spillages occurred, the water could not be used for drinking, so the company sued for their loss. Although the chemicals *could* amount to non-natural user D was found not liable. The HL held that **The Wagon Mound** test of foreseeability also applied to both nuisance and **Rylands**. This meant D was not liable if damage could not have been foreseen, as was the case here.

Key principle: **The Wagon Mound** test also applies to both nuisance and **Rylands** so the damage must be foreseeable.

Is liability strict?

Rylands v Fletcher is called a strict liability tort because D will be liable even if not at fault. In the HL, Lord Cranworth said, *"If it does escape, and cause damage, he is responsible, however careful he may have been, and whatever precautions he may have taken"*. This means that C need not prove D was negligent, merely that something has escaped and caused damage.

Example

Mary takes great care of her lamb. She trains it properly and keeps it tied up very firmly when in the garden. She also builds a wall to make sure it can't escape. Despite all these precautions the lamb manages to get out and eats the plants in the garden centre next door. Although Mary was careful she is liable for the *mischief* caused by the *escape*. This is because liability is strict so the garden centre does not have to prove that she is at fault. They can prove all the **Rylands** elements and causation, as it is *foreseeable* that damage to the plants could occur, so it is not too remote.

Task 38

Using the example of Mary and her lamb, go through and apply each of the **Rylands** elements as restated in **Gore v Stannard**.

Although liability is strict in that if damage *is* foreseeable then D is liable regardless of the amount of care taken, **Cambridge Water** limits this by saying if the damage is *not* foreseeable D will avoid liability.

It is also possible for D to avoid liability by using a defence. Let's take a brief look at these. There are several so you don't need a lot of detail.

Defences

Statutory authority: It was confirmed in **Transco** that where something is permitted under an Act of Parliament this may be a defence to an 'escape'.

Act of a stranger: an unforeseeable act by someone else means D may avoid liability because it breaks the chain of causation. In **Rickards v Lothian 1913**, D was not liable not only because water was natural, but also because an unknown person had blocked up the basin and overflow pipe causing the flooding. In **Perry v Kendricks 1956**, two boys had thrown a match into the petrol tank of a coach on D's land. A boy walking on wasteland nearby suffered burns and sued D. The court agreed that the rule in **Rylands v Fletcher** applied. The petrol and vapour in the tank was inflammable so could be classed as a 'dangerous thing', that thing escaped in the form of the fire and it caused damage. However, D was not liable because the fire was caused by a third party. However, in **Hale v Jennings 1938**, the defence failed as it was foreseeable that a passenger might tamper with the chair, so this did not break the chain of causation.

Act of God: this also breaks the chain of causation and is used where D has no control over some force of nature. In **Nichols v Marsland 1876**, C created artificial lakes on her land, but it was an exceptionally heavy rainfall which caused them to flood and damage neighbouring land. She was not liable.

Default of the claimant: Blackburn J continued his comments in **Rylands** with the words *"He can excuse himself by showing that the escape was owing to the plaintiff's default"*. This means that if C has done something, or more accurately *failed to do something*, which has led to the damage, D will not be liable.

Contributory negligence: if C is partly to blame for the damage the amount of compensation may be reduced in relation to C's 'contribution'.

Consent: if C consents to the accumulation by D, then D will not be liable for damage caused by its escape.

Note: Contributory negligence and consent are dealt with in the chapter on defences as they apply to other torts.

Common benefit: if the accumulation benefits C as well as D then there is unlikely to be liability.

Example

Harry and Tom are neighbours. They are worried about a spate of burglaries in the area. They decide to get a guard dog and Harry has the most space. The dog is kept in Harry's garden during the day. Tom has a very old and decrepit fence and the dog gets through and causes a lot of damage to his plants. If Tom sues he will argue that Harry *brought on* the dog and that it *escaped* and did *mischief*. Harry can argue that Tom *consented* to him 'bringing on' the dog. He can also argue *contributory negligence* in that Tom was partly to blame by not mending his fence. Then, even if found liable, Harry would pay less compensation. It may even amount to Tom's *'default'* so Harry avoids liability altogether. Finally, Harry can argue that the dog was of *common benefit* to them both. Harry should be OK.

Summary of the rules

- *D brings onto land*
- *Something non-natural*
- *Which is likely to do mischief*
- *Which escapes onto other land*
- *Which causes foreseeable damage*
- *To property belonging to C*

Task 39

Find a case to illustrate each of the issues in the summary and make a chart for your file.

Links to the non-substantive law

ELS: For links to the English legal system, look back at the diagram and examples in the introduction to Part 1. In particular, where a principle of law has been established the system of appeals is relevant, as these principles are established in the higher appeal courts, i.e., the CA and SC. ADR is always relevant to tort cases too, as is access to justice, because cases can be expensive to take to court so alternatives or help with expenses may be needed. As with nuisance, **Rylands** is particularly relevant to ADR as the dispute is often between neighbours and going to court can make the relationship worse.

The nature of law: The role of law is to mediate between the parties in a case and provide a fair remedy where appropriate. The remedy will be based on the level of fault, or blameworthiness. If someone is found to be at fault then this justifies the court imposing a penalty. In civil law, this is done by way of compensation but more often in a **Rylands** case an injunction.

Fault is particularly relevant here because although **Cambridge Water** confirms that harm must be foreseeable. **Rylands** is still a strict liability tort, i.e., liability does not require proof of fault. As Lord Cranworth said in the case itself, *"he is responsible, however careful he may have been, and whatever precautions he may have taken"*. This can be compared to negligence, which requires proof of breach of duty, and nuisance which has a lower level of fault than negligence but still requires unreasonableness. There are also a great many defences to the tort under **Rylands**, so although D can be liable without fault if the fault is seen as that of a third party, or of nature, D will not be liable for the escape.

Balancing interests applies here in the same way as for nuisance.

Self-test questions

1. *What were the facts in **Rylands**?*
2. *Why, on similar facts, was D not liable in **Transco**?*
3. *Explain 3 of the defences*
4. *What was the importance of **Cambridge Water**?*

Answers to the tasks and self-test questions are on my website at www.drsr.org. Please click on 'Answers to tasks'. For a range of free interactive exercises, click on 'Free Exercises'.

Chapter 12 Vicarious liability

"Vicarious liability is a species of strict liability ... an employer who is not personally at fault is made legally answerable for the fault of his employee" – Lord Millett

By the end of this chapter you should be able to:

- **Explain how far one person can be liable for the actions of another**
- **Show how the law applies to particular situations by reference to cases**
- **Identify problems with the law and/or discuss its development in order to evaluate it**

The nature and purpose of vicarious liability

Vicarious liability essentially means liability for someone else. It applies to all torts. Most commonly, it applies in employment situations, where an employer is liable for the torts of an employee. This means that the employer rather than the employee can be sued. The person committing the tort, e.g., being negligent or causing a nuisance, is called a *tortfeasor*.

The main reason for making an employer liable for the actions of employees is purely a matter of economic reality. An employer is normally in a better position to pay compensation and is usually insured. If it was not for the fact that an employer can be sued, in many cases C may not be compensated at all. Few employees would be able to meet a claim for personal injury from their salary or wages and are much less likely to be insured.

Evaluation pointer

The main argument against vicarious liability is that an employer will be liable even if not at fault. On the other hand, it can be said to be fair because an employer has a certain amount of control over what an employee does.

Task 40 (there is no answer to this, just make some notes)

As you read this chapter make a few notes on the cases, adding a comment of your own as to whether you agree with the decision. When you get to the recent cases, note what has changed over the years and consider how far the law of tort relies on proving fault (or doesn't).

There are two essentials to showing that the employer is liable:

- **that the tortfeasor is an employee (rather than an independent contractor)**
- **that the tortfeasor is acting in the course of employment (rather than on what the courts have referred to as a 'frolic of his own')**

Note the word *tortfeasor*. If the employee has not committed a tort, e.g., has not been negligent, *no one* will be liable.

Examination pointer

It is a common mistake to discuss only vicarious liability and nothing more. However, C will have to prove that the employee has committed a tort. This will require applying the usual rules for that particular tort. Thus, if the case is one of negligence, there will be no liability if the employee has reached the standard expected of the reasonable person. This will involve looking at the usual factors such as degree of risk and cost of precautions.

Example

Julie is stacking shelves in Tesco and drops a bottle of oil. She puts a warning sign in front of it and immediately goes to get a cloth to clear it up. Beth is shopping but doesn't notice it; she slips and injures herself. Tesco is unlikely to be vicariously liable because Julie has not been negligent. However, if Julie had left the spillage and gone for her tea break, Beth is likely to succeed in proving Julie was negligent. There is quite a high likelihood of someone slipping and the cost of putting out a warning or taking other precautions is very low. Beth can sue Tesco on the basis of *vicarious liability* for Julie's *negligence*. If she wins, she is more likely to be able to get the money from the supermarket than a shelf-stacker, who will be on limited wages. Also note that an employer can be both vicariously and primarily liable, e.g., for having poorly trained staff. In both cases, Beth will sue Tesco, but in the first, she must prove Julie was negligent, in the second that Tesco was.

It is important to distinguish between an *employee* and an *independent contractor*, for whom an employer is **not** liable.

Independent contractors

The reason it is important to establish the status of the worker, is that a person is not usually liable for independent contractors. These would include people 'employed' for a particular job, like a plumber or electrician called in make repairs. We saw when looking at occupier's liability that if the occupier did not take care in selection, or did not check on the work, then they may be liable. This type of liability is not *vicarious* (on behalf of another) but *primary* (the employer is personally at fault). This will apply to other people, not just occupiers. Much will depend on whether the contractor is competent, whether the work is supervised and what type of work is involved.

selection and supervision

If the status test for an employee is satisfied then the employer is vicariously liable. If it is not satisfied there is no *vicarious* liability, but there may be *primary* liability due to the choice of the contractor or lack of proper supervision. Primary liability means the employer is sued due to their *own* negligence (in not choosing a competent contractor or not supervising the work properly) rather than sued for the negligence *of the employee*.

In **Haseldine v Daw 1941,** the person hiring the contractor was not liable because:

- **he gave the job to a competent lift engineer**

- he could not be expected to have the expertise to supervise such specialist work

In **Woodward v Mayor of Hastings 1945,** a pupil was injured slipping on an icy step, which a cleaner had left in a dangerous state. Here it was easy to check that the snow had been properly cleared so the 'employer' was liable for the cleaner's negligence.

Another way of looking at this is to say the duty owed by the employer is *'non-delegable'*. It means the employer has a duty, e.g., to ensure people's safety, and cannot escape liability by delegating the work to someone else. This would be particularly true in the case of unusually hazardous activities. There are many Acts imposing a duty in respect of activities involving, e.g., the use of nuclear power, fire and hazardous chemicals. This type of duty would be 'non-delegable'. It is no good arguing that you delegated the storing of dangerous chemicals to an independent contractor but the contractor failed to do as asked, if you used an unqualified person or hadn't bothered to check. However, if you choose a competent person and supervise their work, as far as is possible in the circumstances, you will have fulfilled your duty.

So, a person can be primarily liable for a contractor and vicariously liable for an employee. Now we need to look more carefully at what constitutes an employee.

Test for an employee

Where people are employed on a casual basis, it may not always be clear whether they are employees or contractors. In **Ready Mixed Concrete v Minister of Pensions 1968**, the 'multiple', or 'composite', test was established. This looks at several factors to assess the economic reality of the situation. These include:

- *whether the work is done in return for a wage*
- *who controls the work done*
- *who pays national insurance*
- *who supplies equipment*

However, this is merely a starting point. In **Cable and Wireless v Muscat 2006**, the CA held that all the circumstances should be considered, although control is a key factor. The control test will be particularly appropriate where there is more than one possible employer, so that the employer with most control over the work will be liable. In **Mersey Docks Harbour Board v Coggins and Griffiths (Liverpool) Ltd 1947**, a crane driver and his crane had been lent to the Harbour Board. The HL said that the original employer was liable when the driver ran someone over, because it was this employer who controlled the method of performance (the way he drove the crane). In **Viasystems (Tyneside) Ltd v Thermal Transfer (Northern) Ltd 2005**, the CA held that two employers may share liability for an employee's negligence.

Finally on this point note should be taken of **Cox v Ministry of Justice 2016** where the SC held that vicarious liability was not confined to employment situations but could 'in principle' be imposed outside such relationships. In this case the prison service was found vicariously liable for the acts of a prisoner who dropped some equipment and injured a kitchen worker. However, the prisoner was helping in the kitchen at the time so it was very close to an employment situation.

Examination pointer

There is not usually a problem with showing someone is an employee in examination scenarios. Look for clues, and if there is any doubt refer to the **Ready Mixed Concrete** factors but note that *all* factors affecting the employment will be relevant (**Cable and Wireless**). Control is an important factor, especially if there are two employers, and liability can now be shared – **Viasystems**. If the question explicitly refers to an employee you do not need to apply the tests and can move straight to the second part, discussed next. In any case you could now cite **Cox** to suggest that the principle can be extended to non-employment cases.

In the course of employment

Traditionally, acting 'in the course of employment' would include not only acts expressly authorised by an employer, but also authorised acts done in a wrongful way, even if specifically prohibited. A comparison of the following two cases illustrates this.

Limpus v London General Omnibus Company 1862	a bus driver was forbidden to race other buses but he did so and his employer was found liable for the resulting damage. This is a *wrongful* way (racing) of doing something *authorised* (driving)
Beard v LGOC 1900	a conductor drove a bus and injured someone. Here the employer was not liable because driving was not within the scope of his job as a conductor, it was not *authorised*

An employer will not usually be liable where the employee is on the way to or from work. However, if that time is paid for then it could come within the scope of employment, as stated in **Smith v Stages 1989**.

An employer may avoid liability if the employee is on 'a frolic of his own'. Again, a comparison will illustrate this.

Twine v Bean's Express 1946	the driver had been told not to give lifts and had done so. The employer was not liable to a hitchhiker for the driver's negligent driving as it was outside the scope of employment and a 'frolic of his own'
Rose v Plenty 1976	despite there being a strict order not to carry children, the employer was liable for a boy's injuries incurred whilst on a milk float. Here the boy was actually assisting in the deliveries and this brought it within the scope of employment

The main difference here (and what to look for in a scenario) is whether the activity is in the employer's interests. In **Twine v Bean's Express 1946** it wasn't, but in **Rose v Plenty 1976** the boy was helping so the activity was in the employer's interests.

Evaluation pointer

These cases are hard to reconcile and make it hard for an employer to know where liability will start and stop. It is also difficult for employers to explain the rules to employees if they don't understand which acts will come within the course of employment.

In **Century Insurance Co v NIRTB 1942**, it was held that an employer could be liable for a careless act of an employee. A tanker driver had lit a match to light a cigarette and thrown it on the floor while transferring petrol to a tank at a petrol station. This was held to be in the scope of his employment. It was not authorised but he was doing what he was employed to do at the time, deliver petrol. A slightly different approach to what comes within the scope of employment was established by the HL in **Lister v Helsey Hall 2001**.

Key case

In **Lister**, unknown to the employer, a warden sexually abused boarders at a school for children with behavioural difficulties. The children sued, alleging the school was vicariously liable. The CA held that the assaults could not be seen as 'authorised acts' so the school was not liable. In allowing the appeal the HL used a different approach. Rather than asking whether the act was *authorised* it was better to concentrate on the *closeness of the connection* between the nature of the employment and the tort. Sexual abuse against pupils, committed by a warden of a boarding school, was sufficiently connected with the work he was employed to do to be within the course of his employment. The HL overruled **Trotman v North Yorkshire CC 1999**, where the employers had been found not to be vicariously liable for a sexual assault by a teacher during a residential school trip.

Key principle: an employer is vicariously liable for the tort of an employee if it had a close connection to the employment.

The principle that comes from **Lister** is that the test is now based on whether the tort has a *'close connection with the employment'*. Lord Millet said it would be "stretching language to breaking point" to describe the warden's actions as "merely a wrongful and unauthorised" method of performance. He also made the defining comments in this Chapter's opening quotation. Many of the older cases would be included in this new definition, but the decision itself is not without its critics.

In **Graham v Commercial Bodyworks Ltd 2015**, an employer was found not to be vicariously liable when a worker lit a cigarette which ignited some flammable liquid and injured another worker. This time the court held that the use of a lighter near the liquid was a reckless act and not within the scope of his employment. The CA combined the old and new tests somewhat. The employer had strict rules in place about working with inflammable material and the worker who lit the cigarette had previously spayed the liquid around as a prank. The CA said the employer could be liable for authorised acts done in a wrongful way or for unauthorised acts which were 'so connected with' acts the employee was authorised to do that they could be deemed to be methods of doing those acts, even though in an improper way. However, on the facts the employee had acted recklessly and in a way that was not connected to his employment.

Task 41

Compare **Century Insurance** with **Graham**. Briefly explain why there was liability in the first case but not the 2015 one.

Evaluation pointer

There are strong and conflicting arguments as to whether **Trotman** or **Lister** is to be preferred. Bill Thomas, in The Legal Executive, (July 2001), argues that the **Lister** case is "illogical" and refers to **Trotman** (which it overruled) as a "bastion of old-fashioned common sense". Terry Kynaston, a practitioner dealing with child abuse cases, replies in October in the same journal. He argues that the House is to be congratulated on its "fair and open-minded approach to a complex issue whilst also adhering to legal principle". Both have valid points. You should make up your own mind as to whether an employer should be liable for assaults by employees whose duties include protecting those in their care

Other types of assault are treated in a similar way. In **Mattis v Pollock 2003**, a club doorman stabbed and seriously injured a man outside the club. The evidence was that he had gone home to get the knife. The injured man claimed that the club owner was vicariously liable. The trial judge referred to **Lister**, but felt that there was not a sufficiently close connection between the employment (as a doorman), and the attack. The CA disagreed and said that as a doorman he was expected to use physical force in his work, and that the stabbing was connected to an earlier argument in the club. The club was vicariously liable.

In **Gravil v Carroll & another 2008**, a rugby player had punched another player following a scrum and fractured his jaw. The victim brought a claim not only against the player, but also against the club which employed that player on a part-time basis. The court decided that the club was not vicariously liable and C appealed. The CA held that the player was an employee even though he only played on a part-time basis, because he had obligations under his contract with the club and he played in a semi-professional capacity. The club had argued that the punch was outside the scope of his employment. The CA approved the case of **Lister** and also referred to **Mattis v Pollock.** The critical factor was again held to be the closeness of the connection between the nature of the employment and the tort. In this case the CA held there was a close connection between the punch and the type of scuffle that often occurs in a game of rugby. He was employed to play rugby and was doing so at the time. There was a scuffle going on of a kind which frequently occurred during rugby matches and it was not unforeseeable that punches would be throw in such a situation; it was quite common in rugby. The punch was therefore sufficiently closely connected to the playing of the game and it was fair to hold the club liable. The appeal was allowed.

In **Mohamud v WM Morrison Supermarkets plc 2016**, the SC considered **Lister** and applied the close connection test. C had been assaulted by a petrol attendant following some verbal abuse and the CA had rejected the claim on the basis that his work was to serve and help customers so the assault was outside the scope of his employment. The SC reversed the decision and held that although D may have abused his position his actions still came within the scope of his employment. The SC made clear there were two questions. The first was what the nature of the job was, and this should be addressed broadly. The second involved whether there was sufficient connection between that job and the wrongful conduct to make it right for the employer to be held liable under the principle of social justice. This shows that policy reasons and moral principles are factors in establishing whether a person is vicariously liable.

In **Armes v Nottinghamshire CC 2017**, the SC reversed a decision by the CA. The CA had held that a council was not vicariously liable in respect of the abuse of a child by foster parents with whom the council had placed the child but made clear that there was a difference between a child in a residential care home and a child with foster parents. In the first case there could be liability in the same way as in **Lister**, in the latter the council has passed over any duty to the foster parents. The SC preferred the decision in **Mohamud** and decided to impose liability.

This case is an example of the way D may be liable in two different ways. *Vicarious* liability is where D is liable for another's wrongdoing. The case was brought on the basis that the council were vicariously liable for the wrongdoing of the foster parents. However, the council could have *primary* liability (i.e., liability in negligence) if the selection process for the foster parents was flawed in some way.

Task 42

Jack is a bouncer in a club. One night he sees Frank, against whom he has an old grudge for stealing his girlfriend. When Frank leaves, Jack follows him up the road and attacks him. Do you think the club owner will be liable? Will **Mattis** be followed or distinguished?

Another case involving a nightclub illustrates both parts of the test for vicarious liability.

In **Hawley v Luminar Leisure Ltd 2006**, a doorman punched a customer and caused serious injury. The CA held that a nightclub was vicariously liable for a doorman even though in this case the doorman was actually employed by a security company, because the club had greater control over the work done. The doorman had worked at the club for years, wore the club's uniform and was told what to do, and how to do it, by the club. The club was therefore vicariously liable for the assault by the doorman outside the club. The CA considered, but distinguished, **Viasystems**. In this case the security firm had no control at all over what the doorman did or how he did it so there was no reason to impose dual liability.

Finally, the two parts to the test were restated in **JGE v English Province of Our Lady of Charity and another 2011**. This was a case of child abuse by a priest. The court confirmed that when deciding if a person was vicariously responsible for the acts of another there was a two-stage test. Firstly, to consider what the relationship between the two parties was and secondly, to consider whether the tortious act in question was within the scope of employment (or other relationship). For the first part of the test whether tools, equipment, uniform or premises were provided were particularly relevant, but were not exhaustive and other factors may be relevant in particular cases. Control was also relevant but was just one of the many factors to be considered. The second part involved consideration of whether there was a sufficiently close connection between the act and the purpose of the relationship, or employment.

This case confirms that the first part of the test requires all the circumstances to be considered and the second requires a close connection between the act and the employment.

Summary of vicarious liability

Is D an employee?	No single test – **Ready Mixed Concrete**
dual vicarious liability possible	**Viasystems**
Is D in the course of employment?	Is there a connection? - **Lister**
or on a 'frolic'	**Twine's**
If D is an independent contractor consider *Occupier's Liability Act 1957*	Occupier may be liable if work not checked s2 (4) (b) – **Woodward**

Links to the non-substantive law

ELS: For links to the English legal system, look back at the diagram and examples in the introduction to Part 1. In particular, where a principle of law has been established the system of appeals is relevant, as these principles are established in the higher appeal courts, i.e., the CA and SC. ADR is always relevant to tort cases too, as is access to justice, because cases can be expensive to take to court so alternatives or help with expenses may be needed.

The nature of law: The role of law is to mediate between the parties in a case and provide a fair remedy where appropriate. The remedy will be based on the level of fault, or blameworthiness. If someone is found to be at fault then this justifies the court imposing a penalty. In civil law, this is done by way of compensation (or sometimes an injunction as you will see with remedies). Fault can be discussed with any vicarious liability cases because they all allow someone to be liable for the wrongdoing of another. This is a particular problem where the wrongdoing is an assault. It is questionable whether an employer should be liable for assaults by employees, especially in cases such as **Lister** where it was sexual abuse which is arguably not very closely connected to the employment. However, the law must provide justice for those harmed. In **Mohamud v WM Morrison Supermarkets plc 2016**, the SC noted that there had to be sufficient connection between the job and D's wrongful conduct to make it right for the employer to be held liable under the principle of social justice. This shows that policy reasons and moral principles are both taken into account when establishing whether a person is vicariously liable. Another example is **Armes v Nottinghamshire CC 2017** where the SC imposed liability on the council for abuse by foster parents. This is perhaps less justifiable but does ensure the victim is not left without compensation.

There is also a matter of policy and public interest in making an employer liable in that employees should be properly selected and trained. Making employers liable may make them take greater care in the future.

Self-test questions

1. Why was the employer liable in one case against the London bus company but not the other?
2. What are the names of these two cases, and which is which?
3. Which case was overruled by the HL in **Lister** and what is the new test for establishing whether an employee is within the scope of employment?

Answers to the tasks and self-test questions are on my website at www.drsr.org. Please click on 'Answers to tasks'. For a range of free interactive exercises, click on 'Free Exercises'.

Chapter 13 Contributory negligence and consent

"The accident is caused by bad driving. The damage is caused in part by the bad driving of the defendant and in part by the failure of C to wear a seat belt" – Lord Denning

By the end of this chapter you should be able to:

- ***Explain how to prove contributory negligence***
- ***Explain how to prove consent, both express and implied***
- ***Show how the defences apply in particular situations by reference to cases and Acts of Parliament***
- ***Identify problems with the law in order to evaluate it***

We will look at the two defences which apply to all the torts discussed in this book in this chapter. They are dealt with together here as they often overlap. If C's own negligence *contributes* to the injury sufficiently it may be said that C *consents* to the injury. The effect of the defences is different however, and it is important to bear this in mind when considering them.

Example

I accept an offer to go water-skiing with a powerboat driver who I know is drunk. He loses control and I am injured. I can claim compensation. He owes *a duty* to passengers in his boat, has **breached** it by driving while drunk and this **caused** my injury. He can argue as a defence that I **contributed** to my injury by getting in the boat knowing he was drunk. He can also argue that I **consented** to the risk of harm by doing so. If the first defence succeeds I may get compensation but it will be reduced to reflect my own negligence. If the second defence succeeds I won't get compensation at all.

Contributory negligence

The main defence used in tort claims is *contributory negligence*. It is not a full defence but can reduce the amount D has to pay to C in compensation. It is called *contributory* negligence because it is based on C being partly to blame by 'contributing' to the harm caused. In **Jones v Livox Quarries 1952**, C was riding on the tow bar of a vehicle when he was injured. He had exposed himself to the risk of harm and so was partly responsible for his own injuries. I have not made any cases key as they all involved successful claims and differ only in the amount by which the compensation was reduced – and why.

The effect of successfully using this defence is that if C is shown to have contributed to the harm, then the amount of compensation (damages) will be apportioned by the court. This is governed by the **Law Reform (Contributory Negligence) Act 1945**.

S 1(1) of the Act allows the court to use its discretion to reduce the damages awarded, *"to such extent as the court thinks just and equitable having regard to the claimant's share in the responsibility for the damage"*

There are two ways C can contribute:

- **by contributing to the amount of damage or loss suffered**
- **by contributing to the accident itself**

Contributing to the damage or loss

In **Froom v Butcher 1976**, a passenger had contributed to his injury by not wearing a seat belt. The court held that damages should be reduced as he had been partly to blame for the amount of harm that occurred. Lord Denning made the comment opening this Chapter in this case.

In **Finch v Smith 2009,** a cyclist had been hit by a motorbike and suffered serious brain injuries. He was not wearing a helmet and D argued he had been contributorily negligent. The judge cited **Froom v Butcher** and said that the same principle could apply. However, it would have to be shown that wearing a helmet would have made a difference. On the facts, given the force of the impact, this was not the case so no reduction in damages should be made. In **Phethean-Hubble v Coles 2012**, on similar facts but where the motorist was driving at 35 mph, the CA ruled a cyclist to be contributorily negligent by not wearing a helmet (and by turning off the pavement onto the road in front of the motorist) and reduced the damages by 50%. These cases indicate that much will depend on the type of accident and that if wearing a helmet would not have made a difference to the harm suffered the defence will fail.

A slightly different example is **Badger v Ministry of Defence 2005**. A man had worked in a dockyard and been exposed to asbestos dust and fibres. He later died from cancer and his widow claimed on his behalf that his death was caused by this exposure. The MOD admitted liability but argued that he was also at fault because his smoking was partly the cause of the cancer. The court agreed that smoking had been a substantial cause of the cancer and that the man had been contributorily negligence in not giving up smoking after being advised to do so. Damages were reduced by 20%.

Contributing to the accident itself

In **Sayers v Harlow 1958**, C got stuck in a public lavatory, she didn't want to wait to be rescued so tried to climb out. She was held to be 25% contributorily negligent in putting her weight on the toilet-roll holder when attempting to climb out of the cubicle. If she had not done so she would not have been harmed. Note that defences don't come into play until C has proved that D's breach has caused harm so here are a few case examples from earlier where there was liability but compensation was reduced due to C being contributorily negligent.

In **Dalling v RJ Heale & Co 2011** (see causation Chapter 4), damages were reduced by a third because C contributed to the accident (falling over) by getting drunk.

In **Ahmed v MacLean 2016**, (see breach of duty Chapter 5) the court found that C had known he lacked the ability to ride the particular slope safely as he done it before and had difficulty. He therefore bore some responsibility for his own safety. There had been 20% contributory negligence on his part and his damages were reduced accordingly.

In **Taylor v English Heritage 2016** (see occupier's liability Chapter 5), C's damages were reduced by 50% for contributory negligence because he did not take any precautions himself (like sliding down on his bottom).

Whichever way C contributes, the court will consider all the circumstances of the situation. The question will be whether C's action is reasonable *in the circumstances*. This includes factors such as C's age, whether it was an emergency or rescue situation etc. The less reasonable C's act then the more likely damages will be reduced by a larger amount. Children are less likely to be found to be contributorily negligent because they are not expected to recognise the risk of harm in their actions. In **Yachuk v Oliver Blais Ltd 1949**, a 9-year-old boy was found not to be contributorily negligent after he bought petrol at a garage and burnt himself. The court held that the child was not expected to see the danger involved in asking for petrol, so the garage which sold it to him was fully liable for the injuries caused by the burns. He should be judged by the standard expected of a 9-year-old child not an adult. This can be compared to **Gannon v Rotherham MBC 1991**, where the court held that a 14-year-old ought to recognise the danger of diving into the shallow end of pool so he was found to have contributed to his injuries when he did so.

In **Jackson v Murray 2015**, a child stepped out from behind a minibus into the path of an oncoming car. The driver hit the child, causing severe injuries. If he had not been driving too fast he would not have hit her and he was found liable. The trial judge assessed her contributory negligence at 90% which was reduced on appeal to 70%. C appealed again to the SC, which refused the appeal despite agreeing that a fairer apportionment would be one-third and two-thirds. The SC made clear that the role of an appellate court was not to substitute its judgment for that of a court below unless that court was plainly wrong.

Evaluation pointer

Consider how fair the defence is. Until the **Act** a claim would fail altogether if C was shown to be partly to blame. This is one area where it can be argued that the law has improved. If C is partly at fault, there is a good argument that the compensation should be reduced accordingly. The **Act** allows the judge to have *"regard to the claimant's share in the responsibility for the damage"*. This means that the circumstances can be taken into account and allowance made for factors such as C's age. On the other hand, it means that D may pay more or less depending on unknown factors like this.

Examination pointer

Look out for clues such as C's age. A young child is less likely to be found to have contributed, as in **Yachuk**. The older the child, the more likely the court will apportion the amount of compensation, as in **Gannon**.

Sometimes C may be contributorily negligent in both ways, to the accident and to the harm caused.

In **Eyres v Atkinson's Kitchens and Bedrooms Ltd 2007**, a driver who had been working long hours lost control of the van he was driving. He was not wearing a seat belt and was seriously injured when he was flung out of the van. The long hours had contributed to the accident happening, and not wearing a seatbelt had contributed to the amount of harm suffered. The CA held that the employer was liable in negligence for allowing him to work long hours and then drive the van back to base. The employer was actually asleep in the back of the van when the incident occurred. However, the driver was partly to blame for continuing to drive knowing that he was tired and also for not wearing a seat belt. His damages were reduced by 33%.

How much the reduction is will depend on C's blameworthiness. The Act gives the judge discretion to apportion damages *"having regard to the claimant's share in the responsibility for the damage"*. The 50% in **Phethean** was quite high but C had ridden in front of the motorist as well as not wearing a helmet. In the next case the court indicated that it would normally be the negligent driver who was seen as most blameworthy.

In **Best v Smyth 2010**, C was a passenger in a van driven by D. They had met earlier in the day and had been drinking together. C was injured due to D's negligent driving, and D argued the defence of contributory negligence on two grounds. C had not been wearing a seat belt, and he had got into the van when he must have known that D had had too much to drink. D proposed a 50% reduction of damages due to contributory negligence. The court commented that a passenger in such a case should not be considered equally to blame with the negligent driver and reduced damages by 30%.

However, in **Belka v Prosperini 2011**, C had crossed a dual carriageway near a roundabout having drunk about four pints of beer. He was hit by a taxi and claimed in negligence for his injuries. The judge found that he was two-thirds to blame and reduced his damages accordingly. He appealed, arguing that even if blame was to be shared he was not more blameworthy than D. The CA held that C was more to blame because, although D had been negligent in not anticipating the risk of hitting someone, C had taken a deliberate risk by running across the road in front of the vehicle. Similarly, in **Jackson v Murray 2015** damages were reduced by an unusually high amount, especially since the case involved a child who is not seen as understanding the risk, so is less blameworthy. Even on appeal it was only changed to a 70% reduction, and the SC refused to alter that decision.

Examination pointer

You can see from the cases that the amount by which damages are reduced will depend on C's blameworthiness, but that the courts are not always consistent. In **Best**, the court commented that a passenger should not be considered equally to blame with the negligent driver and reduced damages by 30%. However, in **Belka**, damages were reduced by 66% and in **Jackson** by 70%. This means you will not be expected to come up with a figure, so apply the rules and decide if contributory negligence is likely to succeed as a defence. Then say the court will apportion damages under the **Law Reform (Contributory Negligence) Act 1945** according to C's blameworthiness.

Breaking the chain of causation

If C's action is extremely unreasonable it may break the *chain of causation*. The effect of this is that it removes D's liability altogether so it is not strictly a defence. However, it overlaps with contributory negligence because a 'contribution' by C which is unreasonable is quite likely to be unforeseeable. If something unforeseeable happens it can break the chain of causation because the harm will be seen as too remote from the breach. This is called *novus actus interveniens*, or 'new act intervening' (see causation Chapter 4). If the act is not sufficient to break the chain it may still amount to contributory negligence, hence the overlap. In **Reeves v MPC 1999,** the police argued that the prisoner's suicide was an intervening act which broke the chain of causation. The HL did not accept this, but they reduced damages by 50% for contributory negligence. Thus, although not strictly a 'defence', *novus actus interveniens* can be discussed either when looking at causation or when looking at the defences.

Consent

The Latin expression for the defence of consent is *volenti non fit injuria*. It means that if C voluntarily accepts a risk of harm any claim for injury will fail. Both terms are still used by the courts but consent is more common these days. For the defence to succeed there must be 'true' consent and this involves two things:

- ***knowledge of a risk of harm***
- ***real consent to that risk***

This means just *knowing* of a risk is not enough in itself; C must also have voluntarily accepted the risk *of harm*. Much will again depend on the particular circumstances. The courts are reluctant to find consent in cases involving employees and rescuers because there is no *real* consent. An employee may consent to a risk of harm only in order to keep a job, and a rescuer may be acting under a moral obligation to take a risk to save another.

An example of an employment situation can be seen in **Smith v Baker 1891**. Here an employee was told by his employer to work under a crane which was moving large stones. He was injured when a stone fell on him. The court held that there was no true consent; he consented only in order to keep his job. The employer's defence failed and he had to pay compensation. However, if C need not have been exposed to danger at all the defence may succeed. In **ICI v Shatwell 1965**, C ignored his employer's instructions and instead did what his brother suggested as regards the handling of explosives. This was an unsafe method and when he was injured the employer successfully argued that he had consented to the risk of harm. The difference here is that far from following his employer's orders he specifically chose to ignore them.

The following cases illustrate the courts' approach to rescuers.

In **Haynes v Harwood 1935**, a policeman was injured when he attempted to stop some horses which had bolted and which were putting others in danger. He was not found to have truly consented because he was under a moral obligation to act. This can be compared to **Cutler v**

United Dairies 1933 where, in similar circumstances, a horse had bolted but was posing no danger to others, having ended up in a field. In this case the 'rescuer' was held to have consented to the risk of harm and so failed in his claim for compensation when he was injured. So if there is a genuine rescue attempt and the rescuer is injured a claim is likely to succeed.

Key case

In **Chadwick v BTC 1967**, a rescuer at a train crash was found not to have consented to the risk of harm. The essence of this is that if the rescuer is under a moral obligation to help then consent is not real consent.

Key principle: consent must be real and if there is a moral obligation for C to act this is not the case and the defence will fail.

Other relevant factors would include the type of risk and how obvious it is. In **Morris v Murray 1990**, C consented to going in a plane with a very drunk pilot. This was a defence to his claim for damages because the risk of harm was obvious. Compare this to **Dann v Hamilton 1939**, where a passenger was not found to have consented to the risk of harm in getting in a car with a driver who had been drinking because he was not obviously drunk.

Road Traffic Act 1988

Note that **Dann v Hamilton** would be decided differently today because it is now impossible for a driver to use consent as a defence in relation to harm to a passenger. This is stated in **s 149** of the **Road Traffic Act 1988**. However contributory negligence is still a possible defence in these circumstances.

Examination pointer

Watch for cases where the **Road Traffic Act 1988** applies. Mention that the defence of consent will fail due to this but then go on to discuss contributory negligence as an alternative. Also note that the **Act** only applies to road transport, in cases like **Morris** the consent defence can still be argued.

Those cases involved situations where D was drunk but the question was whether C knew that. Where it is C who is drunk there may be a successful plea of consent to a claim against D, or, if consent fails there may be a possibility of using contributory negligence. In **Ratcliff v McConnell 1999** (see occupier's liability Chapter 5), a 19-year-old student was seriously injured diving into a swimming pool at his college. He had been drinking but the evidence was that he knew what he was doing. The court found that the risk of hitting his head on the bottom was obvious so the defence of consent succeeded. In **Barrett v MOD 1995**, the defence of contributory negligence succeeded. C's employer had been negligent in not looking after him when he passed out through drink. However, damages were reduced by two thirds because C had been drinking heavily so was partly to blame for his own death.

Implied consent

There is *implied consent* in certain situations. This is commonly seen in sports, where participants are deemed to have consented to the risk of some harm, especially in contact sports like boxing and rugby. It will generally only apply where the harm occurs within the rules of a game. Thus in **Condon v Basi 1985**, the defence failed. A rough tackle broke a footballer's leg and he sued the other player. As the tackle was found by the referee to be foul play, the injured player had not consented to it. The CA said the test was whether a player had taken reasonable care in the circumstances. In **Woolridge v Sumner 1963**, a photographer at a race who was injured by a horse failed in his claim against the organisers of the event. Diplock LJ said, *"a person attending a game or competition takes the risk of any damage caused to him by any act of a participant done in the course of and for the purposes of the game or competition"*.

Evaluation pointer

How far spectators at sporting events may be shown to have consented is somewhat unclear. There is an overlap here between consent and breach of duty. In **Woolridge**, the court was of the opinion that the organisers had not been negligent and Diplock LJ continued what he said above by saying *"unless the participant's conduct is such as to evince a reckless disregard of the spectator's safety"*. This indicates that there was no breach of duty; rather than that the spectator had consented to harm.

Examination pointer

Note that if D can show C consented to a risk of harm, the effect is that D does not have to pay any compensation even though duty, breach and causation have been proved. This is also the case if the chain of causation is broken. However, contributory negligence merely leads to a reduction in the amount D has to pay. Show that you understand the effect of using these defences by pointing this out in your answer, especially if asked to advise D. Any advice should include what is best so if appropriate explain both defences but add that consent would be a better choice for D. Alternatively, if there is a possibility the chain of causation has been broken this will have the same effect.

Example

Both the defences, and the chain of causation argument, were seen in **Reeves v MPC 1999**. D's argument that C *consented* to his own suicide failed, as did the argument that C's actions broke the *chain of causation* between the breach of duty and the suicide. However, *contributory negligence* was accepted and damages apportioned fifty-fifty between his estate and the police.

Task 43

Explain whether contributory negligence or consent, or both, was used in the following cases and what the effect was (reduction in damages, no liability or full liability).

Jones v Livox Quarries 1952

Sayers v Harlow 1958

Barrett v MOD 1995

Yachuk v Oliver Blais Ltd 1949

Smith v Baker 1891

Gannon v Rotherham MBC 1991

Morris v Murray 1990

Condon v Basi 1985

Froom v Butcher 1976

Other than consent and contributory negligence, there are special defences available with particular torts, such as nuisance and **Rylands v Fletcher**. These are discussed along with those torts.

Summary

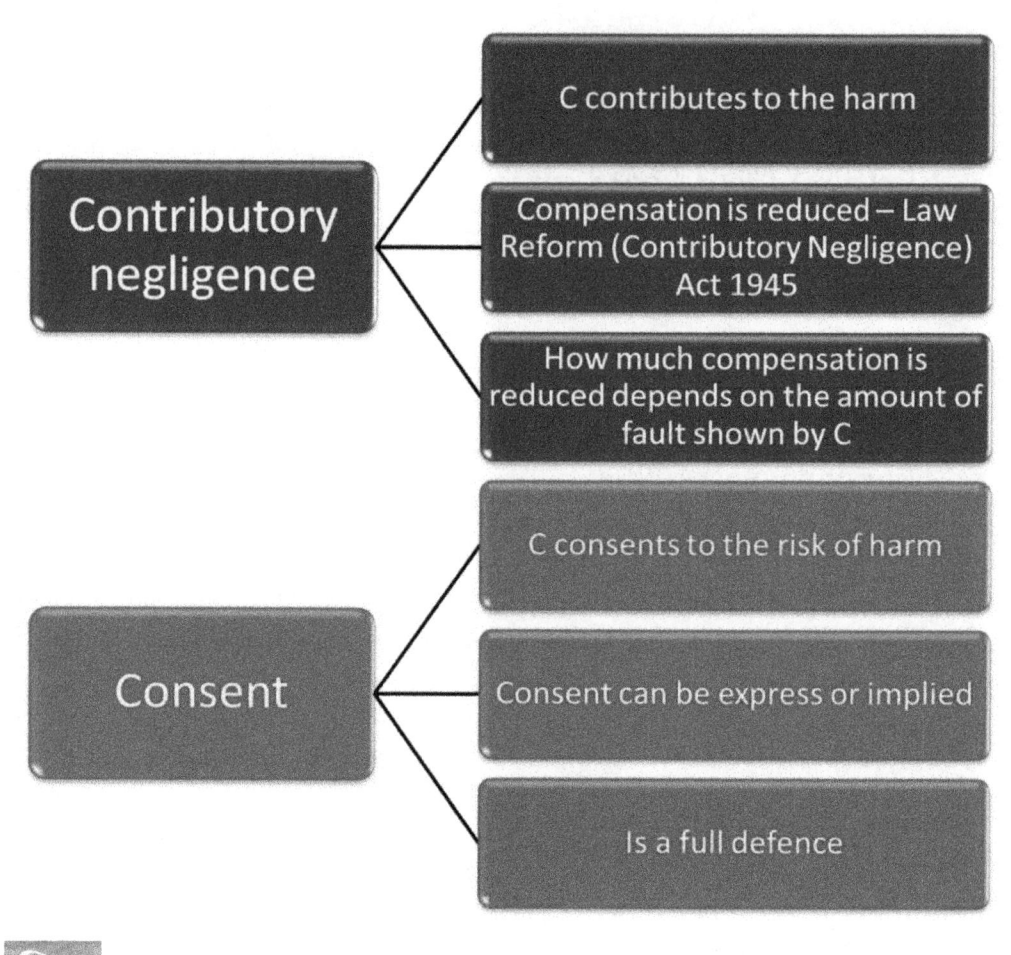

```
                              ┌─────────────────────────────────┐
                              │   C contributes to the harm     │
                              └─────────────────────────────────┘
┌──────────────────┐          ┌─────────────────────────────────┐
│   Contributory   │──────────│  Compensation is reduced – Law  │
│    negligence    │          │ Reform (Contributory Negligence)│
└──────────────────┘          │            Act 1945             │
                              └─────────────────────────────────┘
                              ┌─────────────────────────────────┐
                              │   How much compensation is      │
                              │ reduced depends on the amount of│
                              │       fault shown by C          │
                              └─────────────────────────────────┘

                              ┌─────────────────────────────────┐
                              │   C consents to the risk of harm│
                              └─────────────────────────────────┘
┌──────────────────┐          ┌─────────────────────────────────┐
│     Consent      │──────────│ Consent can be express or implied│
└──────────────────┘          └─────────────────────────────────┘
                              ┌─────────────────────────────────┐
                              │        Is a full defence        │
                              └─────────────────────────────────┘
```

Links to the non-substantive law

ELS: For links to the English legal system, look back at the diagram and examples in the introduction to Part 1. In particular, where a principle of law has been established the system of appeals is relevant, as these principles are established in the higher appeal courts, i.e., the CA and SC. ADR is always relevant to tort cases too, as is access to justice, because cases can be expensive to take to court so alternatives or help with expenses may be needed.

The nature of law: The role of law is to mediate between the parties in a case and provide a fair remedy where appropriate. The remedy will be based on the level of fault, or blameworthiness. If someone is found to be at fault then this justifies the court imposing a penalty. In civil law, this is done by way of compensation (or sometimes an injunction as you will see with remedies).

All cases on contributory negligence can illustrate a discussion of fault. The principle is that if C is partly to blame D should not pay full compensation. A useful case is **Jackson v Murray 2015** because although the SC felt that a fairer apportionment would be one-third and two-thirds the appeal was refused. The principle that the role of an appellate court was not to substitute its judgment for that of a court below unless it was plainly wrong provides certainty in the law, but it lacks morality. Also damages were reduced by a much larger amount than normal even though the case involved a child. Any reduction usually relates to blameworthiness, and a child is less likely to see the risk of harm so is usually less likely to be found contributorily negligent (as in **Yachuk**), let alone 70% to blame. However, the benefit of this defence is that damages can be apportioned and the court can make any award after taking into account the blameworthiness of both parties. This provides a fairer result than the all-or-nothing nature of the defence of consent.

Morality can be connected to consent cases involving rescue situations. The courts have made it clear that where there is a moral duty to act the defence of consent will not succeed because there is no real consent, as in **Chadwick**.

Self-test questions

1. What does s 1(1) of the **Law Reform (Contributory Negligence) Act 1945** provide?
2. What were the facts of **Sayers v Harlow 1958**?
3. Compare **Yachuk v Oliver Blais Ltd 1949** to **Gannon v Rotherham MBC 1991**. In which did the defence of contributory negligence succeed and why?
4. Why is the defence of consent likely to fail in rescue cases? Give an example.
5. In what other cases is it likely to fail, and why?

Answers to the tasks and self-test questions are on my website at www.drsr.org. Please click on 'Answers to tasks'. For a range of free interactive exercises, click on 'Free Exercises'.

Chapter 14 Remedies

"I just want to be allowed to live in peace. Have we got to wait until someone is killed before anything is done?" – **Miller v Jackson 1977**

By the end of this chapter you should be able to:

- **Explain the monetary remedy of damages**
- **Explain how the courts decide on this remedy with reference to cases**
- **Explain the alternative remedy of injunction**

The most usual remedy in tort is an award of money, called damages. This is intended to compensate the claimant for any injury or damage to property, rather than to punish the defendant. The aim is to return the claimant, as far as possible, to the position he or she would have been in if the tort had not occurred.

Damages: Compensation for the harm caused

Damages are only claimable in respect of foreseeable loss; this is as for causation and based on **The Wagon Mound 1966** test for remoteness of damage.

Examination pointer

Be careful not to confuse 'damage' with 'damages'. Although both relate to foreseeability of harm the term 'damage' relates to the actual loss, the harm or damage to property caused by D. The expression 'damages' is a legal term used for the monetary award, the compensation to C. Read the question carefully to make sure you are answering it correctly.

The amount awarded by the court may be a once-and-for-all payment, i.e., the full amount is paid as a lump sum, or by way of a structured settlement, where an annuity is taken out and the compensation paid as regular instalments. These are most commonly used for the larger awards and/or long-term loss, e.g., where C is unable to work again.

There are two types of damages, called special and general damages. Apart from loss of future earnings the first is quantifiable and is included in the claim. The second, plus any loss of future earnings, is assessed by the court.

Special damages

Special damages include loss of earnings and expenses paid out because of the harm or damage caused. They cover all losses from the time of the breach of duty to the date of the trial. These are reasonably straightforward and can usually be agreed between the parties.

They are easy to quantify as pay slips and receipts can be produced to cover loss of earnings and things like repairs to a car or other belongings, transport costs, medical expenses etc.

Loss of future earnings is assessed by the court. It is calculated by taking the current earnings and multiplying it by a figure (called the multiplier) representing the number of likely working years but reduced to account for investment income and the possibility of reduced employment for other reasons. No allowance is made for inflation or tax. The multiplier is usually a maximum of 18 years but in certain employment situations may be less, as in **Collett v Smith 2008**. In this case a footballer injured his leg while playing for Manchester United reserve team at age 18. He retired a few years later because of the injury. The court had to decide whether he would have succeeded in making a career in professional football and, if so, at what level and for how long. There was evidence that he would have gone on to play at Championship and Premiership level. He was awarded nearly four million pounds based on the lost chance of a successful career, with the multiplier set at 11 years. This would have taken him to the normal age for a footballer retiring of 35 years.

Loss of earnings capacity may be awarded if the harm caused has meant C has less chance of getting a job. In **Smith v Manchester Corporation 1974**, C was injured and, because she then had a reduced chance of getting further employment, an award was made in respect of this.

Damages are further classified as *pecuniary* or *non-pecuniary*. Pecuniary loss means financial loss so pecuniary damages are things like expenses and loss of earnings as discussed above. Thus, pecuniary loss comes within special damages. Non-pecuniary loss is any loss which does not have a quantifiable monetary value. It therefore has to be assessed by the court. It includes compensation for the injury itself, distress, pain and suffering and loss of amenity. These all come within general damages discussed below.

General damages

General damages cover pain and suffering, loss of amenity and the injury itself. The court will assess this by reference to other recent cases and information supplied by the Judicial Studies Board. No award for pain is awarded if the claimant is unconscious or cannot feel pain. Distress at disfigurement, reduced life expectancy etc. may be included in suffering. Loss of amenity relates to quality of life. This is also based on conventional sums, provided by the Judicial Studies Board, but may be increased if the injury affected a special interest or hobby.

Example

My hobby is cycling and due to someone's negligence I am badly injured. I have to have a leg amputated. In addition to any claim for compensation for loss of earnings and expenses, I can claim for the *pain and suffering* caused by the injury and a set amount for the *injury itself*, the loss of a leg. I can claim a further amount to compensate me for not being able to carry on with my hobby – this would come under *loss of amenity*.

Examination pointer

If you are asked to discuss damages in relation to a particular scenario you should look carefully for clues to see whether loss of amenity may be applicable. Reference to, e.g., C being a keen cyclist would indicate that if the injury prevented cycling then an extra amount would be awarded for loss of amenity to compensate for this, as in my example.

Most social security benefits are deductible from the award. Private insurance, charity, gifts etc. are not deductible.

Mitigation of loss

The final point on damages is that C is expected to take reasonable steps to minimise or 'mitigate' any loss. D is not expected to pay compensation for any harm or damage that could have been avoided by C taking reasonable steps, or to pay for loss of earnings where that loss is unnecessary. Thus, if the harm caused means C can no longer perform the same job there will be a claim for loss of earnings. However, the claim for loss of earnings will be reduced if C can do work of some kind but fails to take reasonable steps to obtain such work, e.g., by refusing to go for interviews when work is available or by refusing to retrain for a different type of work.

Example

Clare is a professional dancer whose leg is injured in an accident caused by Dan's negligence. If the injury is temporary it would be reasonable for her not to seek alternative employment. However, if the injury is permanent and means she cannot dance again then she would be expected to seek alternatives. Clare cannot just do nothing and wait for her loss of earnings to grow. She should try to find a different type of employment, or perhaps retrain as a teacher so she can earn money teaching others to dance. Alternatively, she should enrol in some kind of college course to learn another skill altogether. If suitable alternative work is available and she refuses to attend any interviews then any calculation based on loss of future earnings will be reduced to reflect the fact that she has not taken reasonable steps to mitigate her loss.

Task 44

Briefly explain the following terms:

Damages

Special damages

The multiplier

Pecuniary damages

Non-pecuniary damages

Loss of amenity

General damages

Injunctions

Another remedy is an injunction. This is a court order used to prevent D carrying out some type of act. It is most commonly used in nuisance cases, as you saw in Chapter 8.

Example

Tim has started a pop group and they practise at home every night. Alan is a neighbour who cannot sleep. Alan doesn't really want compensation; that won't help him to sleep. He could sue Tim in nuisance and if he wins he should apply to the court for an injunction.

An injunction may be total or partial. In my example, the first would stop Tim practising at home; the second would stop him doing so at certain times, after midnight for example.

In **Tetley v Chitty 1986**, a *total injunction* was granted to stop the go-kart racing altogether. In **Kennaway v Thompson 1981**, a *partial injunction* was granted to stop the noise on a lake caused by speedboat racing, but it was limited to particular times.

An injunction is a *discretionary* remedy. This means it is granted at the court's discretion. Even if C wins the case, the court may decide not to grant an injunction. This is different from damages, which are granted as a right if C wins. Therefore, sometimes the court will award damages rather than an injunction, even in nuisance cases. This stems from the case of **Shelfer v City of London Electric Lighting Co 1895**, although the court made clear it only applied in exceptional circumstances and the norm would be to grant an injunction. **Shelfer** allows for the court to award damages rather than an injunction where the harm to C is minor and an injunction would be oppressive to D. This can be seen in **Miller v Jackson 1977**. Mrs Miller claimed an injunction and the opening quote is what she said to the judge. The CA felt that the public interest outweighed hers and refused it. They would not order the club to stop playing cricket, but awarded damages to compensate Mrs Miller for the inconvenience of having cricket balls landing in the garden. However, in **Regan v Paul Properties Ltd 2006** (see nuisance Chapter 10), the CA confirmed the rule in **Shelfer** that the discretion not to award an injunction should only be exercised in exceptional circumstances. In **Regan**, an injunction would not be oppressive and it would be unfair not to grant one as this would force him to accept money instead of solving his problem. However, as we saw when looking at nuisance remedies, there has been a retreat from **Shelfer** and **Regan**. Here is the case again.

Key case

In **Lawrence v Fen Tigers Ltd (No 2) 2014**, the SC suggested that in a modern world the principle was out of date. Lord Neuberger said, "it is unfortunate that it has been followed so recently and so slavishly" and noted that it had been devised at a time when there was less property and fewer statutory controls. He also indicated that the whole area should be reviewed because so few cases had reached the highest court that "for authoritative statements at the highest level on this area of the law one has to go back almost 150 years, to the landmark case of St Helen's Smelting Co v Tipping (1865)".

Key principle: an injunction may not always be appropriate and damages should be considered as an alternative (rather than slavishly following traditional principles).

Examination pointer

You won't need to discuss remedies in a lot of detail in an examination. The main thing, once you have shown D is liable, is to note which remedy is most appropriate with a very brief explanation of it.

Task 45

Look back at Chapter 10 on nuisance. Chose three cases and decide how an injunction could help C in each of them.

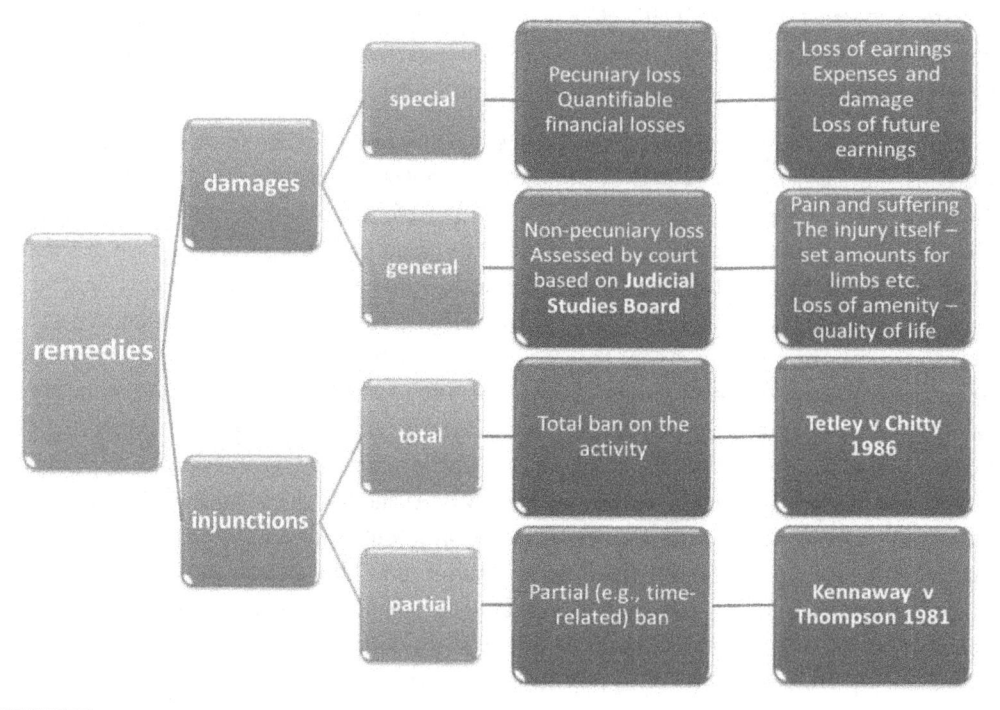

```
remedies
├── damages
│   ├── special — Pecuniary loss / Quantifiable financial losses — Loss of earnings / Expenses and damage / Loss of future earnings
│   └── general — Non-pecuniary loss / Assessed by court based on Judicial Studies Board — Pain and suffering / The injury itself – set amounts for limbs etc. / Loss of amenity – quality of life
└── injunctions
    ├── total — Total ban on the activity — Tetley v Chitty 1986
    └── partial — Partial (e.g., time-related) ban — Kennaway v Thompson 1981
```

Links to the non-substantive law

For links to the English legal system, look back at the diagram and examples in the introduction to Part 1. In particular, ADR and access to justice link to remedies, because cases can be expensive to take to court so alternatives or help with expenses may be needed before a remedy can be sought.

As with causation, damages is based on **The Wagon Mound** test of foreseeable loss. Thus what D is liable to pay reflects the level of blameworthiness, or fault.

Mitigation of loss provides a fair balance. It would be morally wrong to make D pay a greater amount than necessary if C could have reduced the loss in some way. In this case C would be at fault for not trying to do so.

As discussed with nuisance and **Rylands**, the remedy of granting an injunction is particularly relevant to balancing interests.

It has long been regarded as morally wrong to refuse an injunction except in exceptional circumstances because it would be forcing C to accept money instead of stopping the wrongdoing. The result of this is effectively that D is able to buy the right to cause a nuisance. However, this idea, as exemplified in **Shelfer** and **Regan**, has more recently been eroded by the decision of the SC in **Lawrence v Fen Tigers**.

Self-test questions

1. Can you explain the difference between special and general damages?
2. Can you explain the difference between pecuniary and non-pecuniary loss?
3. What is a structured settlement and when is it most appropriate?
4. What does mitigation of loss mean?

Summary 3 Nuisance, Rylands v Fletcher, vicarious liability, defences and remedies

Comparison of nuisance and Rylands

nuisance		Rylands v Fletcher
public	**private**	
a crime but also a tort if C suffers special damage		
now rare	a tort	a tort
Goldstein; Rimmington 2005		
affects a class of people	affects C's enjoyment	something likely to do mischief escapes and causes damage
C need not have interest in land	C must have an interest in land	C must have an interest in land
needs to occur more than once		can be a one-off event
D must act unreasonably		D need not be at fault, but use of land must be 'non-natural'
Causation: **Wagon Mound** test applies to all — **Cambridge Water**		
defences are contributory negligence and consent plus:		defences are contributory negligence and consent plus:
• statutory authority		• statutory authority
• act of God		• act of God
• act of a stranger		• act of a stranger
• prescription		• default of claimant
		• common benefit

Task 46

Look up the tests mentioned above. Draw your own diagram adding a case for each point, and the factors affecting liability. Keep this for revision.

Key criticisms of nuisance and Rylands

- *The effect of Sturges is that C can effectively 'self-inflict' the nuisance*
- *A person can be liable for the actions of a third party as in Sedleigh Denfield*
- *Interference with television reception and electromagnetic interference is not actionable – Hunter/Network Rail*
- *The overlap with nuisance and negligence means Rylands is arguably unnecessary – Crown*
- *Courts have been reluctant to develop Rylands – Cambridge Water – but are also reluctant to abolish it – Transco*
- *There are so many defences and limits that a Rylands action rarely succeeds*

Summary of vicarious liability

Is D an employee?	No single test – **Ready Mixed Concrete**
dual vicarious liability possible	**Viasystems**
Is D in the course of employment?	Is there a connection? - **Lister**
or on a 'frolic'	**Twine's**
If D is an independent contractor consider *Occupier's Liability Act 1957*	Occupier may be liable if work not checked s2 (4) (b) – **Woodward**

Key criticisms of vicarious liability

- *D is liable even if not at fault*
- *What comes within the scope of employment is now treated very widely*
- *Lister arguably goes too far in saying the acts of the employee were connected to the employment*
- *A balance must be found between ensuring the victim is compensated and overburdening an employer*
- *One development that can be said to be improving fairness is Viasystems, where dual vicarious liability was made possible so that blame can be fairly apportioned at the discretion of the court*

Before looking at whether D has a defence to a claim, a quick recap of some essentials using the diagrams from Part 1. C first has to prove:

Duty of care

- Duty of care
  - Donoghue v Stevenson
    - Proximity
    - Foreseeability
    - It is fair just and reasonable to impose a duty
  - Duty is restricted in cases of Nervous shock — McLoughlin / Alcock
  - Duty is restricted in cases of Economic loss — Hedley Byrne / White v Jones
  - Occupiers' liability: duty to a visitor — Occupiers' Liability Act 1957
  - Occupiers' liability: duty to a non-visitor — Occupiers' Liability Act 1984

Whether a duty is shown at common law, or under the **Occupiers Liability Acts**, both breach of duty and causation must then be proved.

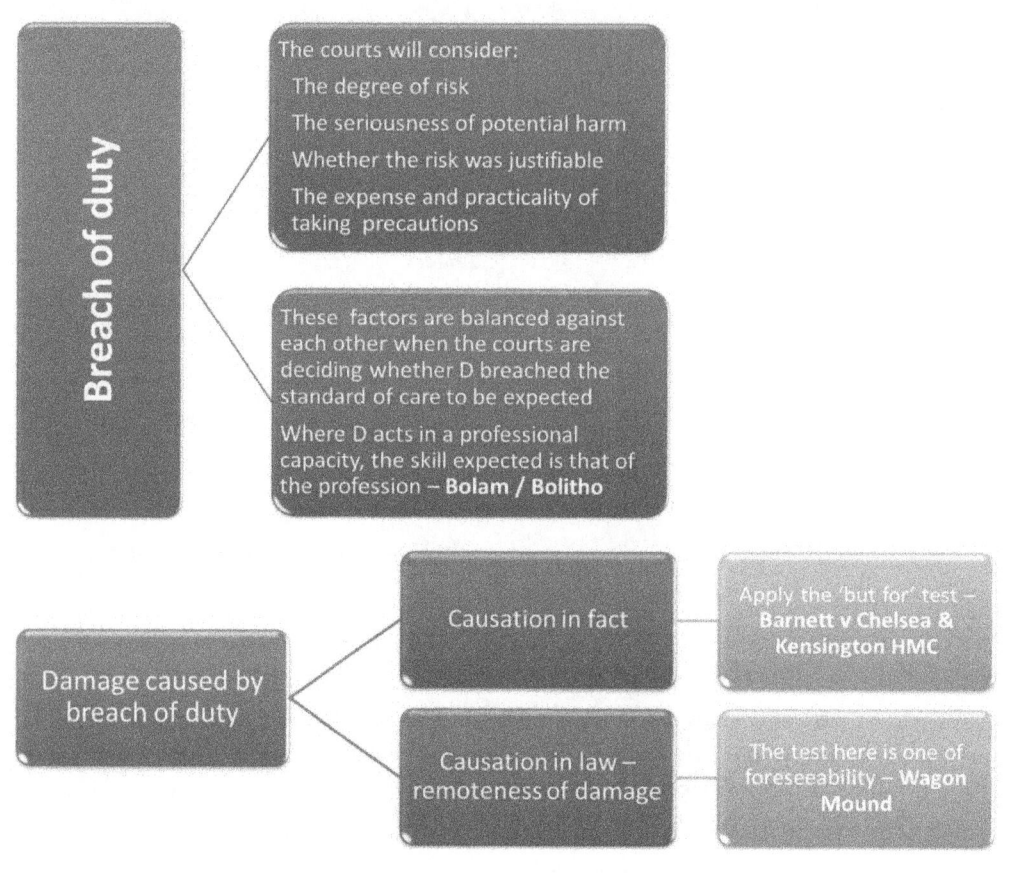

Breach of duty

The courts will consider:
- The degree of risk
- The seriousness of potential harm
- Whether the risk was justifiable
- The expense and practicality of taking precautions

These factors are balanced against each other when the courts are deciding whether D breached the standard of care to be expected

Where D acts in a professional capacity, the skill expected is that of the profession – **Bolam / Bolitho**

Damage caused by breach of duty

Causation in fact — Apply the 'but for' test – **Barnett v Chelsea & Kensington HMC**

Causation in law – remoteness of damage — The test here is one of foreseeability – **Wagon Mound**

Summary of the two defences which apply to all torts

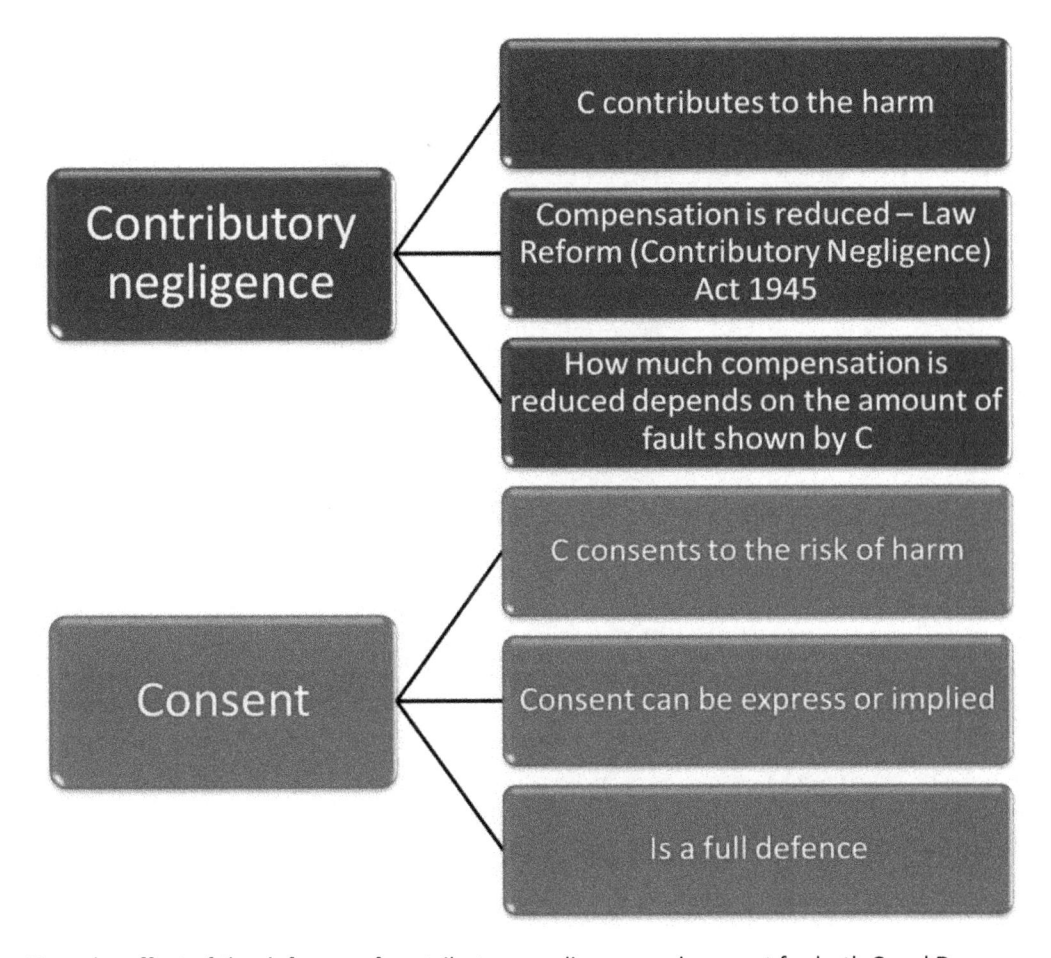

Contributory negligence
- C contributes to the harm
- Compensation is reduced – Law Reform (Contributory Negligence) Act 1945
- How much compensation is reduced depends on the amount of fault shown by C

Consent
- C consents to the risk of harm
- Consent can be express or implied
- Is a full defence

Note the effect of the defences of contributory negligence and consent for both C and D.

The first reduces the amount of compensation paid by D to C, the second means D pays no compensation and C has no remedy.

Summary of remedies

An award of damages is the most common remedy in tort, an amount of money to compensate the claimant. However, as you saw, an injunction may be of more help in certain situations.

Examination pointer

As I said earlier, you won't normally need to discuss damages in a lot of detail in an examination. However, more may be needed if the case is one of nuisance or under **Rylands** as what type of injunction will depend on the given circumstances and there may be policy reasons to refuses an injunction, as in **Miller v Jackson 1977**.

Here is a diagram summary showing both damages and injunctions.

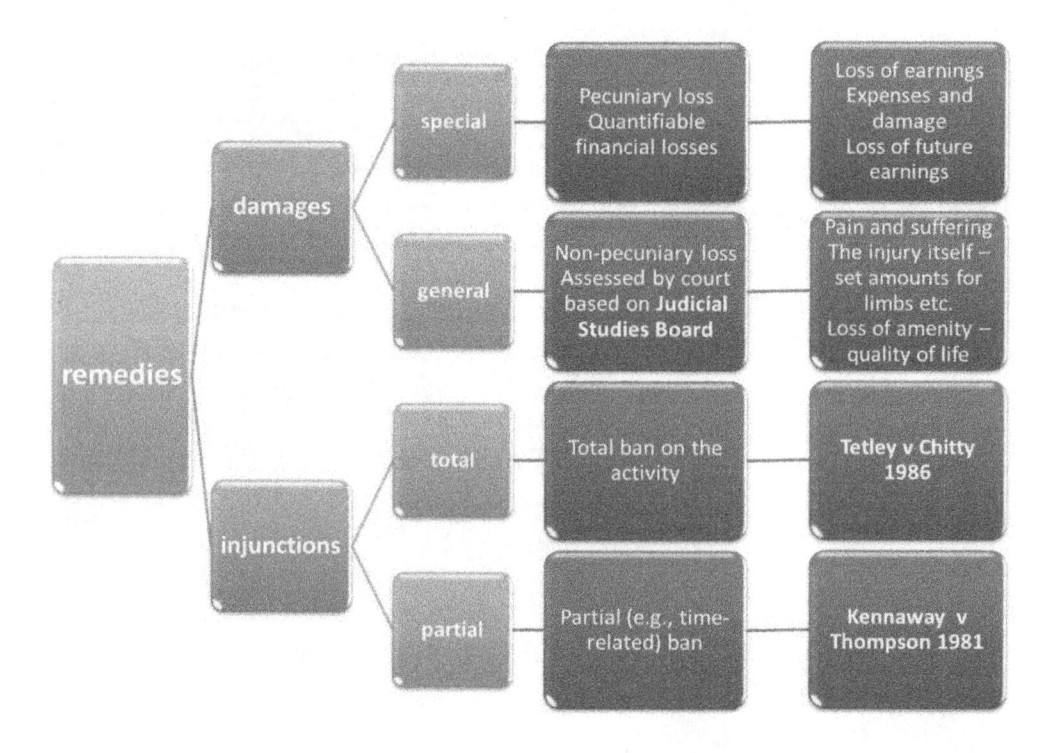

```
remedies
├── damages
│   ├── special — Pecuniary loss / Quantifiable financial losses — Loss of earnings / Expenses and damage / Loss of future earnings
│   └── general — Non-pecuniary loss / Assessed by court based on **Judicial Studies Board** — Pain and suffering / The injury itself – set amounts for limbs etc. / Loss of amenity – quality of life
└── injunctions
    ├── total — Total ban on the activity — **Tetley v Chitty 1986**
    └── partial — Partial (e.g., time-related) ban — **Kennaway v Thompson 1981**
```

Chapter 15: The A-level Examination (7162)

About the exams

This Chapter covers information for all three papers so you will have a complete idea of what is required. The guidance and actual paper are just for Paper 1.

The A-level is a two-year course with an external examination at the end of it (the first being in May/June 2019). There are three papers. Each is 2 hours long, worth 100 marks and is a third of the A-Level.

All papers are a mix of multiple-choice, short answer and extended writing questions. The nature of law and the English legal system come into all three (see table below for what goes where), the difference being the core substantive law.

Paper 1: The nature of law and the English legal system (25 marks) plus criminal law (75 marks)

Paper 2: The nature of law and the English legal system (25 marks) plus tort (75 marks)

Paper 3: The nature of law and the English legal system (25 marks) plus contract OR human rights (75 marks)

The assessment objectives (AOs)

These apply to all A-level courses and all examination boards. The examination will test you in the following ways.

AO1 tests your knowledge and understanding of the English legal system and legal rules and principles (13.33%)

AO2 tests your ability to apply legal rules and principles to given scenarios in order to present a legal argument using appropriate terminology (9%)

AO3 tests your ability to evaluate and analyse legal rules, principles, concepts and issues (11%)

Weighting is the same for all three papers and is given as a percentage (of 33.33% for each paper) in brackets. You should be aware of these weightings so that you plan your time accordingly. AO1 for the three papers together is 40%, AO2 is 27% and AO3 is 33%. This makes a total of 100% of the A-level.

For specimen papers and mark schemes visit the AQA site at www.aqa.org.uk.

For teachers: Please visit my website at www.drsr.org for a Guide for teachers including the changes to the specifications and examinations.

The English legal system and the nature/role of law: What goes where for A-level 7162?

Paper 1 Crime	Paper 2 Tort (including balancing competing interests)	Paper 3 Contract or Human rights (HR)
Statutory interpretation	Parliamentary law-making	The rule of law
Precedent	Law Reform	Delegated legislation
Criminal courts	Civil courts	The European Union
Lay people	Alternative dispute resolution	
Legal personnel	Judges and their role in civil courts	Judges and their role in civil (contract) or criminal courts (HR)
Judges and their role in criminal courts	Access to justice and funding in the civil system	Independence of the judiciary
Access to justice and funding in the criminal system	Law and society - fault	Access to justice and funding in the civil (contract) or criminal (HR) system
Law and society - fault	Law and morality	Law and society – balancing conflicting interests
Law and Justice		Law and Justice
		Law and morality

Note that where the English Legal System fits in has changed slightly from the AS papers.

Statutory interpretation was on Tort Paper 2 and is now on Crime Paper 1.

Law reform was on Crime Paper 1 and is now on Tort Paper 2.

Independence of the judiciary was on Crime Paper 1 and is now on Contract or Human Rights Paper 3.

The European Union was on Tort Paper 2 and is now on Contract or Human Rights Paper 3.

The rule of law was on Crime Paper 1 and is now on Contract or Human Rights Paper 3.

Delegated legislation was on Tort Paper 2 and is now on Contract or Human Rights Paper 3.

As for the nature of law, here is a quick summary

Law and society – fault: Papers 1 and 2

Law and society – balancing competing interests: Paper 3 (but note it is included in the substantive law for tort in relation to injunctions as a remedy)

Law and morality: Papers 2 and 3

Law and Justice: Papers 1 and 3

Although the non-substantive law is assigned to a particular paper, you are not limited to using only that area of law to illustrate the concept.

Types of question and apportionment of marks

For each paper, there are 5 multiple-choice questions on the substantive law and the English legal system (total 5 marks). There are 2 short answer questions at 5 marks each one on the substantive law and one on the English legal system (total 10 marks). There is one 10-mark question on the substantive law (total 10 marks). There is one 15-mark extended writing question on BOTH substantive and non-substantive law (ELS or nature / role of law) total 15 marks. Finally, there are two extended writing questions at 30 marks each (total 60 marks). One of these is only substantive law, the other mixes substantive and non-substantive law (ELS or nature / role of law).

It looks like this:

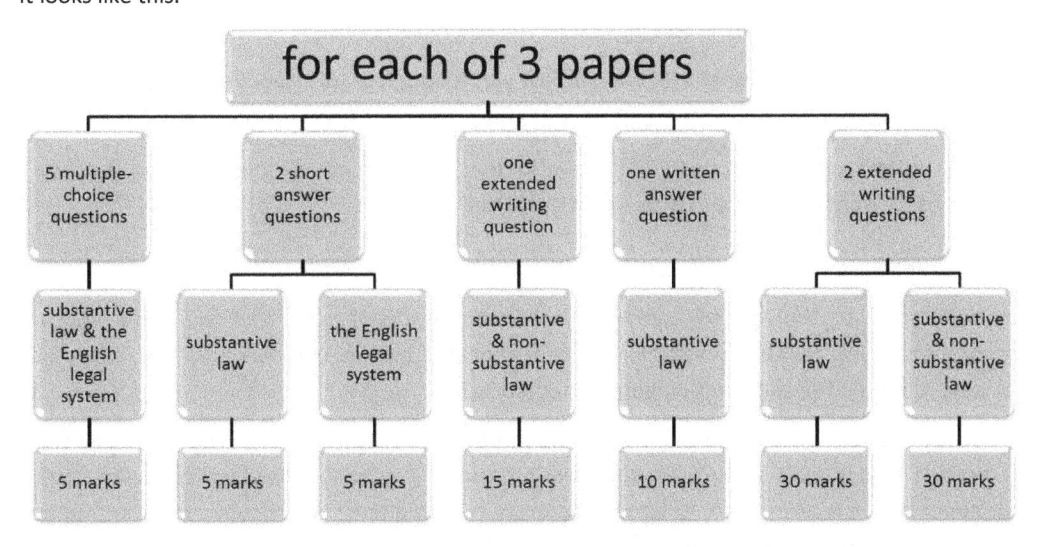

for each of 3 papers

- 5 multiple-choice questions → substantive law & the English legal system → 5 marks
- 2 short answer questions → substantive law → 5 marks; the English legal system → 5 marks
- one extended writing question → substantive & non-substantive law → 15 marks
- one written answer question → substantive law → 10 marks
- 2 extended writing questions → substantive law → 30 marks; substantive & non-substantive law → 30 marks

Note that where for AS there were two extended writing questions, there are three for A-level.

In each of the papers, you have to answer **all** questions. Two questions are a mix of tort and either the English legal system or the nature of law. Look back at the introduction diagram and the links at the end of each chapter for guidance on these.

Examination guidance

As you see there is a mix of questions and sometimes a question will include both application and evaluation of the law. What you need for application and essay questions cannot be divided completely but there is a difference. For both, it is important to know and understand cases and principles well. This is because the examination is not merely a test of knowledge, it is also testing your ability to *use* that knowledge, whether in applying what you know to a set of facts, or in evaluating what you know and connecting it to other areas of law.

In either case, you should structure your answer. As this is a test of **law** you need to state the legal principles involved and apply them to the particular question. A solid start is worth a lot and gets the examiner on your side.

Don't be tempted to write all you know about the area. Being selective is a skill in itself and an examiner won't be able to give you marks for stuff that isn't relevant, even if it is correct. If you ask a solicitor for advice, they won't tell you everything they know, they will pick out the law that suits your case. You have to do the same in answering an examination question.

In precedent, you learnt that the important part of a case is the *ratio decidendi*, the reasoning behind the judge's decision. As you revise a case, think about this and look for the legal principle.

It is important to:

> **Explain a case briefly but show that you understand the principle**
>
> **Show that you understand the relevant law well enough to be selective**

Before going on to look at an examination paper here is some general guidance for the two types of extended writing questions. See also the AS examination guidance for the two summaries for application and evaluation in the mixed questions.

Application advice

For application of the law to scenarios (problem questions) you need the same logical approach as for AS. Some of my earlier advice is repeated here as you may not have looked at it if you did not do the examination paper as practice.

Read the scenarios carefully to make sure you understand the questions. Sometimes you will be directed to a specific area of law and sometimes not. It may be necessary to discuss more than one as there is an overlap. However, if you are told to discuss a particular area you cannot get marks for discussing any other.

Try to summarise the facts in a few words. This is valuable when time is short. The principle of the case is the important part, although you may need to discuss the facts briefly to show why you have chosen that particular case.

Example

In **Reeves v MPC 1999**, one principle was that where there was a close proximity between the police and the victim the principle from **Hill v CC for West Yorkshire 1988** did not apply, so it was fair, just and reasonable to impose a duty. A second principle was that a foreseeable act will not break the chain of causation. You don't need all the facts, just what is relevant. If the scenario involves, e.g., a hospital and a patient, **Reeves** can be used to suggest that a duty may be owed and the relevant fact is the close relationship (police and prisoner is like hospital and patient). If the scenario involves something that D argues breaks the chain **Reeves** is an appropriate case to support the point that an act will not do so if it is foreseeable. Here the relevant fact is that he was a known suicide risk as this is the fact that relates to foreseeability.

If you can't remember the name of a case that is relevant don't leave it out but refer to it in a general way, e.g., 'in one decided case...' or 'in a similar case...'

You need to use *current* and *relevant* legal rules, which come from statutes or cases. **Key cases** highlight cases which are particularly important. Also use the ***examination pointers*** plus the ***diagrams*** or ***summaries*** at the end of each chapter as a guide. An answer should be rounded off with a conclusion as to liability where possible. You should never start an answer with "D will be liable ...." What you need to do is to use the law to prove it:

Identify the appropriate area of law – this will tell the examiner you have understood the focus of the scenario and will shape your answer.

Apply the relevant rules in a logical way to the facts – this will be the substance of your answer. Define the area of law then take each part of the definition in turn. Do this for each area if there is more than one. If you do this logically you won't leave anything out. If the area is covered by a statute, quote the law from that statute accurately and with section numbers if possible.

Add a little more detail if there is a particular issue shown by the facts – there will often be something particular to focus on so look for clues in the given facts to see if you need more on anything, e.g., causation.

Support your application with relevant cases – only use cases which are relevant to the particular scenario, and only state those facts that are essential to show the examiner why you have chosen that case e.g., because the facts are similar.

Conclude in a way that is sustainable and supported by what you have said and the cases you used – it is useful to look back at the question at this point. If it says, "Advise Mary ...", then make sure that your answer does so. In your conclusion, you should pull together the different strands of your answer and the say that based on that application "I would advise Mary that ...".

Try to refer to the facts of a scenario as often as you can when applying the law. This indicates that you are answering the specific question and have a sound enough knowledge to know which cases are relevant to the facts. It also helps to keep you focused. Examiners will include some pointers either to what the tort is or a particular issue in that tort, or possibly to a defence, always look for clues.

Task 47 Application practice

Briefly say what the following phrases suggest to you, i.e. which tort you think would be most appropriate and whether any particularly issues are raised. Add cases in support where possible.

Sue turned her stereo up loud every night in retaliation as she was fed up with the neighbour's continuous noise from …

A tree fell over in Tom's garden during a storm. He left it lying there and it …

Andrew was having a firework party, and a firework landed in the next garden and …

Tony is employed as a delivery driver. Whilst making a delivery and against the orders of his employer he gives someone a lift and while taking a corner too fast …

Theo stored several gallons of petrol in his garden shed, next to machinery which was known to get very hot, and …

Evaluation advice

Essays require more discussion and evaluation of the law or legal issues. The **key criticisms** in the summaries are designed to help with this, along with the **evaluation pointers**. The '**links to non-substantive law**' should help you see how a particular area of law connects to the English legal system and the various concepts of law. The law is not cut up into sections that can be dealt with in isolation; the topics you cover in your course are interwoven and you will need to show you understand the link between various areas of the substantive and non-substantive law.

In an essay question, you may need to form an opinion or weigh up arguments about a particular area of law, or a certain principle or issue. Here a broader range of knowledge is needed, showing you understand any problems with the law and can assess these and discuss possible reforms. You should always round off your answer with a short concluding paragraph, preferably referring back to the question. This shows the examiner you are addressing the given question and not one you would have preferred to have been asked! Planning an answer on an area of law is fine, as long as you are prepared to adapt it to the specific question. Not doing so is a common failing which examiners' reports frequently comment on.

Example

If the examination question asks you to discuss both criticisms and reforms, make sure both these words are included in your concluding paragraph. An example for a question on psychiatric harm could be to discuss the problems and proposals for reform and then conclude something like this: "*As can be seen from the above there have been many criticisms of the law in this area for some time. Despite the calls for reform, especially those of the Law Commission, little has been done to clarify matters. The law in this rea is still unnecessarily complex and case decisions are unpredictable. If the law is not clear and accessible it cannot achieve justice.*"

Examination practice Task 48

Look back at some of the evaluation pointers and links to the non-substantive law. Make a few notes on the problems with the law and how far it is based on an appropriate level of fault. Also note any areas which are insufficiently clear or where there are conflicting cases. Keep these for revision for an essay question and for using when answering the mixed question on tort and the concepts of morals and/or fault.

As with application of the law, you should try to take a logical approach. The beginning, should introduce the subject matter, the central part should explain/analyse/criticise it as appropriate, and the conclusion should bring the various strands of argument together with reference to the question set. Where possible, try to consider alternative arguments. A well-rounded essay will bring in other views even if you disagree with them. Here is an idea of how you might structure an essay. This is only a rough guide; in the central part you will of course need to cover any specific issues raised by the question e.g., a discussion of reforms, or of the development of an area of law, or of whether the particular law achieves justice.

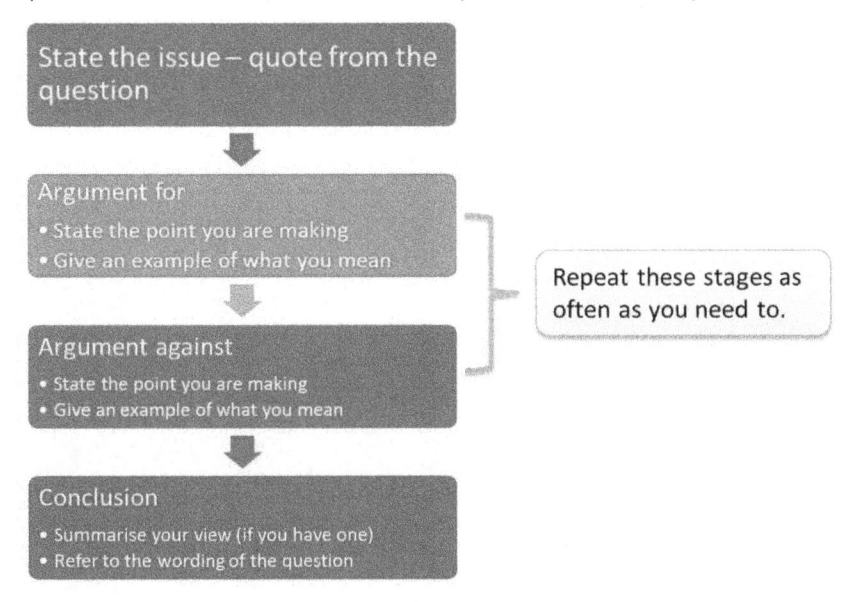

State the issue – quote from the question

⬇

Argument for
- State the point you are making
- Give an example of what you mean

⬇

Argument against
- State the point you are making
- Give an example of what you mean

Repeat these stages as often as you need to.

⬇

Conclusion
- Summarise your view (if you have one)
- Refer to the wording of the question

Finally, if you are confused by a case, or you see cases which conflict, don't despair. Just think 'I can use this to illustrate an argument that the law has not achieved justice'. If there is confusion or uncertainty then there will be a valid case for arguing that the law is not fully satisfactory so does not achieve justice.

Examination practice Task 49

Look back at any of the tasks that you had trouble with. Do these again and then check your answers before attempting the examination paper.

Examination paper Task 50

For each of the three papers that make up the A-level examination there are 100 marks in total and a time of 2 hours. Each paper is worth 33% of the full A-level.

What's assessed in Paper 2?

The nature of law and the English legal system (25 marks out of 100)

Tort law (75 marks out of 100)

It is unlikely an examination paper will cover everything but I have included a wide range here so that you get practice on as many topics as possible.

A-Level law Paper 2

Answer all questions

Tick the correct answer for multiple-choice questions

A-Level law Paper 2

Answer all questions

Tick the correct answer for multiple-choice questions

[1] If established by the defendant the defence of consent has the following effect on a claim in negligence? **1 mark**

A Damages will be reduced by half

B No damages will be awarded

C Damages will be reduced taking into account the amount of fault shown by the claimant

D Damages will be reduced taking into account the amount of fault shown by the defendant

[2] Which **one** of the following statements about special damages is **most accurate**? **1 mark**

A Special damages cannot be quantified

B Special damages are assessed by the court

C Special damages are those up to the date of the trial

D Special damages include loss of amenity

[3] Which **one** of the following statements is **false**? **1 mark**

A All Bills start in the House of Commons

B All Bills start in the House of Lords

C Most Bills start in the House of Commons

D Most Bills start in the House of Lords

[4] Which **one** of the following statements best describes consolidation of the law by the Law Commission? **1 mark**

A Combining all law from all sources

B Combining several Acts of Parliament

C Combining all case law

D Repealing several Acts of Parliament

[5] The High Court has three divisions, in which division is the Administrative Court? **1 mark**

A The Family Division

B The Chancery Division

C The Queen's Bench Division

D None of the above

[6] Briefly explain the role of Tribunals as an alternative to bringing a court case. **5 marks**

[7] Brad has been injured by Ivan's negligence. Assuming both duty and breach can be proved suggest to Brad what he will have to establish in order to prove that Ivan's negligence caused his injury. **5 marks**

[8]

Peter lives in a house with a huge garden and his hobby is bee-keeping. Recently a new house has been built on the land adjacent to his. The new owners have complained that the bees are a nuisance as they cannot use their gardens for fear of being stung. His new neighbour, Stan, is so fed up he takes to having large bonfires near the bee hives to make them nervous and stop them producing honey.

Advise Stan as to his rights and remedies against Peter in regard to the bees. **10 marks**

In question 9 you are required to provide an extended answer which shows a clear, logical and sustained line of reasoning leading to a valid conclusion.

[9]

Rylands v Fletcher is sometimes called a strict liability tort. Examine the significance of fault in establishing liability in civil law and discuss how far liability in Rylands v Fletcher is based on fault. **15 marks**

In question 10 you are required to provide an extended answer which shows a clear, logical and sustained line of reasoning leading to a valid conclusion.

[10]

Dan is tired after a long day and wants to get home. He is driving too fast and crashes into another car, seriously injuring both the driver and passenger and narrowly missing a cyclist. The cyclist, Pascal, suffers post-traumatic stress disorder as a result. Sadie is waiting at a bus stop around the corner. She hears the crash and goes into shock. Tarquin passes by and stops to give first aid. He is suffers severe depression following this experience. Consider the rights and remedies of Sadie, Pascal and Tarquin against Dan. **30 marks**

In question 11 you are required to provide an extended answer which shows a clear, logical and sustained line of reasoning leading to a valid conclusion.

[11]

Jack has an old shed in his garden and is worried about the local kids getting in and hurting themselves as there are gaps in his fence and he lives near a school. Before he gets round to doing anything Kanye is walking home from school when he sees that there is a tree covered in apples in Jack's garden. He gets through the fence and climbs onto the roof of the shed so he can reach some ripe apples, and the roof collapses. He badly injures his leg when he falls and tears a big hole in his trousers. A piece of wood from the roof falls on Ben, a homeless man who is sleeping in the shed, and injures him.

Consider the rights and remedies available to Kanye and Ben. Assess the options that might be available to Ben who has no money to pay for legal advice. who has no money to pay for legal advice. **30 marks**

Total 100 marks

END OF QUESTIONS

Index of cases

Adams v Ursell 1913 .... 127, 132
AG v PYA Quarries 1957 123
Ahmed v MacLean 2016 .... 31, 161
Alcock v CC of South Yorkshire 1991 109, 110
Allen v Gulf Oil 1981 132
Armes v Nottinghamshire CC 2017 155, 158
Atkinson v Seghal 2003 113
Badger v Ministry of Defence 2005 160
Bailey v Ministry of Defence and another 2008 41
Barker v Corus UK Ltd 2006 40
Barnett v Chelsea & Kensington HMC 1968 .... 38, 71
Barr v Biffa Waste Services Ltd 2011 127, 132
Barrett v MOD 1995 165
Belka v Prosperini 2011 162
Best v Smyth 2010 162
Blair-Ford v CRS Adventures Ltd 2012 29
Blyth v Birmingham Waterworks Co. 1856 27
Bolam v Friern HMC 1957 .... 33, 34, 39
Bolitho v City & Hackney HA 1998 33, 35, 39, 71, 121
Bolton v Stone 1951 13, 29, 30, 32, 36, 123, 124, 125, 126, 128, 131, 132
Bottomley v Todmorden Cricket Club 2003 55
Bourhill v Young 1943 .... 20, 109, 120
Bourne Leisure Ltd v Marsden 2009 58
British Railways Board v Herrington 1972 63
Brown 1994 .... 88, 90
Brown v Richmond upon Thames LBC 2012 116
Burton Hospitals NHS Trust 2017 44
Cable and Wireless v Muscat 2006 152
Calvert v William Hill Credit Ltd 2008 ... 102
Cambridge Water Co Ltd v Eastern Counties Leather plc 1994 132
Cambridge Water Co. v Eastern Counties Leather plc 1994 146
Caparo plc v Dickman 1990 97
Caparo v Dickman 1990 17, 21, 23, 24, 25, 71, 98, 101, 108, 109, 113, 120

Carty v Croydon LBC 2005 100
Castle v St Augustine's Links 1922 124
Century Insurance Co v NIRTB 1942 154
Chadwick v BTC 1967 .... 112, 164
Chaudhry v Prabhakar 1989 99
Christie v Davey 1893 .... 128, 132
CLG v CC of Merseyside Police 2015 22
Collett v Smith 2008 .... 44, 170
Condon v Basi 1985 165
Coope v Ward 2015 130
Corby Group Litigation v Corby Borough Council 2008 143
Corr v IBC Vehicles Ltd 2008 45
Coventry Promotions v Lawrence 2014 .... 124, 129, 130, 136
Cox v Ministry of Justice 2016 153
Crown River Cruises Ltd v Kimbolton Fireworks Ltd 1996 144
Customs and Excise Commissioners v Barclays Bank 2006 .... 101, 102
Cutler v United Dairies 1933 164
Dalling v RJ Heale & Co 2011 .... 39, 160
Dann v Hamilton 1939 164
Darby v National Trust 2001 56
Darnley v Croydon NHS Trust 2017 24
Daw v Intel Corp (UK) Ltd 2007 28
De Keyser's Hotel v Spicer 1914 .... 126, 136
Delaware Mansions Ltd v Westminster City Council 2001 137
Donachie v Chief Constable of Greater Manchester 2004 111
Donoghue v Folkestone Properties 2003 .... 57, 65
Donoghue v Stevenson 1932 16, 18, 19, 25, 96, 120
DS v Northern Lincolnshire and Goole NHS Trust 2016 39
Dulieu v White 1901 109
Edwards v London Borough of Sutton 2016 56
Esso Petroleum v Marden 1976 97
Evans v AG 2015 14
Evans v Wolverhampton Hospitals NHS Trust 2015 34
Eyres v Atkinson's Kitchens and Bedrooms Ltd 2007 162

192

Fairchild v Glenhaven Funeral Services Ltd 2002 .... 40, 121
Fardon v Harcourt-Rivington 1932 28
Fernquest v Swansea CC 2011 22
Finch v Smith 2009 160
Froom v Butcher 1976 160
Frost v CC of South Yorkshire 1998 111
G4S v Manley 2016 51
Gannon v Rotherham MBC 1991 161
Geary v Weatherspoon 2011 58
General Cleaning Contractors v Christmas 1953 54
Giles v Walker 1890 142
Gillingham Borough Council v Medway Docks 1993 133
Glasgow Corporation v Taylor 1922 52, 56, 62, 65
Goldman v Hargrave 1967 .... 130, 133
Gore v Stannard 2012 145
Graham v Commercial Bodyworks Ltd 2015 155
Grant v Australian Knitting Mills 1935 17
Gravil v Carroll & another 2008 156
Gray v Workington Golf Club 2016 29
Greatorex v Greatorex 2000 112
Gregg v Scott 2005 44
Grimes v Hawkins 2011 58
Gwilliam v West Hertfordshire Hospitals NHS Trust 2002 55
Hadlow v Peterborough CC 2011 47
Hale v Jennings 1938 .... 145, 147
Hall v Simons 2000 24
Halsey v Esso Petroleum Co 1961 125
Hambrook v Stokes 1925 109
Harris v Perry 2008 27
Haseldine v Daw 1941 .... 55, 151
Hawley v Luminar Leisure Ltd 2006 157
Haynes v Harwood 1935 164
Hedley Byrne v Heller 1963 96
Henderson v Merrett Syndicates 1995 . 100
Henegham v Manchester Dry Docks Ltd 2016 42
Higgs v Foster 2004 63
Hill v CC for West Yorkshire 1988 21, 23, 77, 183
Hirose Electrical UK Ltd v Peak Ingredients Ltd 2011 .... 124, 127, 132

Holbeck Hall Hotel v Scarborough Borough Council 2001 131
Hollywood Silver Fox Farm v Emmett 1936 128
Hughes v Lord Advocate 1963 .... 46, 47
Hunter v Canary Wharf 1997 .... 125, 129
ICI v Shatwell 1965 164
Jackson v Murray 2015 .... 161, 162, 167
Jain v Trent Strategic Health Authority 2009 101
JEB Fasteners Ltd v Mark Bloom 1983 97
JGE v English Province of Our Lady of Charity and another 2011 157
Jolley v Sutton LBC 2000 .... 46, 47, 53
Jones v Livox Quarries 1952 159
Junior Books v Veitchi 1983 103
Kennaway v Thompson 1981 .... 136, 172
Kent v Griffiths 19
Keown Coventry NHS Trust 2006 ...... 66, 67
Khorasandjan v Bush 1993 129
King v Phillips 1952 109
Kolasa v Ealing Hospital NHS Trust 2015 63, 67
Latimer v AEC 1952 .... 30, 71
Law Society v KPMG Peat Marwick 2000 98
Lawrence v Fen Tigers Ltd (No 2) 2014 *See* Coventry Promotions v Lawrence 2014, *Coventry Promotions v Lawrence 2014*
Laws v Florinplace 1981 127
Leakey v National Trust 1980 .... 130, 133
Lear v Hickstead Ltd and WH Security Ltd 2016 51
Lejonvarn v Burgess 2017 99
Lennon v MPC 2004 97
Lister v Helsey Hall 2001 154
Liverpool Women's Hospital NHS Trust v Ronayne 2015 115
LMS International Ltd v Styrene Packaging & Insulation Ltd 2005 143
Maguire v Harland & Wolff plc 2005 . 28, 71
Malone v Laskey 1907 129
Mann v Northern Electric Distribution Ltd 2010 64
Marcic v Thames Water Utilities Ltd 2003 133
Mason v Levy Autoparts 1967 142
Mattis v Pollock 2003 156
Mayne v Atlas Stone Company Ltd 2016 41

McDonnell v Holwerda 2005 34
McFarlane v Caledonia Ltd 1993 112
McKinnon Industries v Walker 1951 ...128, 132
McLoughlin v O'Brien 1982 109
Mersey Docks Harbour Board v Coggins and Griffiths (Liverpool) Ltd 1947 152
Michael v CC of South Wales 2015 22
Miller v Jackson 1977 ...87, 126, 128, 132, 135, 136, 169, 172, 178
Milton Keynes Borough Council v Nulty 2013 42
Mohamud v WM Morrison Supermarkets plc 2016 .... 156, 158
Moloney v Lambeth LBC 1966 52
Monk v Harrington 2008 112
Morris v Murray 1990 164
Mullin v Richards 1998 .... 32, 71, 121
Murphy v Brentwood DC 1990 104
Mutual Life and Citizen's Assurance Co v Evatt 1971 97
Nettleship v Weston 1971 ...32, 34, 71, 121
Network Rail v Morris 2004 .... 125, 128
Nichols v Marsland 1876 147
North Glamorgan NHST v Walters 2003 115
Ogwo v Taylor 1988 .... 54, 58
Orange v CC of West Yorkshire Police 2001 21
Orchard v Lee 2009 32
Owers v Medway NHS Trust 2015 115
Page v Smith 1995 .... 108, 110, 119
Palmer v Cornwall CC 2009 32
Paris v Stepney BC 38
Paris v Stepney BC 1951 .... 29, 71
Peires v Bickerton's Aerodromes Ltd 2017 .... 126, 133
Performance Cars Ltd v Abraham 1962 .. 39
Perrin and Another v Northampton BC 2007 137
Perry v Kendricks 1956 147
Phelps v Hillingdon BC 2001 100
Phethean-Hubble v Coles 2012 160
Phipps v Rochester Corporation 1955 ...52, 65
Platt v Liverpool City Council 1997 64
Poppleton v Trustees of the Portsmouth Youth Activities Committee 2008 .50, 58
R v R 1991 90

R v Royal National Orthopaedic Hospital NHS Trust 2012 33
Ratcliff v McConnell 1999 ...56, 64, 65, 67, 165
Read v Lyons 1947 142
Ready Mixed Concrete v Minister of Pensions 1968 152
Rees v Skerrett 2001 131
Reeves v MPC 1999 ...21, 25, 45, 77, 163, 166, 183
Regan v Paul Properties Ltd 2006 .135, 172
Rickards v Lothian 1913 .... 142, 147
Ritz Hotel Casino v Al-Daher 2014 102
Robinson v Kilvert 1889 .... 128, 132
Roe v Ministry of Health 1954 28
Roles v Nathan 1963 54
Rondel v Worsley 1969 24
Rose v Plenty 1976 154
Ross v Caunters 1980 99
Rylands v Fletcher 1868 141
Salmon v Seafarer's Restaurant 1983 54
Sayers v Harlow 1958 160
Scott v Gavigan 2016 28
Scullion v Bank of Scotland plc 2011 98
Sedleigh Denfield v O'Callaghan 1940 .. 129
Shelfer v City of London Electric Lighting Co 1895 .... 135, 172
Shiffman v Grand Priory of St John 1936 144
Shorter v Surrey & East Sussex NHS Trust 2014 115
Sidorn v Patel 2007 66
Sion v Hampstead AHA 1994 115
Smith v Baker 1891 163
Smith v Bush 1989 98
Smith v CC of Sussex Police 2008 21
Smith v Leech Brain 1962 47
Smith v Littlewoods 1987 .... 25, 45
Smith v Manchester Corporation 1974 .170
Smith v Stages 1989 153
Spartan Steel and Alloys Ltd v Martin & Co 1973 103
Spicer v Smee 1946 126
Spring v Guardian Assurance plc 1993 98
St Helen's Smelting Co v Tipping 1865 127, 132
Stone & Rolls Ltd v Moore Stephens 2009 98

Sturges v Bridgeman 1879......................134
Sturges v Bridgman 1879................127, 132
Swynson Ltd v Lowick Rose LLP 2017......98
Taylor v A Novo (UK) Ltd 2013 114
Taylor v English Heritage 2016 ....56, 161
Tetley v Chitty 1986........................130, 172
The Wagon Mound 1966...44, 71, 121, 131, 169
Tomlinson v Congleton Borough Council 2003................................57, 66, 68
Topp v London County Bus Ltd 1993.......19
Transco Plc v Stockport BC 2004 142
Trotman v North Yorkshire CC 1999 154
Twine v Bean's Express 1946..................154
Ultramares v Touche 1931 95
Uren v Corporate Leisure 2013..........29, 30
Vernon Knight Associates v Cornwall CC 2013 ....23, 30
Viasystems (Tyneside) Ltd v Thermal Transfer (Northern) Ltd 2005 153
Vowles v Evans 2003 ....23, 27
Wandsworth LBC v Railtrack 123
Wandsworth LBC v Railtrack 2001 123, 130

Watson & Ors v Croft Promo-Sport Ltd 2009 ....134, 136
Watson v British Boxing Board 2000.......23
Watt v Hertfordshire CC 1954 ....31, 71
Webster v Burton Hospitals NHS Trust 2017 35
Wells v Cooper 1958..........................33, 59
Wells v University Hospital 2015 115
Wheat v Lacon 1966 51
Wheeler v Saunders 1995......................133
White v CC of South Yorkshire 1999 111
White v Jones 1995..........................99, 100
Williams v The Bermuda Hospitals Board 2016 42
Williams v University of Birmingham 2011 28
Woodward v Mayor of Hastings 1945...55, 152
Woolridge v Sumner1963......................165
Wright v Cambridge Medical Group 2011 39
Yachuk v Oliver Blais Ltd 1949 161
Young v Kent CC 2005........................66, 67

List of abbreviations

All these abbreviations are commonly used. You may use them in an examination answer, but should write them in full the first time e.g., write 'actual bodily harm (ABH)' and then after that you can just write 'ABH', similarly with the defendant (D) and the victim (V).

Case names should be in full the first time but can be shortened in later use if they are lengthy.

General

Draft Code – A Criminal Code for England and Wales (Law Commission No. 177), 1989

CCRC Criminal Cases Review Commission

ABH actual bodily harm

GBH grievous bodily harm

D defendant

C claimant

V Victim

CA Court of Appeal

HL House of Lords

SC Supreme Court

Acts

S – Section (thus s1 Theft Act 1968 refers to section 1 of that Act)

s1 (2) means section 1 subsection 2 of an Act

OAPA – Offences against the Person Act 1861

OLA – Occupiers Liability Act

In cases (these don't need to be written in full)

CC (at beginning) chief constable

CC (at end) county council

BC borough council

DC district council

LBC London borough council

AHA Area Health Authority

Judges and other legal personnel (these don't need to be written in full)

J Justice

LJ Lord Justice

LCJ Lord Chief Justice

LC Lord Chancellor

VC Vice Chancellor

AG Attorney General

CPS Crown Prosecution Service

DPP Director of Public Prosecutions

AG Attorney General